Thoreau's Maine Woods

A Legacy for Conservation

by

Dean B. Bennett

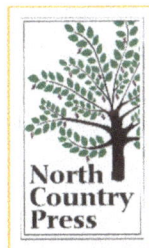

North
Country
Press

Thoreau's Maine Woods: A Legacy for Conservation

Design, digital art, illustrations, and words by Dean B. Bennett

ISBN 978-1-943424-65-8
LCCN 2021931243

North Country Press
Unity, Maine

To those who work to protect the Maine woods Henry David Thoreau traveled through.

Contents

THE ALLEGASH AND EAST BRANCH

Preface

I began my writing career by producing curriculum materials in my field of science and environmental education and editing a textbook on the study of Maine for middle school students. One of my curriculum projects was a kindergarten-through-grade-twelve study of the natural history of Maine. This led to an offer in 1979 to write a book using the scientific reports produced by Maine's Critical Areas Program. The book was published in 1988 as *Maine's Natural Heritage: Rare Species and Unique Natural Features*. Two more books followed in 1994 and 1996, also with conservation messages: *Allagash: Maine's Wild and Scenic River* and *The Forgotten Nature of New England: A Search for Traces of the Original Wilderness.*

In the year 2000, I left my long-held faculty position at the University of Maine at Farmington to write and illustrate books full time. By then I had built an extensive library of references on art, writing, nature, and history, including many books by and about Henry David Thoreau. In the first decade of this century, I produced five more published books on nature and wilderness, including three for children, which I illustrated in watercolor. It was also my pleasure to work with two good friends, Phyllis Austin and Robert Kimber, both distinguished authors, to produce and edit a book on wilderness in Maine.

My bookwork during these years included research and writing about Thoreau, who was born on July 12, 1817, and died on May 6, 1862, in Concord, Massachusetts. Thoreau was, foremost, a writer, but also a "naturalist, a philosopher, a political theorist, and a scientist," in the words of Thoreau scholars Walter Harding and Milton Meltzer.[1] To these areas of endeavor, we must add the observation of Boston University Professor Emeritus Edward Wagenknecht: "Thoreau was one of the pioneer American conservationists, functioning long before most of his countrymen had begun to grasp the fact that our resources are not inexhaustible."[2] Meltzer and Harding also concluded that Thoreau was "one of the few American literary figures [that achieved] world-wide significance and stature."[3] Among his admirers and those who acknowledged his influence on their lives are Bernard Baruch, Robert Frost, Martin Bubar, Sinclair Lewis, Ernest Hemingway, Lewis Mumford, E. B. White, N. C. Wyeth, Andrew Wyeth, Stewart L. Udall, William O. Douglas, Mohandas Gandhi, Martin Luther King, Jr., and Franklin D. Roosevelt.[4]

My deepening understanding of Thoreau was also accompanied by other events during the early twenty-first century that helped spawn this book. First, I was invited to a meeting by Roxanne Quimby, who later gave land in the East Branch of the Penobscot country to the federal government for a new national monument. At the meeting I learned about the Thoreau-Wabanaki Trail, a project of Maine Woods Forever, a non-profit organization dedicated to protecting the legacy of the north woods. The organization aims to raise public awareness of the wilderness and recreational heritage of the north woods and especially of the trips of Henry David Thoreau and the ancient Wabanaki canoe routes he followed. As part of this effort, two beautiful and detailed maps of the Thoreau-Wabanaki Trail were published. Second, J. Parker Huber, former director of the Henry D. Thoreau School of Wilderness Studies at Eastern Connecticut State College, sent me a striking new edition of his book *The Wildest Country: Exploring Thoreau's Maine*. The book is beautifully illustrated by the photographs of Bridget Besaw. These initiatives spawned a renewed consciousness about the country in northern Maine that Thoreau wrote about more than a century and a half ago, and in 2010, I began planning and illustrating this book.

Acknowledgements

First, I thank two professors who steered me into the conservation field, Professor Robert Miller, University of Southern Maine, and Professor William Stapp, University of Michigan. Both became advisors, mentors, and friends. I also thank Harry (Hank) R. Tyler, Jr., formerly the head of Maine's Critical Areas Program, for giving me the opportunity to write my first book about conservation, *Maine's Natural Heritage*. I am grateful, too, for the instruction and advice I've received from the many art teachers I have had, both within and outside the formal course program setting. They include Doris Holman for initiating me in the wonders of watercolor painting; J. Thomas (Tom) Higgins for teaching me drawing and plein-air painting with oils, and giving me the benefit of his experience in reviewing my initial illustrations for this book; Jan Piribeck for teaching me how to use acrylics in painting; Ellen Roberts for instructing me about two-dimensional design; Sheila Garrett at the Portland School of Art for her insightful course on children's book illustration; and Karen Ackoff, scientific illustrator for the Smithsonian Institution, for her wonderful week-long course on sharp focus watercolor illustration at the Eagle Hill Wildlife Research Station in Steuben, Maine.

Regarding Henry David Thoreau and his connection with the Maine woods, I have benefited from the extraordinarily creative work of J. Parker Huber in his researching and writing of both editions of his book *The Wildest Country: Exploring Thoreau's Maine*. His maps and descriptions of Thoreau's three excursions to the Maine woods were most helpful. I thank him for turning his knowledge and experience into such a valuable and inspiring publication. In my preparation of this book, I also express my thanks to Marion (Mimi) McConnell and Paul Johnson of Maine Woods Forever for their support and advice.

As for my many trips following Thoreau's steps in Maine's north woods, I wish to say how much I enjoyed the companionship of my family on these excursions, and especially how grateful I am to my wife Sheila for her company on my trips and for the enthusiasm, enjoyment, and encouragement she expressed as we shared these adventures. I also thank her for giving me insightful critiques of my illustrations, valuable perspectives on conservation, and critical editing comments on the book's design and manuscript.

Regarding the book's illustrations, I should add that all images of natural features and animals drew on elements of my own photographs with the exception of a flying kingfisher from the public domain in the files of the United States Fish and Wildlife Service, with no attribution required, and a black bear taken with a trail camera by Charles Martin and used by permission.

As for the book's maps, I greatly appreciate the enormously important effort of the Maine Bureau of Parks and Lands and Director Andy Cutko to consolidate years of land conservation in Maine into a map. Because of this, I was able to complete my effort to identify the conservation of land areas near Thoreau's three routes through the Maine woods.

I am indebted to Scott Herrick for keeping my computer in good condition and operating efficiently. This book was very dependent on his skills.

I thank Patricia Newell, my publisher, for bringing this book and its message of the conservation of Maine's natural environment to the public.

Introduction

Thoreau's Maine Woods

Throughout history we have discovered places on this earth that inspire us, that connect us to the natural world, that give us an identity—wild places that reveal nature in a condition relatively unaffected by our presence, that possess a vulnerability to the powerful impact of human settlement, and that impress on us a moral responsibility to walk quietly and gently over the land, aware of where we go and what our footsteps do. This is an exploration of one such place—the Maine woods.

This vast forest blankets a gently rolling landscape of spruce and fir and northern hardwoods through which mountains randomly rise; a landscape embroidered with strands of bright, rippling streams and rivers linking sparkling lakes and ponds; a landscape teeming with life and surprises; a landscape that I came to know and love. Here, I explored most of the places Thoreau visited on his three trips to the Maine woods, as well as many others.

What Thoreau brought to the public was word images of this north woods country. His writing evoked an appreciation for its wildness and an awareness of the character of its raw nature, while conveying a connection to the natural world and suggesting a moral responsibility for its care. These elements of his writing inspired me and countless others to explore directly and vicariously this land and the spirit of conservation that Thoreau conveyed in his book, *The Maine Woods*, as well as other writings.

Conservation—Spirit and Issues

Conservation, as I have used it in this book, means the preservation, protection, and restoration of the natural environment, including its life, its wild state, and its ecological balance; the prevention of wasteful use of a resource; and the preservation and restoration of historical and cultural sites. For the purposes of this book, I define the "spirit" of conservation as a vital essence in one's life and a will and motivation to practice conservation, along with enthusiasm and courage. By "issues" I mean conflicts in values. Thoreau was not afraid of expressing his differences with others about the value of nature. For example, Thoreau strongly proclaimed at times that the highest value of some object or natural feature, such as the much sought-after white pine, could not be measured simply in dollars and cents. In this book, the issues surrounding the conservation of nature will appear in many of the fifty-four essays about the living things, natural objects, and features of land and water that Thoreau encountered. However, despite disagreements in such issues as preserving land for its scenic beauty, study, and some forms of recreation vs. harvesting it for timber, or mining it for minerals, or developing it for human settlement, most will agree that our decisions on conservation issues have taken on greater meaning as our human population has grown in face of a finite planet.

Conservation of the Maine Woods

This is a story of conservation in the Maine woods. Thoreau traveled more than 200 miles in the Maine woods after he left the more settled areas. On his trips, he voiced thoughts that were but ripples of what would become waves of land protection—waves that would lie in the wake of his canoe and be felt by those who followed him far into the future. Through his words, both spoken and written, he called for the protection of the land and its wild character, he deplored the wasteful use of natural resources, including wildlife, and promoted the preservation of indigenous cultures.

The extent of Thoreau's influence through his book *The Maine Woods* and his journals on the protection of Maine's woods can only be conjectured. What is inescapable, however, is the amount of land that has come under some kind of protection since his time, land within a few miles of the routes he took. Thoreau's descriptions of the natural features on these routes, his feelings about them—their beauty and natural order and the ethical responsibilities he saw associated with them—could not help but affect thoughtful readers. His passion for the conservation of nature was, at times, clear and direct in some of his writings. Near the end of his life, he wrote that we should preserve our beautiful natural features that "have a high use which dollars and cents never represent . . . So, if there is any central and commanding hilltop, it should be reserved for public use."[1]

There is such a hilltop in Maine, and it was reserved for public use—Mount Katahdin in Baxter State Park, Maine's highest mountain. And along the east side of this park, adjacent to it, is a more recently preserved land area, Katahdin Woods and Waters National Monument. It was established in 2016 and protects approximately 87,500 acres, including miles of the East Branch of the Penobscot River that Thoreau paddled on his third and final trip to the Maine woods. One of the least developed watersheds in the northeastern United States, it contains a "stunning concentration" of waterfalls and rapids and a diverse natural character, including some of the state's oldest geological features, a significant biodiversity among plant and animal species, striking views of the surrounding country, and a noteworthy human history.[2] Today, protection of this remarkable natural area will allow generations to follow in the footsteps of those whose lives it touched in the past, to see it as they saw it.

Preservation of Indigenous Cultures of the Maine Woods

Native peoples are known to have inhabited the area of Thoreau's journey through the Maine woods for some 11,000 years. They were attracted here because of their dependency on waterways for seasonal searching for food, furs, medicines, and other resources used directly or for trade. The Wabanaki people, as they are called, "consider the Penobscot River a centerpiece of their culture and spiritual values."[3]

Thoreau held a deep and lifelong interest in indigenous peoples and especially in their relationship with the land. Around the time of his Katahdin trip, he began compiling notes on his reading of native peoples and eventually accumulated twelve "Indian Books."[4] When he took his Chesuncook trip in 1853, he hired Joseph Aitteon, a Penobscot Native, as his guide. Aitteon was twenty-four years old and had previously guided moose hunters in the area. He died sixteen years later in a boating accident in the Penobscot River, but in the years before his death, he achieved recognition as the Penobscot Nation's first elected Chief.[5]

In 1857, Thoreau employed forty-eight-year-old Joseph Polis, another Penobscot, to guide for him. Thoreau wrote that he was stoutly built, perhaps above the middle height, and had a broad face. He was known as "particularly steady and trustworthy." He could read and write, owned land, and once represented his tribe in the state capital and in Washington.[6] A good relationship developed between the two men. They exchanged banter throughout the trip, covering all manner of subjects—history, woodcraft, Indian customs, canoe making, hunting, fishing, and natural history. After his return to Concord ten days later, Thoreau wrote: "I . . . think I have had a quite profitable journey . . . I have made a short excursion into the new world the Indian dwells in."[7]

At the end of his second trip to the Maine woods, Thoreau wrote: "Why should not we . . . have our natural preserves, where no villages need be destroyed, which the bear and panther, and some even of the hunter race, may still exist, and not be 'civilized off the face of the earth,'—our forests . . . for inspiration and our own true recreation?"[8]

Protection of Natural Beauty

Thoreau appreciated the aesthetic landscape. He once wrote: "As in many countries precious metals belong to the crown, so here more precious natural objects of rare beauty should belong to the public." His many writings are sprinkled with references to beauty, such as the following from his journal in 1855: "We get only transient and partial glimpses of the beauty of the world. Standing at a right angle, we are dazzled by the colors of the rainbow in colorless ice. From the right point of view, every storm and every drop in it is a rainbow. Beauty and music are not mere traits and exceptions. They are the rule and character. It is the exception that we see and hear." Nature to Thoreau imparted an artistic element with its beauty: "She has her luxurious and florid style as well as art." He often wrote about the need to protect the beauty of the natural features and objects of the land. He spoke of waterfalls, lakes, hills, even rocky cliffs and individual rocks— "such things are beautiful," he said. "It would be wise to seek to preserve these things."

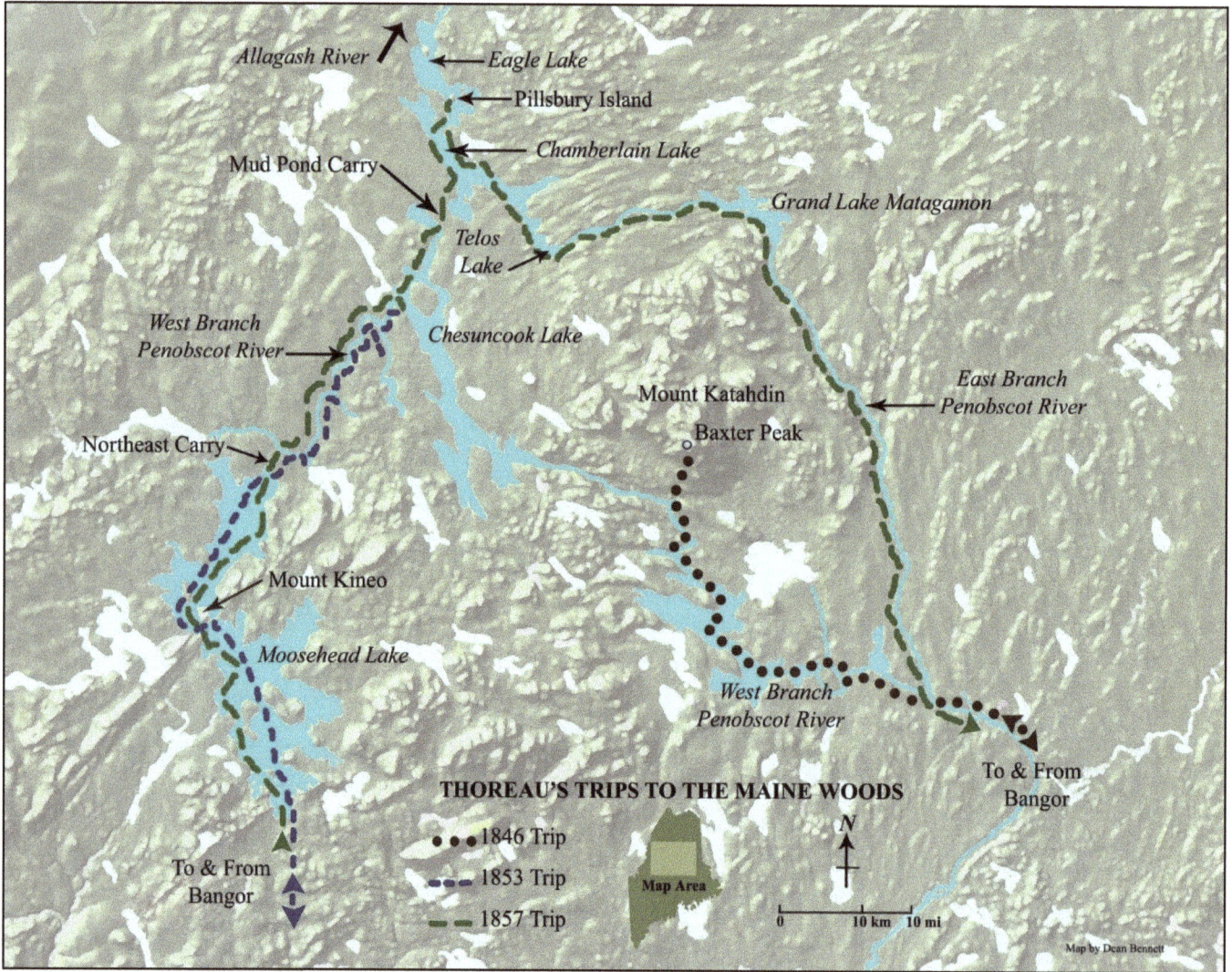

Allagash River

Eagle Lake

Pillsbury Island

Chamberlain Lake

Mud Pond Carry

Telos Lake

Grand Lake Matagamon

West Branch Penobscot River

Chesuncook Lake

Mount Katahdin

Baxter Peak

East Branch Penobscot River

Northeast Carry

Mount Kineo

Moosehead Lake

West Branch Penobscot River

To & From Bangor

To & From Bangor

THOREAU'S TRIPS TO THE MAINE WOODS

●●● 1846 Trip

▪▪▪ 1853 Trip

▬ ▬ 1857 Trip

Map Area

N

0   10 km   10 mi

Map by Dean Bennett

KTAADN

The 1846 Trip

On Monday, August 31, 1846, Henry David Thoreau left his home in Concord, Massachusetts, and caught a train for Boston. Sometime later that day, he boarded a steamer for Bangor, Maine. His purpose: "to make excursions to Mount Ktaadn, . . ."[1] Upon his arrival, he went to the home of his relatives, George and Rebecca Thatcher. The next day, with George Thatcher as his trip arranger and companion, he traveled to Enfield, mostly by horse and buggy. Resuming their journey the next morning, the two spent their next night in Mattawamkeag. From there, Thoreau traveled with Thatcher and others approximately fifty miles on foot and by bateau up the Penobscot River and its lower West Branch to Mount Katahdin. Thoreau never made it to the highest point on the mountain, since named Baxter Peak. Close to the summit, he found himself "deep within the hostile ranks of clouds, and all objects obscured by them." He felt that a "vast, Titanic, inhuman Nature . . . had caught him alone . . . She seems to say sternly, why came ye here before your time? This ground is not prepared for you." With mists blowing around him, tantalizingly revealing the mountain and surrounding vistas for a few moments then obscuring them as quickly and "knowing that the clouds might rest on the mountain for days," he began his descent.[2] Thoreau returned home September 11 with a new understanding and respect for wilderness that would remain with him the rest of his life.

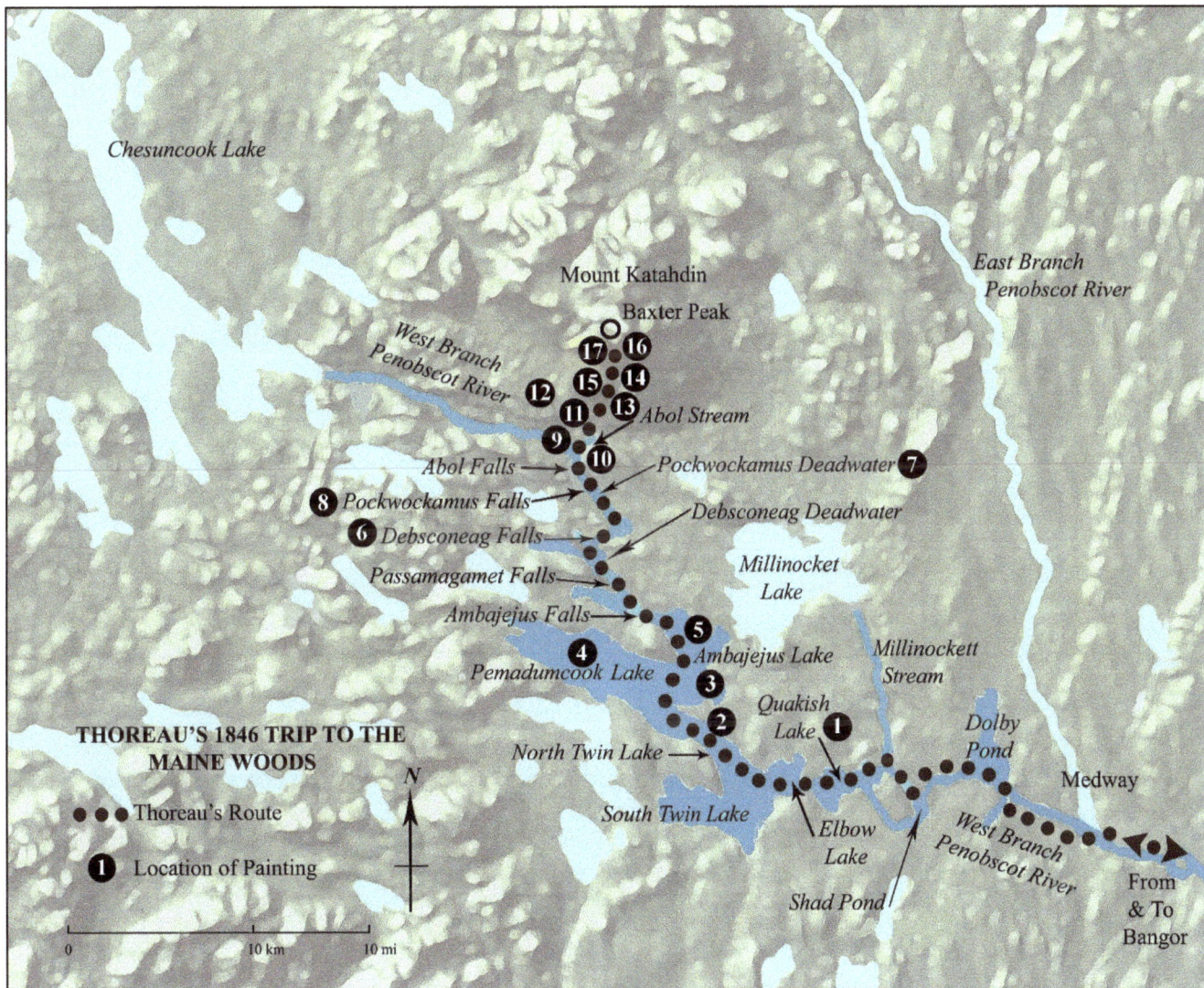

THOREAU'S 1846 TRIP TO THE MAINE WOODS

Chesuncook Lake

Mount Katahdin

Baxter Peak

West Branch Penobscot River

East Branch Penobscot River

17 16
15 14
12
13 Abol Stream
11
9
10
Abol Falls Pockwockamus Deadwater 7
8 Pockwockamus Falls
6 Debsconeag Falls Debsconeag Deadwater
Passamagamet Falls
Millinocket Lake
Ambajejus Falls 5
4 Ambajejus Lake Millinockett Stream
Pemadumcook Lake 3
2 Quakish Lake 1 Dolby Pond
North Twin Lake Medway
South Twin Lake Elbow Lake West Branch Penobscot River
Shad Pond From & To Bangor

THOREAU'S 1846 TRIP TO THE MAINE WOODS

N

•••• Thoreau's Route

1 Location of Painting

0   10 km   10 mi

7

1. QUAKISH LAKE

"We had our first, but partial view of Ktaadn"

September 5, 1846

It was late in the day when Henry David Thoreau reached "the smooth water of the Quakish Lake."[1] Here, from the south, he saw for the first time the summit of Katahdin "connecting the heavens with the earth."[2] Thoreau doesn't explain the odd name of Quakish Lake, but Lucius Hubbard, another nineteenth-century explorer of the Maine woods, included it in his 1883 book, *Woods and Lakes of Maine*, a reference to "Quakish: a pond on the Penobscot above Nicketow [now Medway, Maine]."[3] Although only 400 acres or so when Thoreau and his party took turns in rowing and paddling across this "sheet of water," he described it as "a small, irregular, but handsome lake, shut in on all sides by the forest, and showing no traces of man but some low boom in a distant cove, reserved for spring use [for containing logs from the river drives]."[4]

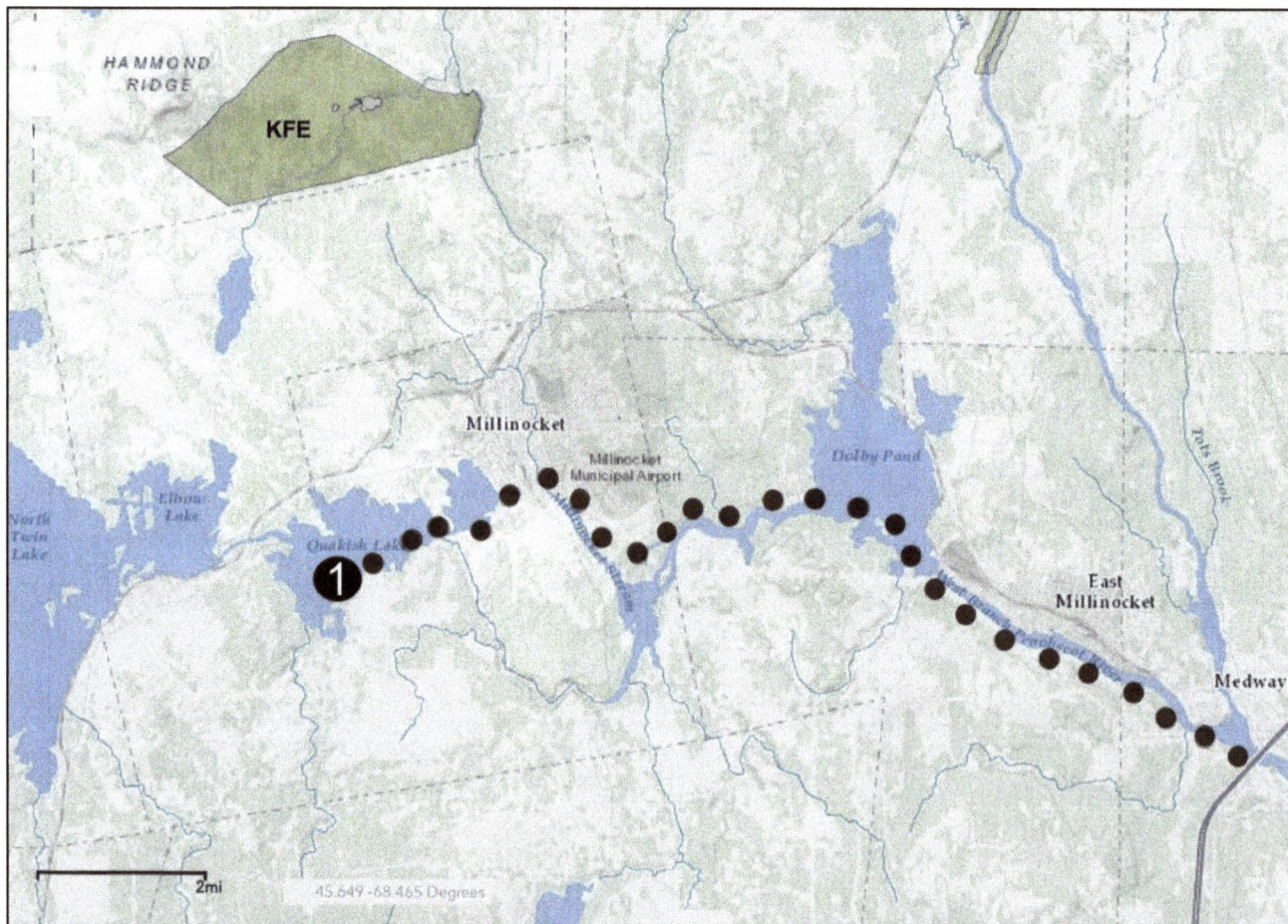

Note: For map keys to Conservation Lands (green), go to Appendix B. For example: The letters KFE mean Katahdin Forest Easement.

Since Thoreau's trip, the lake and its surroundings have undergone dramatic change. At its outlet, the lake was dammed in 1899 by the newly created Great Northern Paper Company and expanded in size to 1,000 acres, diverting water from the Penobscot to the paper mill and continuing to be used as a holding reservoir for logs with booms, as the one Thoreau had mentioned. We now know that use of aquatic systems for the transportation and storage of logs creates physical and chemical disturbances to biotic communities in its effect on substrates where logs contact the bottom, as well as on shading of light, deposition of the logs, bark, and wood debris, and disruption of the water column. Today, there are studies of these disturbances that have led to conservation measures that can be taken with the construction and operation of booms and handling of logs contained by them.

Over the years, since the log drives of Thoreau's day, many logs stored in booms at Quakish Lake have sunk to the bottom of the lake. Wood from these trees, much of it virgin timber, some of which began growing back in the 1500s, is now salvageable, enticing entrepreneurs to harvest it for such products as wall paneling and wood flooring—a form of long-term conservation.[5] But despite the events and changes in and around Quakish Lake, one thing hasn't changed: the view of Katahdin still lures visitors to admire its scenic beauty as it did Thoreau in 1846.

2. NORTH TWIN LAKE

"rambled along the sandy shore in the moonlight,
hoping to meet a moose . . . dark, fantastic rocks, rising here and there."
September 5, 1846

If you travel some eight miles south on Route 11 from the center of Millinocket, you will come to a boat launch and picnic area on the shore of Partridge Cove of South Twin Lake. Here, if you sight northwest by the eastern edge of North Twin Ridge, you will see in the distance beyond the north shore of North Twin Lake. It was here in a small cove where a brook drains from Wadleigh Pond that Thoreau camped on September 5, 1846, after leaving Quakish Lake.

Thoreau and his party had arrived around nine o'clock on a moonlit night to a natural haven between some rocks where a small brook flowed from Wadleigh Pond more than a mile away. "We heard the sound of the rill," he wrote, "which would supply us with cool water emptying into the lake." That night he went to sleep "with the moon and stars shining in [his] face."[1]

In the middle of the night, Thoreau was awakened to find that others in his party couldn't sleep. He got up, added some wood to the fire, "and then rambled along the sandy shore in the moonlight, hoping to meet a moose, come down to drink, or else a wolf." While he walked, "the little rill tinkled louder . . . and the glassy smoothness of the sleeping lake, laving the shores of a new world, with the dark, fantastic rocks rising here and there from its surface, made a scene not easily described." He wrote that it "left such an impression of stern, yet gentle, wildness on my memory as will not soon be effaced."[2]

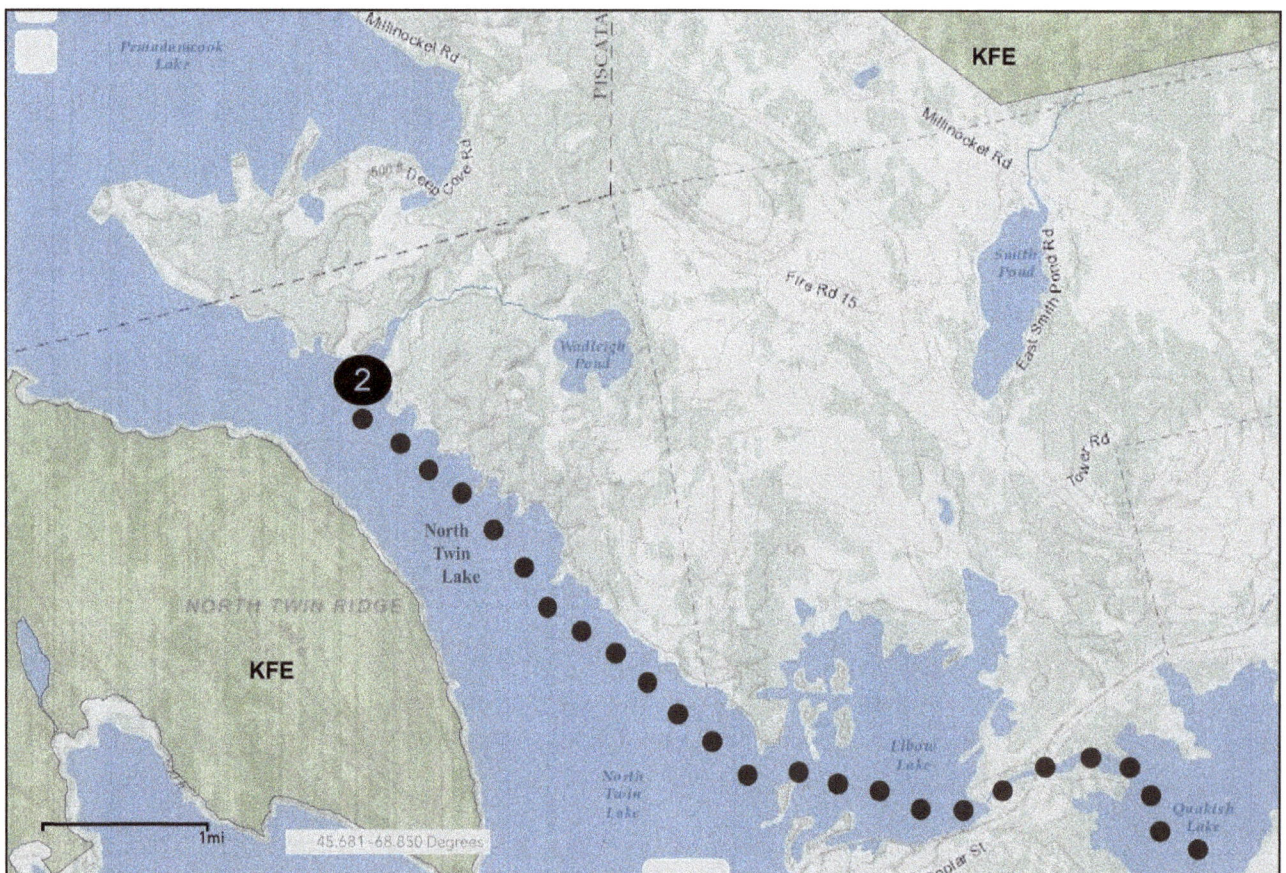

Dean B. Bennett

Wilderness was a constant theme in Thoreau's writing. It would be sixteen years later that he made what may be his most often quoted statement on the subject. It appeared in his essay *Walking*, published posthumously in 1882, the year he died: "In wildness is the preservation of the world."

If Thoreau could once again walk along the beach in front of his campsite on North Twin Lake and look across the narrow lake to North Twin Ridge, he would still see some of the gentle wildness he wrote about. It is part of the 195,000-acre Katahdin Forest Easement (**KFE**), the result of an agreement in 2002 between The Nature Conservancy and Great Northern Paper Company. The agreement "guarantees public access, traditional recreational uses, sustainable forestry, and no future development." In 2006, the Conservancy transferred the **KFE** to the state of Maine, along with a stewardship endowment of $500,000.[3] So today, if you follow Thoreau's rambles down the shore from his 1846 campsite, you will still see an undeveloped shoreline across the lake and a bit of the wildness that Thoreau came to Maine to see.

3. MOOSE TRACKS

"the track of a full-grown moose is like that
of a cow, or larger"
September 7, 1846

The author discovered the tracks pictured here of a large moose on a gravelly-sandy lake shore in the vicinity of one of Thoreau's journeys in the Maine north woods. For the philosopher-naturalist, such a sign of Maine's great mammal added to his fascination with this region. He reported seeing moose tracks on several occasions during his 1846 trip: on a small island below Pockwockamus Falls,[1] on the sides of Katahdin where the tracks "covered every square rod,"[2] and "on the shore of the pond" in a secluded meadow during his return from Katahdin.[3]

Despite all the tracks he saw, Thoreau didn't see a moose on that trip. This appeared to whet his interest in a moose encounter, for early in his 1853 trip, he declared: "Though I had not come a-hunting, and felt some compunctions about accompanying the [moose] hunters, I wished to see a moose near at hand . . . ."[4] On that trip down the Upper West Branch of the Penobscot River to the Chesuncook Lake area , he was successful in having several sightings in close encounters with the moose. In great part, this was due to his choice of his Native American guide, Joe Aitteon, who had experience in guiding moose hunters and with whom Thoreau accompanied on a successful hunt.

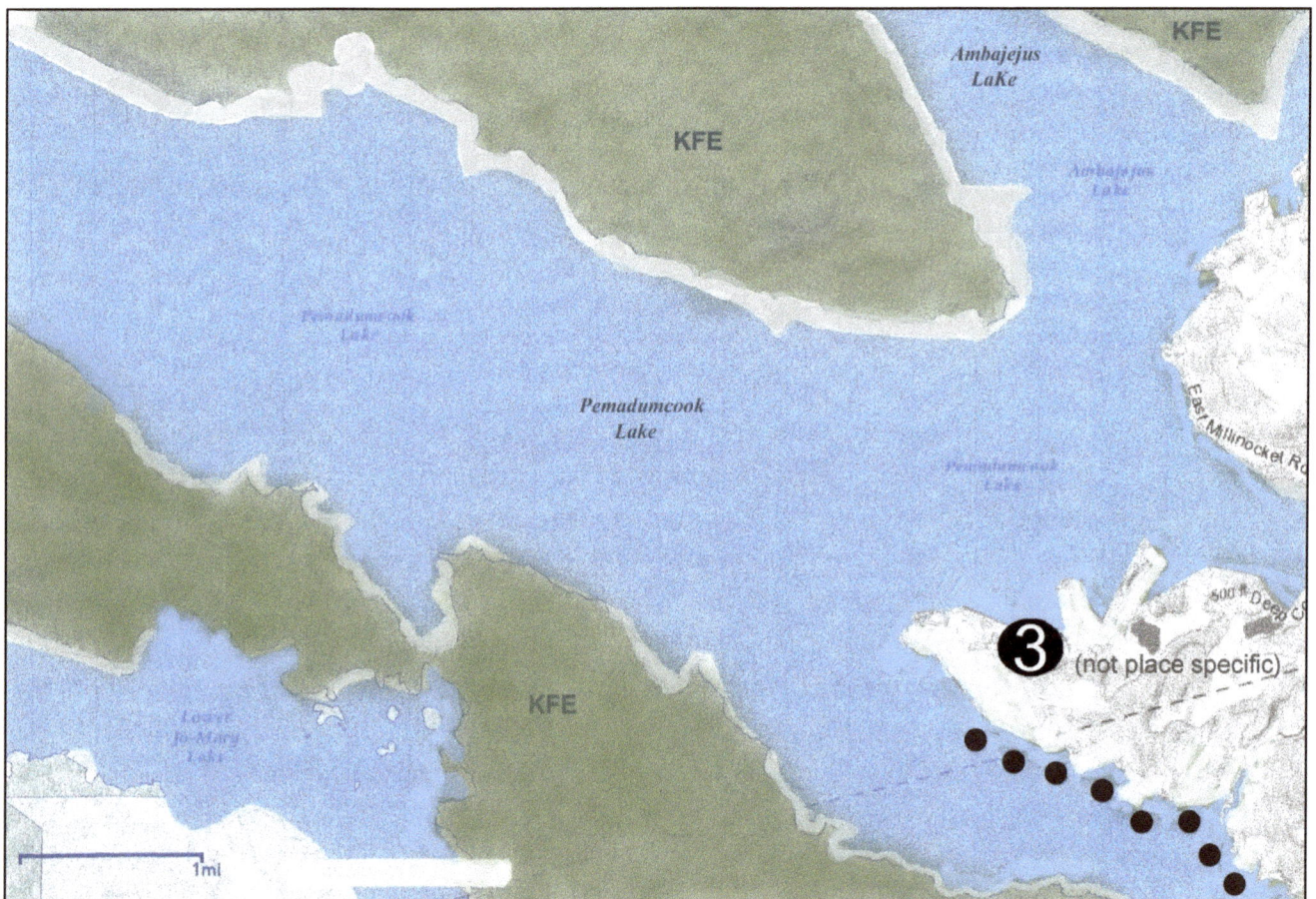

Dean B. Bennett

Through the years after Thoreau's Maine woods trips to the present, there came an increasing recognition of the aesthetic and other nonconsumptive values of wildlife, including the moose. These values were discussed in a paper published in 1975, *Moose as a Nongame Recreational Resource*, given by David Lime at the Tenth North American Moose Workshop held in Minnesota. Lime wrote: "Encounters with moose and other wildlife should be thought of as more than simply viewing animals, even though this might be the most preferred form of encounters . . . Some get enjoyment from tracking animals through snow and over wet ground or simply from seeing fresh tracks."[5] The paper also discussed the changes in attitude being increasingly exhibited toward wildlife, from thinking of game as a source of food and a target for the hunter to game and wildlife having a wide spectrum of nonhunting recreational purposes.[6]

Today, in Maine's Baxter State Park, portions of which Thoreau passed through on his 1857 trip, "wildlife is one of the most popular activities . . . and moose are the number one species visitors hope to see. [Not only is it] exciting to see a moose in its native habitat [but it is] an opportunity to demonstrate respectful behavior toward these wild animals."[7] Such behavior of respect was often a theme underlying Thoreau writings about the wildlife he encountered, including the moose, and it was also a theme in the broader context of nature itself. Indeed, in a very fundamental way, it is about ethics—the ethics of conservation—summed up succinctly by the United States Forest Service in its "Wildlife Watchers Code of Ethics: Respect wildlife, Respect wildlife habitat, Respect the 'wildness' of wildlife, Respect other wildlife viewers and property."[8]

4. THE LAKES
"the lakes are something which you are unprepared for"
(written following the trip)

On August 9, 1854, Thoreau's book *Walden* was first published. In it he wrote: "A lake is a landscape's most beautiful and expressive feature. It is the Earth's eye; looking into which the beholder measures the depth of his own nature."[1] By the time he had published this insightful passage, he had paddled across several lakes on his way to climb Katahdin, including North Twin Lake where he was about to enter Pemadumcook Lake, one of Maine's largest lakes. At that time he observed that "the country is an archipelago of lakes—the lake country of New England."[2]

After the 1846 Katahdin trip, he wrote: "The lakes are something which you are unprepared for; they lie up so high, exposed to the light, and the forest is diminished to a fine fringe on their edges, with here and there a blue mountain, like amethyst jewels set around some jewel of the first water,--so anterior, so superior, to all the changes that are to take place on their shores, even now civil and refined, and fair as they can ever be."[3] In the 1980s, more than a hundred years after Thoreau's death, some of the lakes he paddled were evaluated and considered for land use controls to protect their scenic character and guide growth toward their capacity for development. Thoreau came close to seeing two rated for their exceptional character: Katahdin Lake and Lobster Lake.[4]

Dean B. Bennett

Today, the State of Maine recognizes that "lakes are an integral part of our landscape, covering more than a million acres of our state . . . [and] provide immensely valuable habitat for fish and wildlife, numerous recreational opportunities for people, and drinking water for nearly two-thirds of our population." Many lakes define communities, and "people relate to lakes in a way that is profoundly important to them and their families." Because of these values, the State "is charged with protecting Maine lakes and regulating certain human activities that affect habitat and water quality," as well as degradation by eutrophication, invasive species, and other factors.[5]

The conservation and protection of lakes, however, takes vigilance on the part of citizens working through their government and organizations at many levels. Maine's lakes, like lakes everywhere, have, from time to time, experienced threats from interests in conflict with or who lack understanding of the public and environmental values of lakes.

Today, from a global perspective, some of the largest lakes in the world are under pressure from threats. An article on the website of the organization Circle of Blue suggests that "while there is an array of symptoms afflicting large lakes—from invasive species to harmful algae to declining water levels—the root cause is water management systems that are slow to put ecological health above industrial and agricultural interests."[6] Or perhaps, as Thoreau said, we need to look into the Earth's eye and measure the depth of our own nature.

5. LOONS

"a solitary loon, like a living wave,--a vital spot on the
lake's surface,--laughed and frolicked"
September 5, 1846

Finding the smooth waters of a lake in the early part of his 1846 trip to Katahdin, Thoreau saw ducks sailing here and there and a loon, "a vital spot on the lake's surface." One "laughed and frolicked, and showed its straight leg for [his] amusement."[1] Thoreau was captivated by the call of the loon, and his book, *The Maine Woods*, contains several references to the presence of this bird. When he was paddling along the eastern shore of Moosehead Lake at the beginning of his Allagash-East Branch trip in 1857, he wrote that he saw and heard loons, which his Native guide Joe Polis called *medawisla* and said that it was a sign of wind.[2] In Abenaki folklore, *medawisla* is a loon who serves as messenger of the gods, and it was perhaps Polis's way of saying that they should be mindful of the dangers of the wind and waves.

Later in that same trip, Thoreau and his party, after settling down to sleep on the shore of Chamberlain Lake, "heard the voice of the loon, from far over the lake. It is a very wild sound," he wrote, "quite in keeping with the place and circumstances of the traveler, and very unlike the voice of a bird. I could lie awake for hours listening to it, it is so thrilling."[3] Indeed, loons continue to thrill a great many who live in Maine and visit the state. Nearly 900 people volunteered to participate in the Maine Audubon annual loon count in 2016 in a survey of more than 300 lakes and ponds. The result was a count of 2,848 adult loons and 384 chicks in the southern half of the state. The count is part of Maine Audubon Society's Maine Loon Project begun in 1977. The project involves education and outreach programs, research, and management activities aimed at protecting loons.[4]

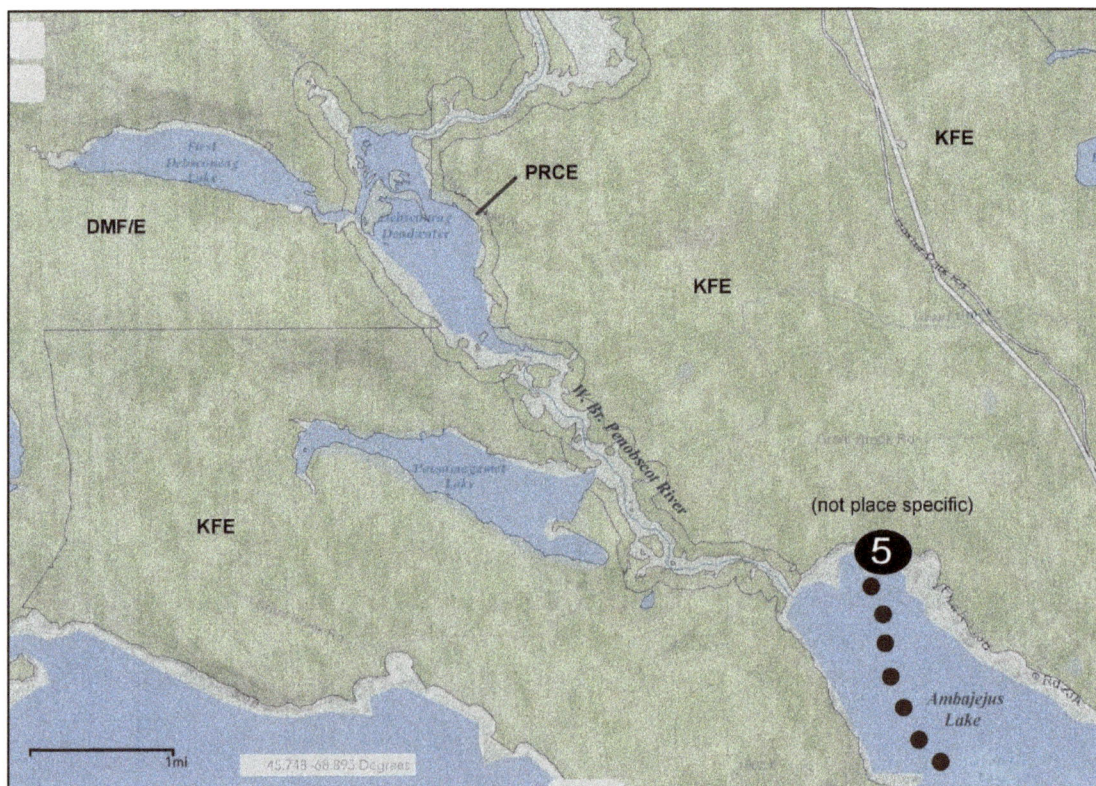

Dean B. Bennett

Major threats to loons in Maine include habitat loss due to development, boating activity that causes disturbance to nesting areas, and lead poisoning. Lead ingested by loons from lost lead sinkers and other fishing equipment is the leading cause of death for loons in Maine and throughout New England. Water quality is also a factor. Clean, clear water is necessary for loons to see and catch their prey fish. Invasive plants, acidification, high levels of mercury, and fluctuating water levels are also detrimental to loons.[5]

When Thoreau entered Second Lake in the waters of the East Branch of the Penobscot, he wrote that "the morning was a bright one, and perfectly still and serene, the lake was smooth as glass . . . the laugh of some loons, sporting in a concealed western bay, as if inspired by the morning, come distinct over the lake to us, and, what was remarkable, the echo which ran around the lake was much louder than the original note. . . we were exactly in the focus of many echoes, the sound being reflected like light from a concave mirror."[6] For many places in Maine today, the call of the loon is a call for conservation, to be echoed throughout the world.

6. DEBSCONEAG FALLS

"The falls . . . [Katepskonegan] where we stopped to dine
are considerable and quite picturesque"
September 6, 1846

After leaving Ambajejus Lake, Thoreau and his party poled up a mile of rapids, portaged around a falls, and paddled through a small lake to another falls, Passamagamet Falls. They warped up the falls, pulling, poling, pushing, lifting, and moving the boat forward any way they could. At the top of the falls, they paddled through a shallow, weedy deadwater before coming to Katepskonegan Falls, now named Debsconeag Falls, which means "carrying place."[1] Here, the party carried around and stopped to dine. Thoreau observed that "The falls are considerable and picturesque."[2]

Thoreau's view of the falls was also one of the conclusions by Janet McMahon, the author of *Maine's Whitewater Rapids*, a planning report for Maine's Critical Areas Program. The program was established by the Maine Legislature in 1974 to encourage and coordinate the conservation of Maine's natural features that have statewide importance because of their unusual natural, scenic, or scientific significance. Because Debsconeag Falls has characteristics of both whitewater rapids and waterfalls, the State's reports for both have been used here to describe the falls, and both concur with Thoreau's observations.[3]

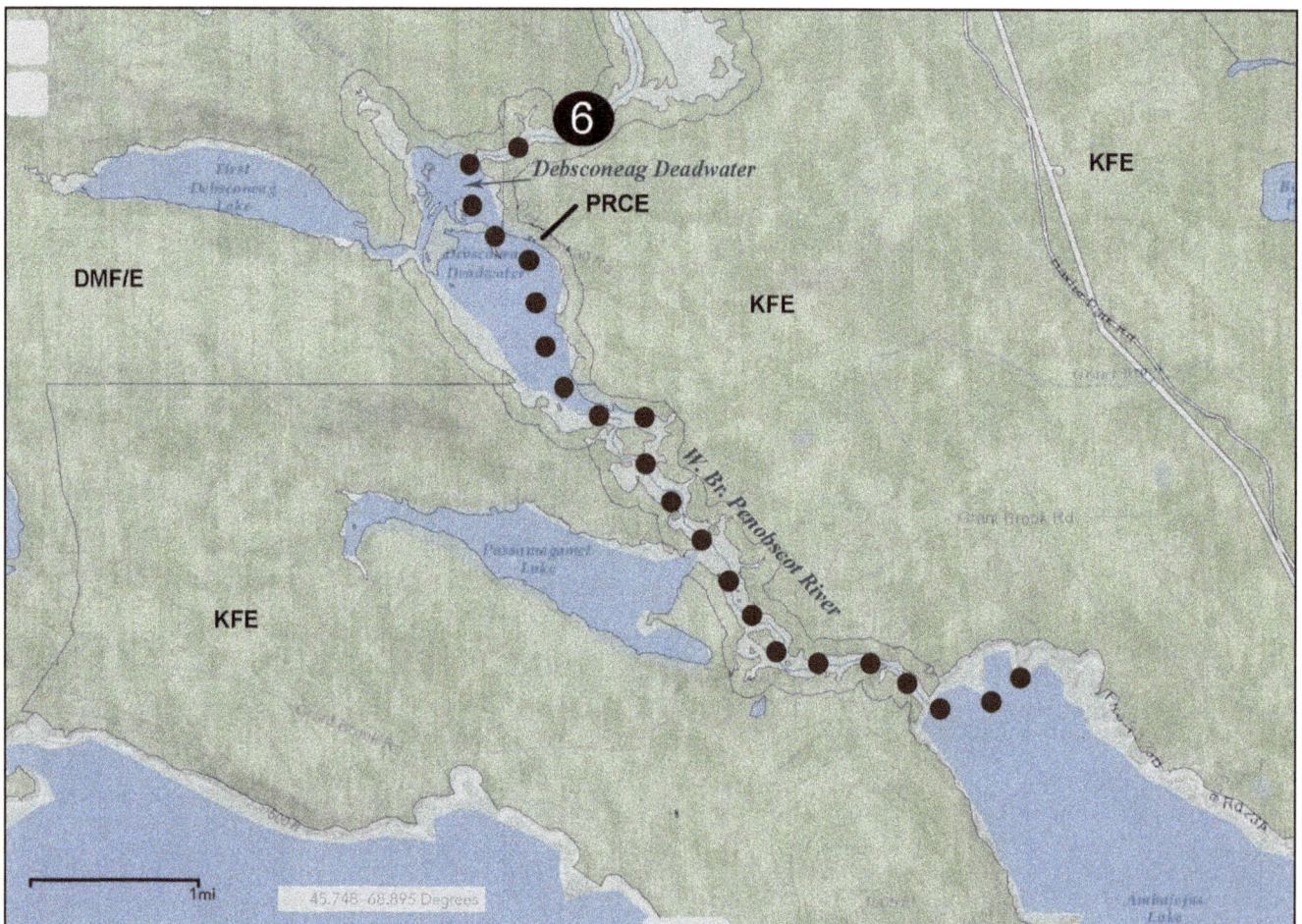

Debsconeag Falls is a magnificent 1,300-foot-long stretch of class IV-V rapids, meaning that they have violent turbulence and range from difficult to extremely difficult to maneuver through. The stretch of falls is steeply pitched, dropping 28 feet in its length. It is about 200 feet wide. Huge boulders in the riverbed contribute to the extreme turbulence. Historically, this was a difficult section of the river for log driving, and many log jams occurred here. The area is also an important nursery for landlocked salmon, as well as an exceptionally scenic area with an outstanding view of Katahdin. The riverbanks are forested with mature stands of white pine, white birch, poplar, and northern white cedar along the water's edge.

In 2002, an easement was negotiated between the Great Northern Paper Company and The Nature Conservancy to protect the natural features in the area and called it **DMF/E** on the map for its name, **Debsconeag Matrix**. The **F** stands for "Fee purchase" and the **E** is for "Easement purchase." A conservation matrix is an environment or natural area in the landscape that supports natural values, such as clean water and important habitat, and cultural values, such as scenic beauty. A conservation matrix also maintains critical ecological connections and supports ecological integrity and landscape sustainability.

And in 1981, a conservation easement for the river corridor in this area was also obtained from the Great Northern Paper Company. So today, if Thoreau were to visit Debsconeag Falls, he would find it little changed and could take some comfort in its recognition and protection for the special natural features he admired on his carry.

7. POCKWOCKAMUS DEADWATER

"the forenoon was . . . serene and placid on this
wild stream in the woods"
September 6, 1846

After portaging around the clamorous and turbulent Debsconeag Falls, Thoreau was struck by the peacefulness of the deadwater above. "We were occasionally startled by the scream of a bald-eagle," he wrote, "sailing over the stream in front of our batteau; or of the fish-hawks, on whom he levies his contributions. There were, at intervals, small meadows of a few acres on the sides of the stream, waving with uncut grass."[1]

We learn from Thoreau that these deadwaters had value for the grass he saw growing in them. The "uncut grass," he said, "attracted the attention of our boatmen, who regretted that they were not nearer to their clearings, and calculated how many stacks they might cut. Two or three men sometimes spend the summer by themselves, cutting the grass in these meadows, to sell to the loggers in the winter, since it will fetch a higher price on the spot than in any market in the State."[2]

Pockwockamus Deadwater was also valued by moose. Landing on a small island covered with this same kind of grass, Thoreau and his party stopped to "consult about our further course, we noticed the recent track of a moose, a large, roundish hole, in the soft wet ground, evincing the great size and weight of the animal that made it. They are fond of the water, and visit all these island-meadows, swimming as easily from island to island as they make their way through thickets on land."[3]

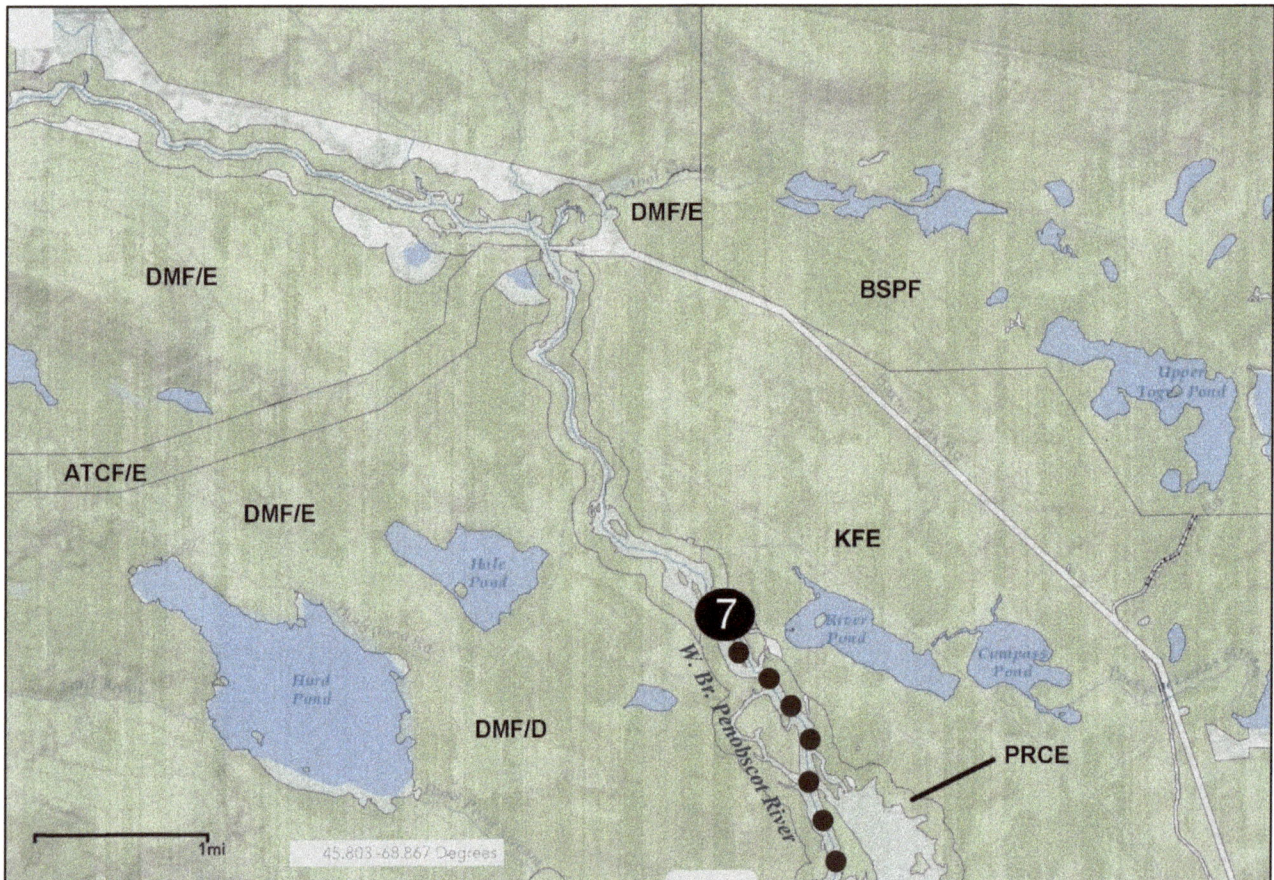

The islands in the deadwater must have created something of a maze for the party to make their way through, for Thoreau noted that "now and then we passed . . . a poke-logan, an Indian term for what the [log] drivers might have reason to call a poke-logs-in, an inlet that leads nowhere. If you get in, you have got to get out again the same way. These, and frequent 'run-rounds' which come into the river again, would embarrass an inexperienced voyager not a little."[4]

Here, in Pockwockamus Deadwater, a delightful conservation education opportunity has been created by Katahdin Forest Management LLC: the River Pond Nature Trail. The trail takes the visitor out into the area Thoreau passed by and about which he wrote. A short access road on the south side of the Golden Road, about 15 miles northwest of Millinocket toward Baxter State Park, leads to an attractive kiosk with a map of the River Pond Nature Trail. The trail is actually several trails that lead to the West Branch of the Penobscot and Pockwockamus Deadwater, a black spruce plantation, the shore of River Pond with its striking views of Katahdin, and, perhaps, even a moose.[5]

As you will note on the accompanying map, conserved land surrounds the nature trail property. The trail and the land, together, suggest a message of conservation and give the visitor an intimate view of this country since Thoreau first described it in 1846.

8. POCKWOCKAMUS FALLS

"the carry . . . was exceedingly rough and rocky"
September 6, 1846

When you first look up the river to Pockwockamus Falls, your eye is drawn to one thing—Katahdin, in the distance, massive, deceivingly rugged in its soft, purplish splendor, its body, broken and worn—parts of it lying in the rubble of Pockwockamus Falls. This is what Thoreau saw. It's what had drawn him here on September 6, 1846.

"The carry around Pockwockomus Falls," Thoreau wrote, "was exceedingly rough and rocky, the batteau having to be lifted directly from the water up four or five feet onto a rock, and launched again down a similar bank. The rocks on this portage were covered with the *dents* made by the spikes in the lumberers' boots while staggering over under the weight of their batteaux; and you could see where the surface of some large rocks on which they had rested their batteaux was worn quite smooth with use. As it was, we had carried over but half the usual portage at this place for this stage of water, and launched our boat in the smooth wave just curving to the fall, prepared to struggle with the most violent rapid we had to encounter. The rest of the party walked over the remainder of the portage, while I remained with the boatmen to assist in warping up."[1]

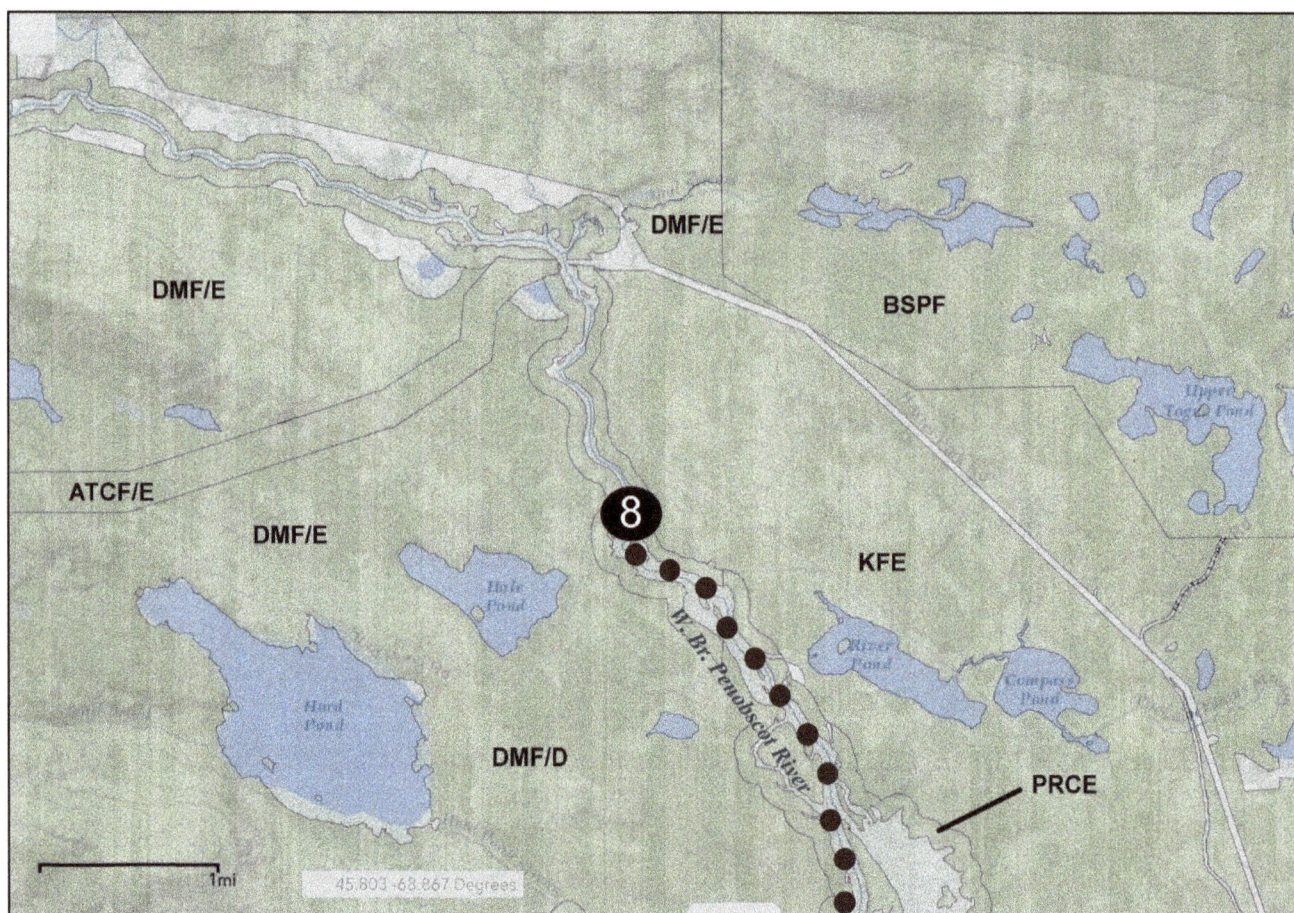

If Thoreau knew the meaning of the name of these falls after that exertion, he might have considered it strange, indeed, for it describes anything but the wild, chaotic rushing of water tumbling down a rocky slope he encountered. To the Penobscot Natives, Pockwockamus meant a lake or deadwater on the Penobscot, thus,

Pockwockamus Falls was named for the two-and-a-half-mile stretch of quieter, calmer waters of the Pock-wockamus Deadwater over which Thoreau and his party had just rowed and poled.[2]

Nearly a century and a half after Thoreau's visit, his observations were confirmed by Maine's recognition of the falls as a natural area worthy of consideration for conservation. The half-mile long Class IV rapids contains two distinct pitches and one exceptionally steep drop. The upper pitch drops 8 feet in a distance of 860 feet, and the lower pitch drops 3 feet in a distance of 260 feet with impressive standing waves. The state's survey of waterfalls found it to be one of the best examples in Maine of falls formed over a lag deposit, an accumulation of coarse rock fragments after finer materials have washed away. The rapids serve as spawning grounds for brook trout and landlocked salmon.[3]

Something that did not escape the eyes of the scientists who evaluated the falls for the Maine's Critical Areas Program and especially did not Thoreau's as he assisted the boatmen over the falls was its "highly scenic and natural locale."[4] This observation, which the state made near the end of the twentieth century, would have probably resonated with the Concord naturalist more than any other about Pockwockamus Falls.

Dean B. Bennett

9. ABOL DEADWATER

"the last half-mile carried us to the Sowadnehunk dead-water
[now called Abol Deadwater]"
September 6, 1846

"As we poled up a swift rapid for half a mile above Aboljacarmegus Falls, some of the party read their own marks on the huge logs which lay piled up high and dry on the rocks on either hand, the relics probably of a jam which had taken place here in the Great Freshet in the spring."[1] It was the lumberman's practice to mark the end of each log with a mark identifying it with the individual or company owning the log. When the log reached the mill or other destination after its journey down a river, it was sorted in a boom with all the other logs having the same mark. On the logging drives, there were opportunities for logs to sink or become stranded on riverbanks, as Thoreau saw, and never reach their destinations.

"The last half-mile carried us to the Sowadnehunk dead-water [now known as Abol Deadwater], so called from the stream of the same name, meaning 'running between mountains,'" Thoreau recorded. Here, he and his party camped on September 6, 1846, somewhere near "Murch and Aboljacknagesic" streams, now called Katahdin and Abol respectively. Thoreau estimated that the deadwater was about a "dozen miles from the summit" of Katahdin. In miles, as the crow flies, the distance was actually only about five miles.[2]

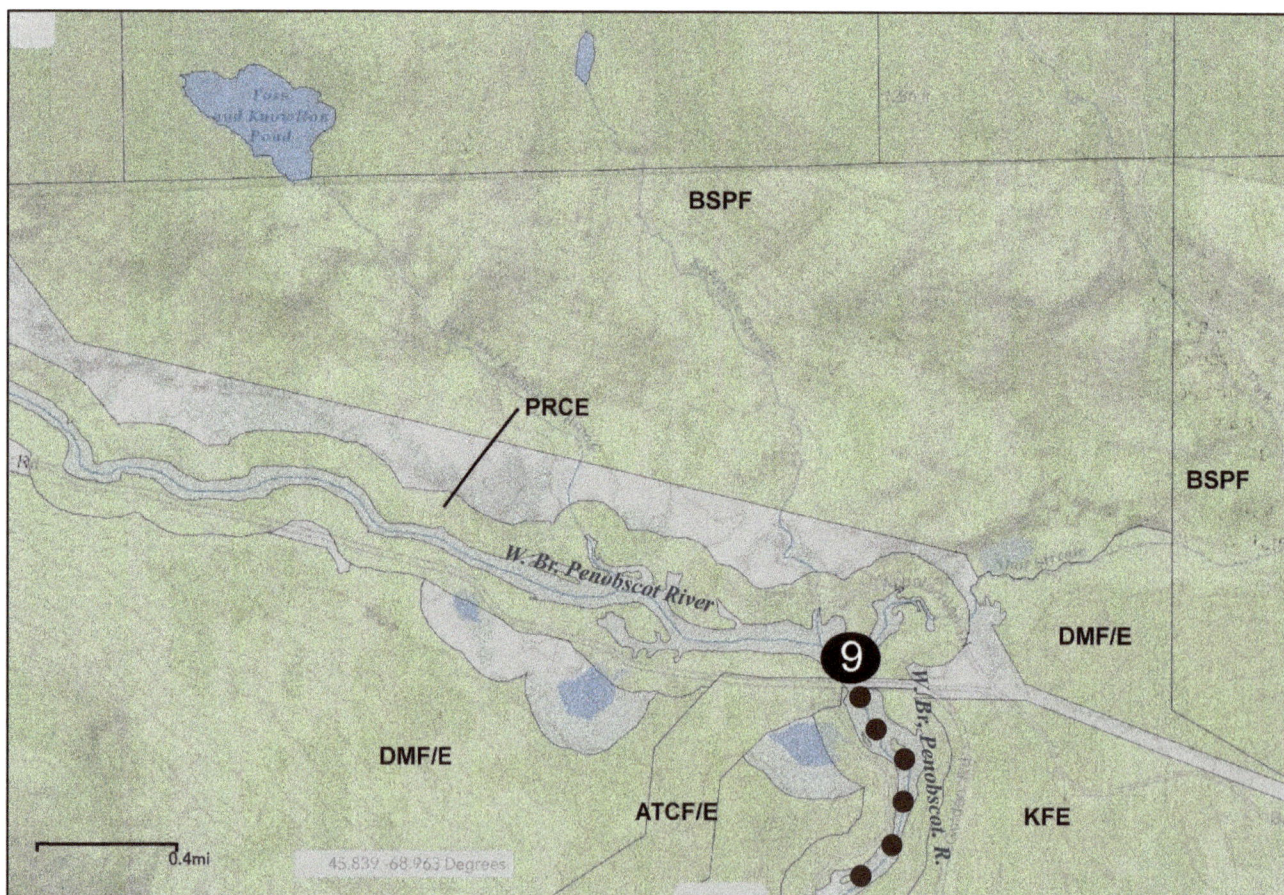

Today, if Thoreau once again ascended the West Branch, the changes he would find upon reaching Abol Deadwater would be enormous—certainly difficult to have imagined from what he saw there in 1846. Just before entering the deadwater, he would have passed under a bridge over the river, known as Abol Bridge. The road passing over the river at the bridge is a 96-mile-long private road built by Great Northern Paper Company to carry logs in large trucks rather than drive them down the river to its mill in Millinocket. The road, called the Golden Road, opened in the early 1970s at a time when log driving ended in Maine, partly, at least, because of environmental concerns. The reasons for the choice of the road's name are not entirely clear. Some believe that it relates to the cost of the road and maintaining the network of roads of which it is a part, but the savings in shipping logs by truck were significant in time and money. What took months to transport timber to the mill took only days after the road was built.

Today, hikers who wish to climb Katahdin arrive at Abol Deadwater by the Golden Road or by the Appalachian Trail, which crosses Abol Bridge. From here, through-hikers and others can access trails that will take them to the top of Katahdin. On the shore of the deadwater there is now a privately operated campground which advertises a variety of outdoor activities, such as, canoeing, kayaking, rafting, fishing, swimming, and wildlife watching. Yet, despite all the changes here, most of the surrounding land is now protected by conservation measures and continues to provide breathtaking views of Katahdin and the river that are similar to what Thoreau first saw.

10. SPECKLED TROUT

"the speckled trout . . . glistened like the fairest flowers,
the product of primitive rivers"
September 6, 1846

Arriving at Abol Deadwater, Thoreau wrote that they had been told that "we should here find trout enough: so, while some prepared the camp, the rest fell to fishing. Seizing the birch-poles which some party . . . had left on the shore, and baiting our hooks with pork, and with trout, as soon as they were caught, we cast our lines into the mouth of the Aboljacknagesic, a clear, swift, shallow stream, which came in from Ktaadn . . . alternately the speckled trout, and the silvery roaches, swallowed the bait as fast as we could throw it in; and the finest specimens of both that I have ever seen, the largest one weighing three pounds, were heaved upon the shore, though at first in vain, to wriggle down into the water again, for we stood in the boat; but soon we learned to remedy this evil; for one, who had lost his hook, stood on shore to catch them as they fell in a perfect shower around him,–sometimes, wet and slippery, full in his face and bosom, as his arms were outstretched to receive them. While yet alive, before their tints had faded, they glistened like the fairest flowers, the product of primitive rivers; and he could hardly trust his senses as he stood over them, that these jewels should have swam away in that Aboljacknagesic water for so long, so many dark ages–these bright fluviatile flowers, seen of Indians only, made beautiful, the Lord only knows why, to swim there! . . . . But there is the rough voice of [one] who commands at the frying-pan, to send over what you've got, and then you may stay till morning. The pork sizzles, and cries for fish."[1]

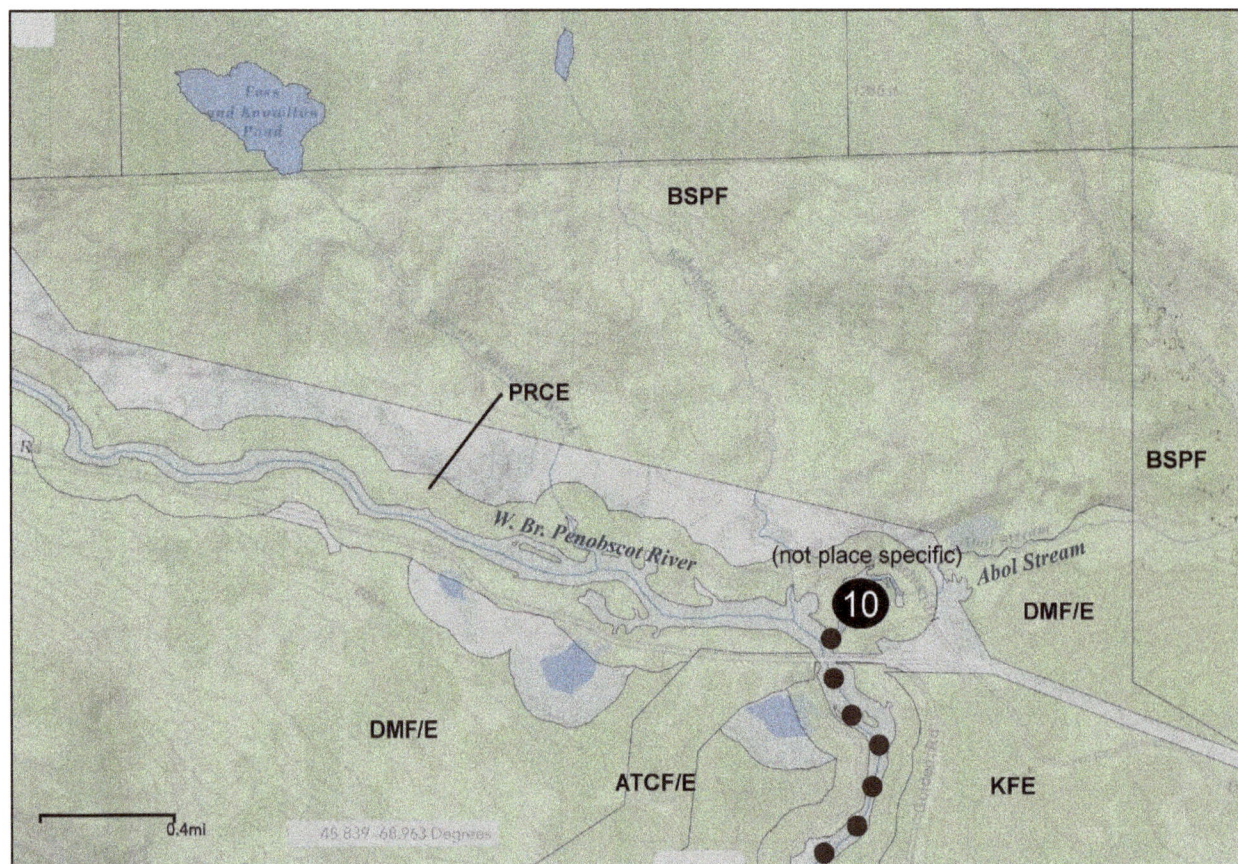

Today, the Maine Department of Inland Fisheries and Wildlife (DIF&W) is actively promoting the conservation of Maine's population of wild and native brook trout. DIF&W reports on its website that almost 10 percent of Maine's 6,000 lakes and ponds, or a total of 555, feature wild and native brook trout, which represent a "unique, valuable, and irreplaceable resource."[2]

The Maine Council of Trout Unlimited (TU) website states that the organization's mission is to conserve, protect, and restore Maine's coldwater fisheries and their watersheds. "Maine is home to the nation's last Atlantic salmon, the last native landlocked salmon and to more than 97% of the nation's native and wild brook trout ponds." The organization states that it carries out its conservation mission "with five Maine chapters and about 1,500 member-volunteers, through on-the-ground restoration projects, advocacy for the waters we love, and education."[3]

Henry David Thoreau's brief but stimulating account of the speckled trout at Abol Deadwater gives even the non-angler pause to consider the importance of this species' conservation.

11. MOOSE SKELETON

"there was the skeleton of a moose here"
September 6, 1846

While at their campsite on Abol Deadwater, Thoreau wrote that "there is the skeleton of a moose here, whose bones some Indian hunters had picked on this very spot."[1] In Thoreau's day, moose skeletons might also have been found in the woods as a result of hunters taking only a few choice parts and leaving the rest of their moose. On occasion, moose skeletons are still found in the north woods as a result of poaching or, in a rare instance, by being mistakenly shot by a hunter and left in the woods. The chance of adult moose being killed by predators other than humans is low in Maine because those capable of killing a large fully-grown moose are rare or absent in the state, although calf moose may be preyed upon by black bears. Of course, moose die of sickness and disease, of which they are especially vulnerable in old age. The average life expectancy for a cow is eight years and for a bull it is seven years.[2]

Toward the end of the twentieth century, climate change became a growing concern for wildlife in the north woods. By a decade and a half into the twenty-first century, the effects of warmer winters and drier summers in the north woods were already being seen. These conditions favored two major parasites that can cause extensive mortality in Maine's moose population: brain worm and winter tick.

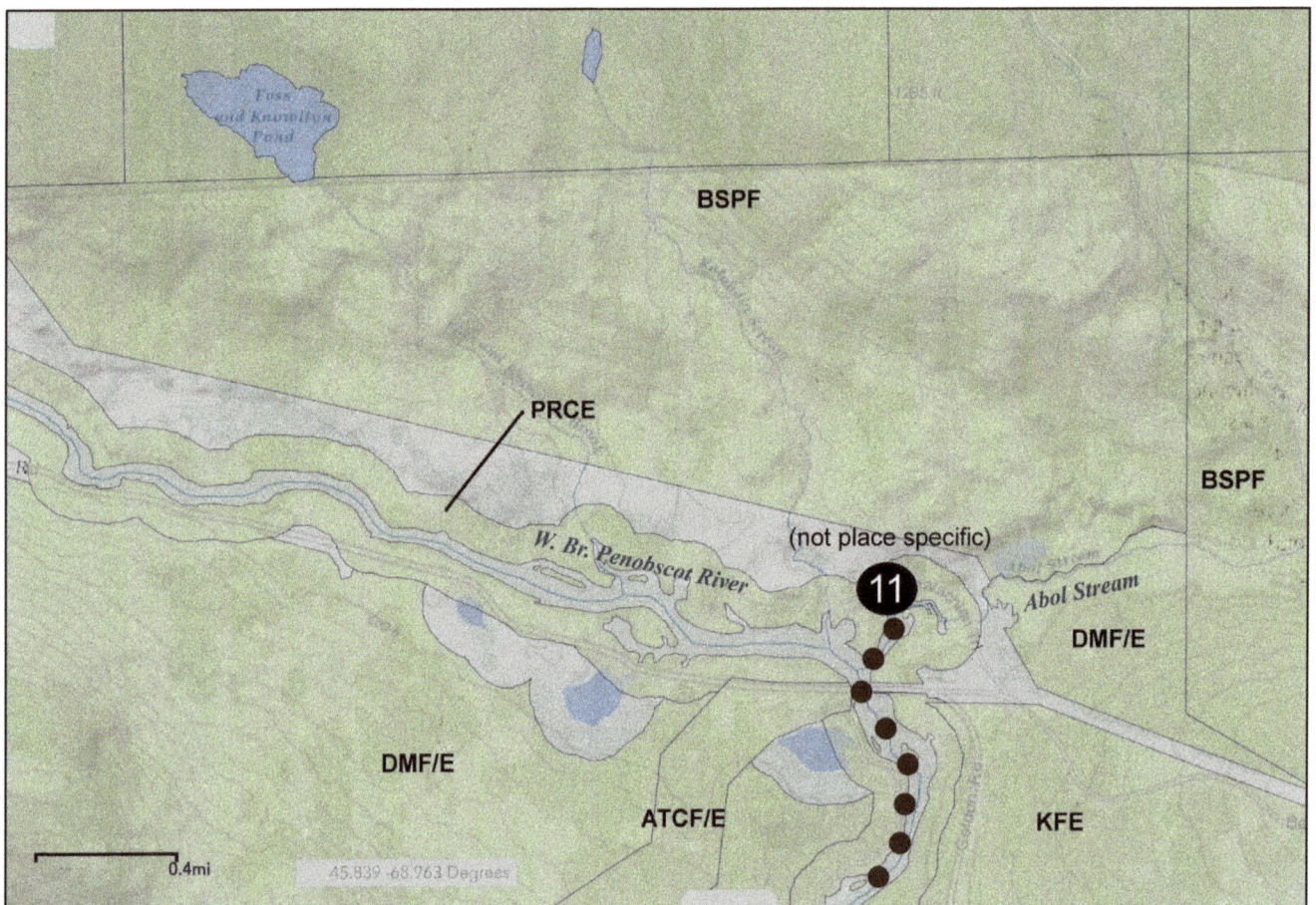

Dean B. Bennett

Brain worm, which commonly infects the white-tailed deer, was gradually introduced into the moose population in the twentieth century as deer moved into southern portions of moose range.[3] In moose it causes a disease of the nervous system and often death. In the twenty-first century as winters continued to warm, winter ticks began taking a hideous toll on moose. For example, researchers in 2014 reported finding more than 100,000 ticks on one moose.[4] In 2016, Maine's leading moose biologist reported that at least 50 percent of moose calves died in their first year.[5] The ticks left ravaged, emaciated, thin, weak, tottery, wretched-looking moose with great bloody patches where hair and skin had been rubbed off, giving rise to the term *ghost* moose. This devastation of the moose herd in the north woods was summed up by the title of an article in *Scientific American* in 2012: "Rapid Climate Changes Turn North Woods into Moose Graveyard." With a majority in the scientific community believing that humans are at least partly to blame for climate warming, we are now facing one of our greatest moral conservation challenges, symbolized, perhaps, by the moose skeleton pictured here.

The skeleton was found floating in the outlet stream of a bog in the late 1990s near where Thoreau passed by on one of his Maine woods trips. It was picked as clean as the one Thoreau saw at Abol Deadwater. Unfortunately, we will never know the exact cause of death.

12. UNBROKEN FOREST

"what is most striking in the Maine wilderness
is the continuousness of the forest"
(written following the trip)

After he had chronicled his 1846 trip to the Maine woods and, in his words, "steaming his way to Massachusetts," Thoreau reflected on what he had seen. "What is most striking in the Maine wilderness," he wrote, "is the continuousness of the forest, with fewer open intervals or glades than you had imagined. Except the few burnt-lands, the narrow intervals on the rivers, the bare tops of high mountains, and the lakes and streams, the forest is uninterrupted. It is even more grim and wild than you had anticipated, a damp and intricate wilderness, in the spring everywhere wet and miry. The aspect of the country, indeed, is universally stern and savage, excepting the distant views of the forest from hills, and the lake prospects, which are mild and civilizing in a degree."[1]

Today, looking north toward Katahdin from the West Branch of the Penobscot River and Abol Deadwater, most of the land and its forest is in Baxter State Park, owned by the State of Maine and held in trust with most of the land to be "forever wild." Here, the first priority for management is to protect wilderness and, secondarily, to provide for recreation. When Governor Percival purchased the more than 200,000 acres and gave it to the State of Maine for a park, most of the acreage was cut-over land. Under its "forever wild" mandate, however, it will eventually return to a state of wildness.

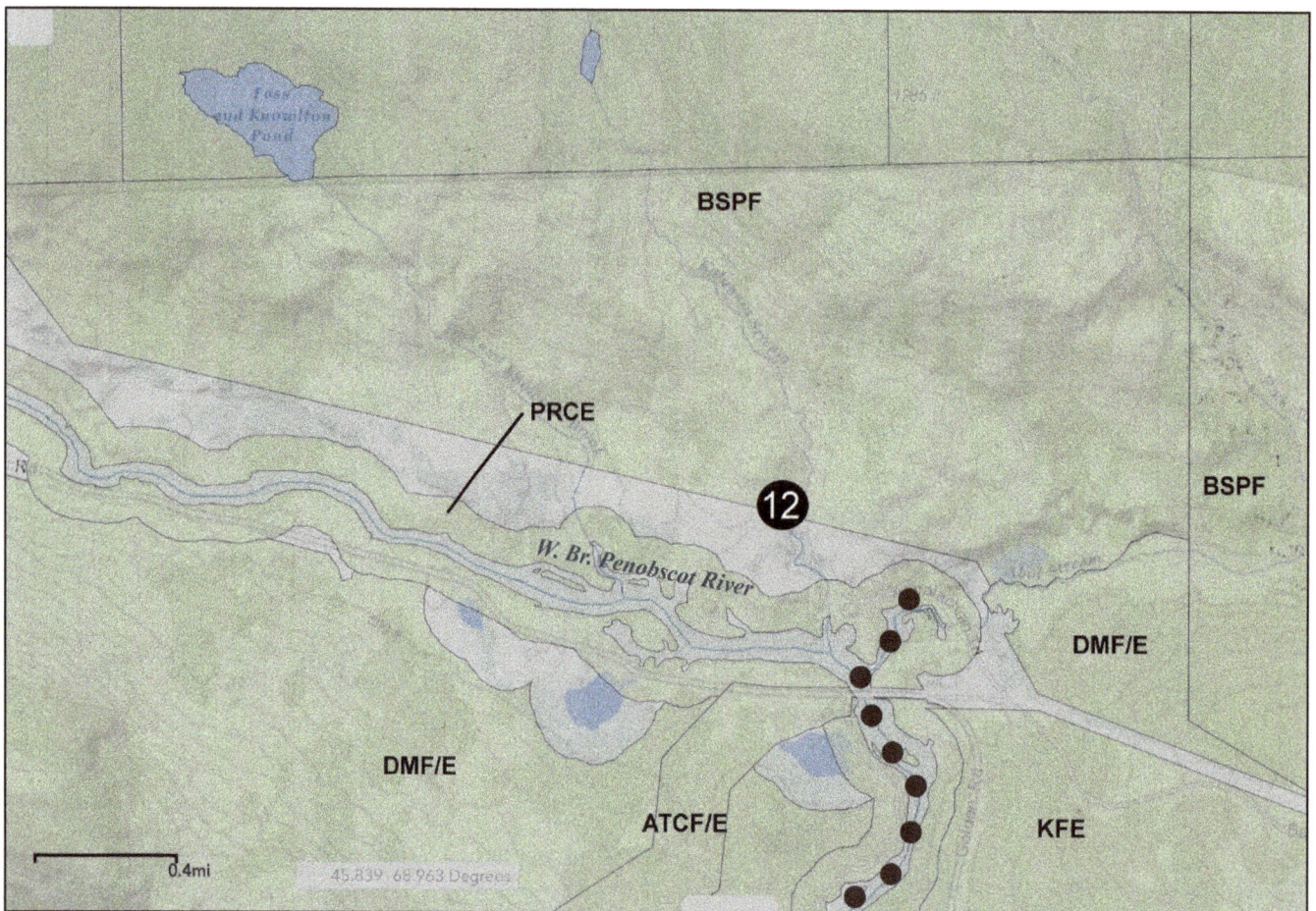

We have in Baxter State Park, which, in size, covers several townships, a large old-growth forest of the future in the making—a demonstration of nature's ability to renew itself. The forested landscape in the park will eventually have what many preserved wilderness areas in the eastern United States do not have: low elevation old-growth forests. Many of the areas set aside as wilderness won the necessary support for wilderness preservation only when they focused on higher elevation areas and areas not as easily harvested for timber. This wasn't the case here: Governor Baxter bought all the land in several townships.

There is no doubt that Thoreau also would have admired what Governor Baxter did: preserving nearly 200,000 acres for wilderness. It was one of the finest demonstrations by one individual of the land ethic espoused by Aldo Leopold, one of the founders of the idea of preserving wilderness in America. Leopold said that "a thing is right when it tends to preserve the integrity, stability, and beauty of the biotic community. It is wrong when it tends otherwise."[2]

Thoreau, undoubtedly, would have also agreed with the Wilderness Act signed into law shortly after Baxter's final acquisition for the park. With this act, we became the first country to make the preservation of wilderness a national policy. Wilderness became defined "as an area where the earth and its community of life are untrammeled by man," where people are visitors only.[3]

13. GRAY LICHENS

"the spruce and cedar . . . hung with gray lichens,
looked . . . like the ghosts of trees"
September 5, 1846

Along the shores of the waters and nearby forests Thoreau encountered, he noted: "The spruce and cedar . . . hung with gray lichens, looked at a distance like the ghosts of trees."[1] The lichen, *Usnea*, the genus name for a shrubby lichen of the fruticose group, is the lichen Thoreau saw. It was probably the Old Man's Beard lichen, a pendulous lichen that drapes the limbs of trees and waves in a breeze. Its yellow or greenish color and appearance in certain situations could suggest that the forest is unhealthy and death close at hand or even present. In the gloom of certain light, the lichen-covered trees tend to impart a mysteriousness. Four years before Thoreau had given his impression of the gray lichen scene, he had written: "Nature is mythical and mystical, always."[2] Perhaps he was thinking of that when he coined the term "ghosts of trees."

Although there is no doubt that Thoreau appreciated lichens on an aesthetic level, the extent of his understanding of them in the context of the study of natural history is not entirely clear. Ray Angelo, author of "Thoreau as Botanist: An Appreciation and Critique," mentioned that "in the winter of 1852, when there were no flowers to observe, he undertook the study of lichens." In 1858, Thoreau, according to Angelo, began "the study of grasses and sedges in earnest . . . Other difficult plants groups, such as lichens, mosses, and fungi resisted study owing to the absence of good regional manuals. Consequently, excepting lichens, his

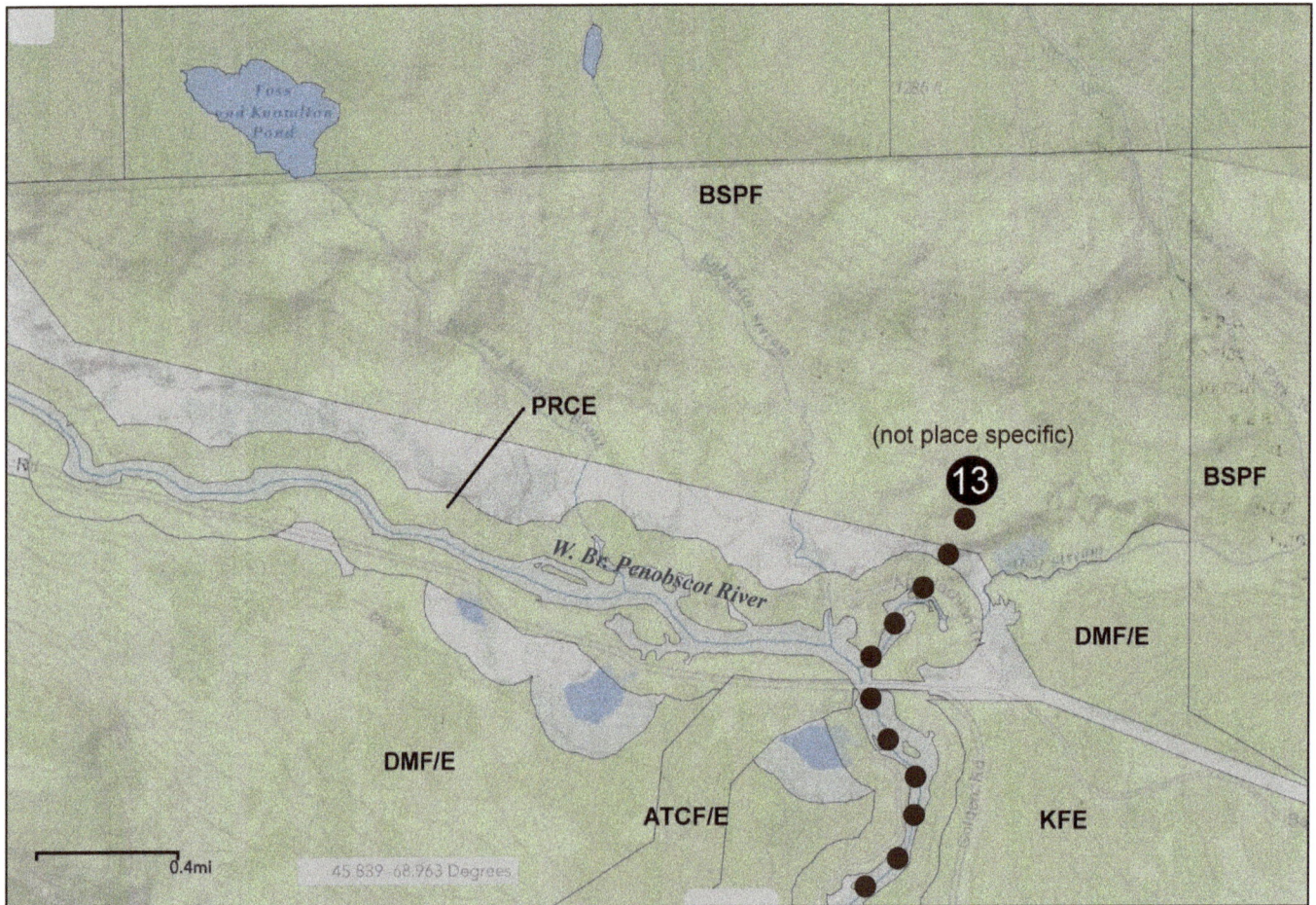

scientific references to these plant groups are minimal. Even with lichens he never came close to acquiring expertise comparable to what he achieved with vascular plants. In a short article entitled 'Thoreau, the Lichenist' lichenologist Heber Howe, Jr., commented that Thoreau's observations of lichens showed 'only a slight knowledge of species, and no technical grasp whatsoever.' But Howe, who studied lichens in Concord about sixty years after Thoreau, noted that Thoreau knew the varied morphological types and appreciated their place in Nature. (See *The Guide to Nature*, volume 5, pages 17-20, 1912.)"[3]

There are about 86 species of *Usnea* and a number of uses, depending on the species. Uses include herbal formulas for sore throats and skin infections, development of dyes, and production of cosmetics as a preservative and deodorant. In environmental conservation efforts, it is used as a bioindicator of air pollution because it seems to grow best where the air is clean. In unpolluted areas the lichen tends to grow longer, 10 to 20 cm, whereas in polluted areas it may grow to only a few millimeters.[4]

Lichens of the *Caliciales* species, also called "stubble lichens" because of their small size, have been used to indicate old-growth and ancient forests. Studies show that older stands of northern hardwoods and spruce-fir contain a greater total number of the species, thus indicating a greater continuity in the forests.[5]

14. DIVERSIFIED COUNTRY

"a country full of evergreen trees, of mossy silver birches,
and watery maples . . . strewn with damp and moss-grown
rocks . . . with the note of the . . . woodpecker"
(written after the trip)

On September 7, 1846, Thoreau and his party left their campsite on Abol Deadwater and, with packs and provisions, began their trek through the woods to the top of Katahdin. With his focus now on the forest instead of his water bound course and gaining elevation, Thoreau began to expand his understanding and appreciation of the natural diversity in the region. Returning home at the end of his trip to Katahdin, he wrote the following:

"It is a country full of evergreen trees, of mossy silver birches and watery maples, the ground dotted with insipid, small, red berries, and strewn with damp and moss-grown rocks,–a country diversified with innumerable lakes and rapid streams, peopled with trout and various species of *leucisci* [minnows], with salmon, shad, and pickerel, and other fishes; the forest resounding at rare intervals with the note of the chicadee, the blue-jay, and the woodpecker, the scream of the fish-hawk and the eagle, the laugh of the loon, and the whistle of ducks along the solitary streams; at night, with the hooting of owls and howling of wolves; in summer, swarming with myriads of black flies and mosquitoes, more formidable than wolves to the white man. Such is the home of the moose, the bear, the caribou, the wolf, the beaver, and the Indian . . . What a place to live, what a place to die and be buried in!"[1]

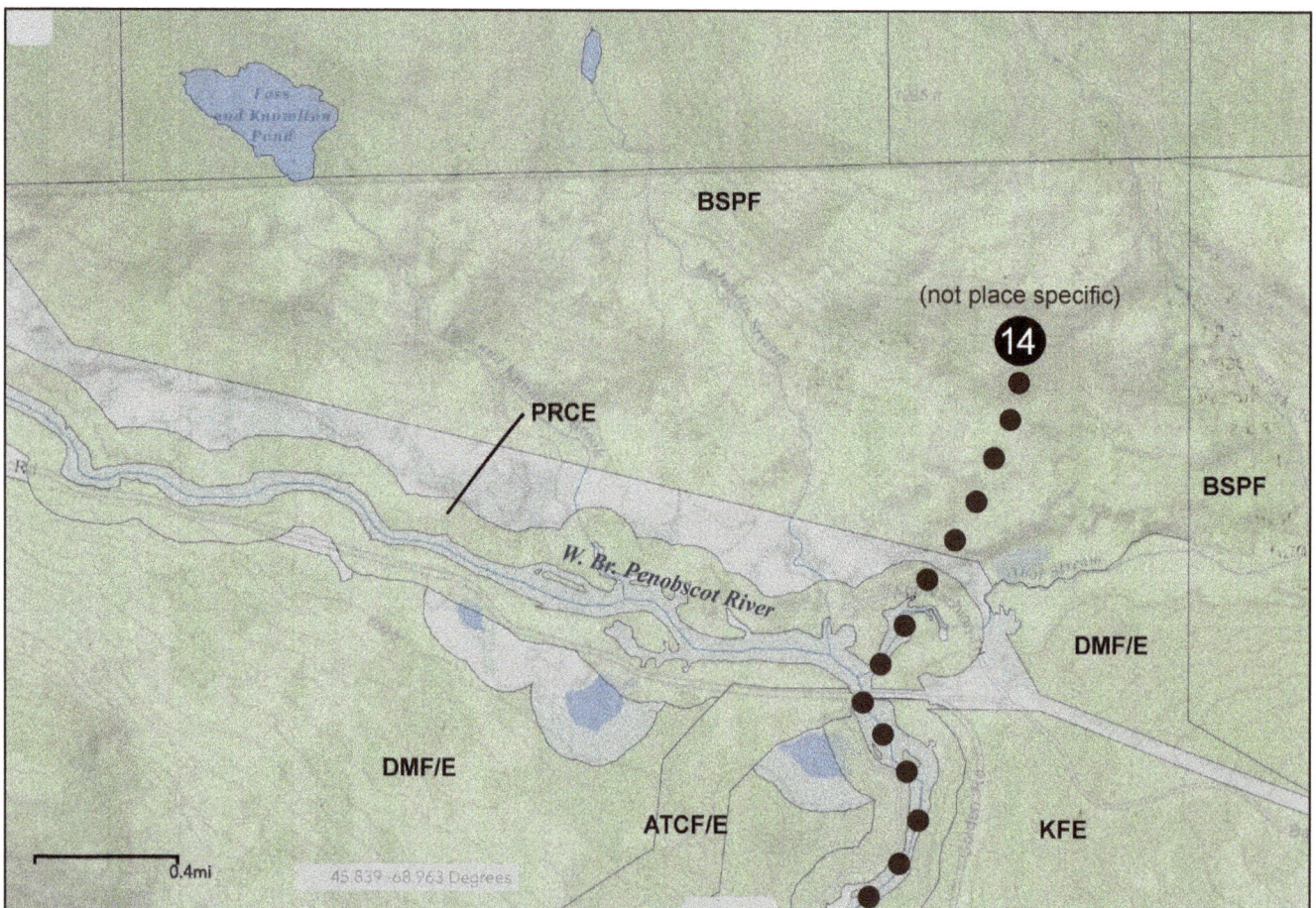

Dean B. Bennett

Thoreau's description of a "country diversified" is an early description of the region's biodiversity, a term that encompasses genes, species, and ecosystems. At an ecosystem level, species diversity, for example, provides renewable resources, increases stability in environmental change, and enhances cultural values associated with nature, *i.e.*, opportunities for study, inspiration, creativity, and leisure activities. However, the diversity of species on our planet is now threatened. The United Nations reported in 2019 that 1 million species on our planet are threatened with global extinction and the rate is accelerating.[2]

In Maine, the mission of the Maine Natural Areas Program (MNAP) in the state's government "is to ensure the maintenance of Maine's natural heritage for the benefit of present and future generations . . . [and to facilitate] informed decision-making in development planning, conservation, and natural resources management . . . With landowner permission, the program inventories lands that support rare and endangered plants, rare natural communities and ecosystems . . ." The program also works with scientists and other professionals in the international NatureServe Network to conserve biodiversity.[3]

Thoreau in *The Maine Woods* gives us a sense of Maine's natural heritage and many of the aspects of the diversity and values found in the north woods more than a century and a half ago. Even then he was well aware of the need for conservation.

15. OVERLOOKING THE COUNTRY

"I had soon cleared the trees, and paused . . . to look back over the country"
September 7, 1846

It is in the opening two paragraphs of *The Maine Woods* that we learn why Henry David Thoreau wished to make his excursion to Katahdin. It is, he said, "the second highest mountain in New England," and the approach from the West Branch of the Penobscot on the mountain's south side would allow him to see more wilderness, though he believed this approach more difficult, and to see the "glorious river and lake scenery," experience "the batteau and boatman's life," and encounter a "primitive forest."[1] From these words, we learn that he wished to experience a wild nature that challenged him physically, awed him aesthetically, enlarged his perspective of the natural world, and educated him about the lives of those who lived in such an environment. The trip also encouraged him to think about his spiritual and ethical relationship with the rest of nature, although this did not expressly appear among his hopes for the trip.

It was early in the morning of September 7, 1846, that Thoreau and his party left their campsite on Abol Deadwater to begin their trek to Katahdin and no trails to guide them. With Thoreau in the lead, they started over partially open, burned land toward the highest peak they could see. "This course," he wrote, "would lead us parallel to a dark seam in the forest, which marked the bed of a torrent, and over a slight spur, which extended southward from the main mountain, from whose bare summit we could get an outlook over the country . . . Seen from this point . . . Ktaadn presented a different aspect from any mountain I have seen, there being a greater proportion of naked rock rising abruptly from the forest; and we looked up at this blue barrier as if it were some fragment of a wall which anciently bounded the earth in that direction. Setting our compass for a northeast course . . . we were soon buried in the woods."[2]

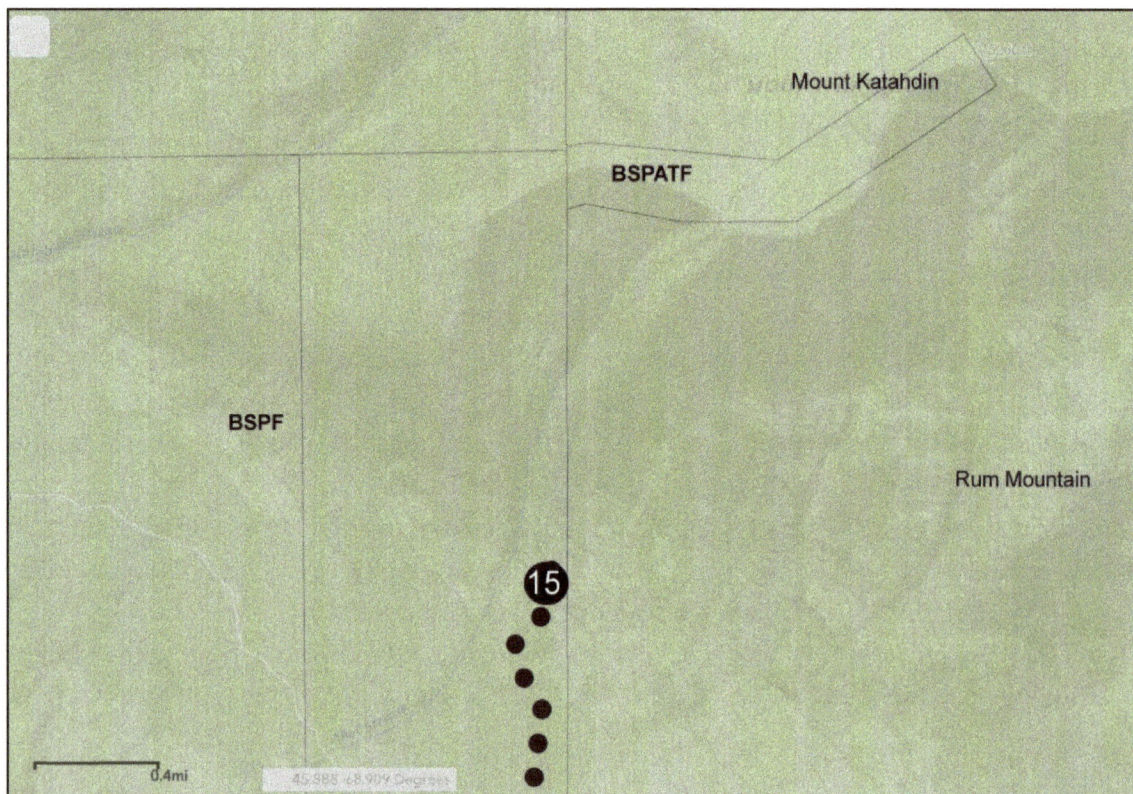

Working upward in the forest, Thoreau and his party stopped at four o'clock to camp in a place where there was water and a view of the summit. While his companions were preparing camp and with daylight still left, Thoreau started alone toward the summit "in a deep and narrow ravine, sloping up to the clouds, at an angle of nearly forty-five degrees," down which rushed a torrent of water in a mountain stream. Pulling himself up by the roots of small trees, scrambling on all fours, and "having slumped, scrambled, rolled, bounced, and walked, by turns, over this scraggy country, [he] arrived upon a side-hill . . . where rocks, gray, silent rocks, were flocks and herds that pastured, chewing a rocky cud at sunset. "They looked at me," he said, "with hard gray eyes, without a bleat or a low. This brought me to the skirt of a cloud and bounded my walk that night." He turned around.[3]

16. THOREAU'S KATAHDIN
"I entered within the skirts of the cloud"
September 8, 1846

You're on a trail just west of Thoreau's attempt to reach the top of Katahdin. A storm is approaching, and the ragged edges of dark clouds are lowering. Beyond them the mountains are still bathed in light and so is the trail crossing the rocky nubble below you. A breeze begins to stir the trailside shrubs—long trained to hunker down or to face away from the wind. Among them a water pipit looks for shelter. As the sky darkens, a raven skims down over the ledges, spots you, brakes, and swoops upward, screaming in surprise and alarm. You watch it soar into the mist enveloping the ridge above, and something catches your eye—a faint outline. You look in disbelief. It must be a boulder or a deformed shrub. In Thoreau's day, it could have been what it appears to be—a caribou.

Thoreau made two attempts to reach the summit of Katahdin. The first was in the late afternoon of September 7, 1846, when he left his companions who were seeking a place to camp, but he was blocked by low clouds and turned around. The next morning, the party began climbing together, but Thoreau soon left his companions behind and headed toward the mountain's peak shrouded in a mist. "The mountain," he wrote, "seemed a vast aggregation of loose rocks . . . They were the raw materials of a planet dropped from an unseen quarry . . . At length I entered within the skirts of the cloud . . . [and] a quarter of a mile farther . . . the summit of the ridge . . . the cloud-line ever rising and falling with the wind's intensity . . ."[1]

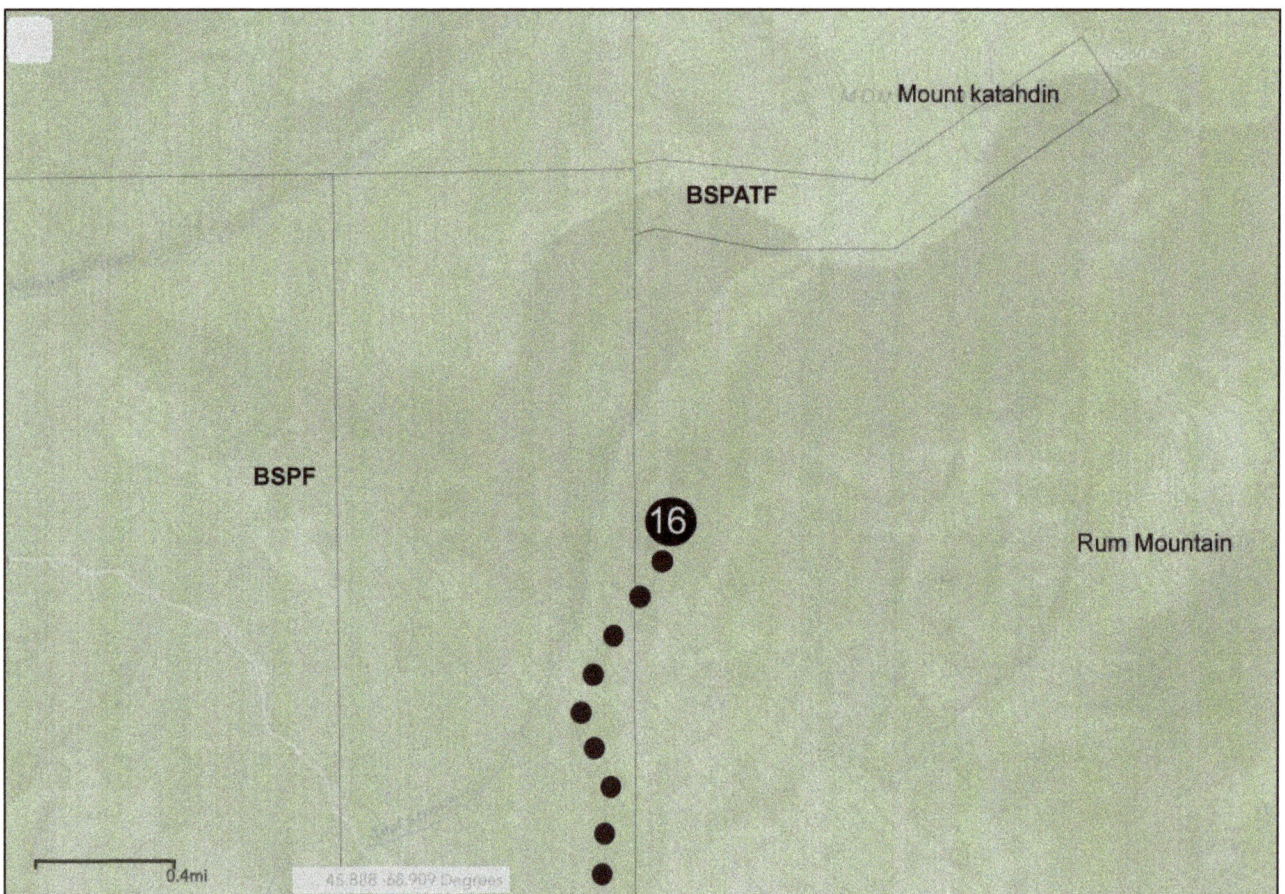

In this environment, Thoreau felt unwelcome. It was, to him, a place where one finds that a "vast Titanic, inhuman Nature has got him at disadvantage, caught him alone . . . [and] does not smile on him. She seems to say sternly, why came ye here before your time?"[2] He felt overpowered, unable to reason. His thinking, even his purpose was being challenged. This is a nature he thought was friendly, that he thought he could even care for and should. It was not the nature familiar to him—"the smiling and verdant plains and valleys [below] . . . . where men inhabit."[3]

On Katahdin, Thoreau had come face to face with a duality of feeling experienced by many who climb mountains. On one hand, some may feel a strong sense of an ability to overcome nature as an obstacle, or domination of nature, or triumphant egoism and, on the other hand, they may also feel greater respect for nature, or a deepening of an environmental ethic, or the acquisition of an ecological conscience as expressed in the literature of the organization Climb for Conservation.

If Thoreau sought to enlarge his perspective on his relationship with nature by journeying to Katahdin, he was successful.

17. BEYOND REACH

"the tops of mountains are the unfinished
parts of the globe"
September 8, 1846

On a ridge below the summit hoping to get sight of it, Thoreau wrote: "Sometimes it seemed as if the summit would be cleared in a few moments, and smile in sunshine; but what was gained on one side was lost on another . . . Occasionally, . . . I caught sight of a dark, damp crag . . . The tops of mountains are among the unfinished parts of the globe . . ."[1] For Thoreau, on that day, nature would not lift her tantalizing scrim of mist through which he attempted to peer at what lay beyond. No. Instead she manipulated how deeply his eyes were allowed to penetrate the scene, leaving him to stare and imagine what was there and denying him a view of the summit. The top of Katahdin would always remain a mystery to him. He had come so close to his goal of reaching the top of this mountain and the moment he had long imagined. Yet, he knew that he had not been unrewarded, for the experience had given him a much deeper view of nature and himself.

"Compelled to descend," he wrote, "occasionally . . . the wind would blow me a vista open, through which I could see the country eastward, boundless forests, and lakes, and streams, gleaming in the sun, some of them emptying into the East Branch."[2] Thus, unknowingly, he viewed the destination of his final trip into the Maine woods a little over a decade later.

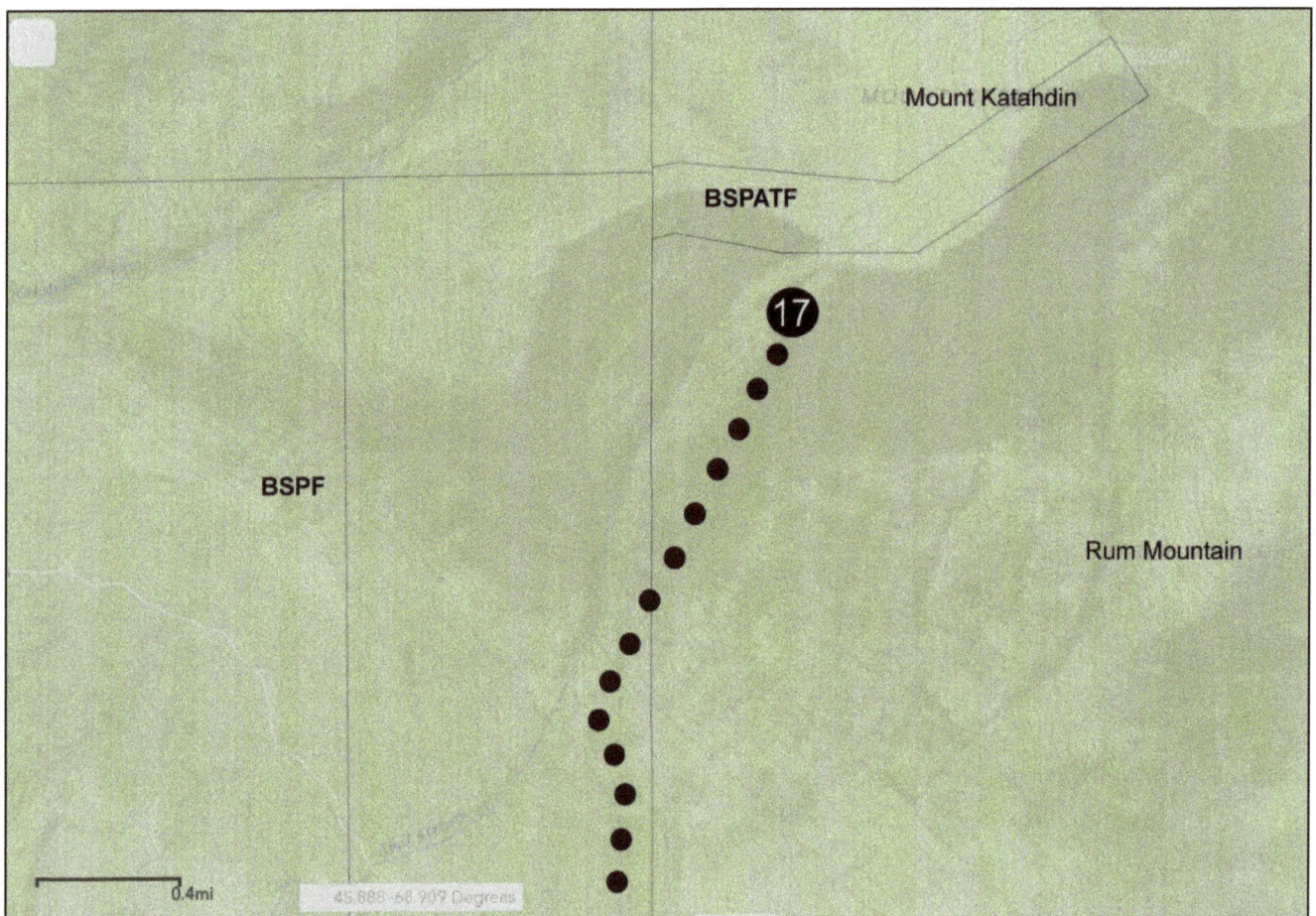

On their way back to Abol Deadwater and the river, Thoreau and his party passed "over 'Burnt Lands,' . . . exceedingly wild and desolate .. . . It is difficult to conceive of a region uninhabited by man. We habitually presume his presence and influence everywhere. And yet we have not seen pure Nature, unless we have seen her thus vast and drear and inhuman, though in the midst of cities. Nature was here something savage and awful, though beautiful. . . It was the fresh and natural surface of the planet Earth . . . Man was not to be associated with it. It was Matter, vast, terrific . . . I stand in awe of my body, this matter to which I am bound has become so strange to me . . . What is this Titan that has possession of me? Talk of mysteries!—Think of our life in nature,–daily to be shown matter, to come in contact with it,–rocks, trees, wind on our cheeks! the *solid* earth! the *actual* world! the *common sense! Contact! Contact! Who* are we? *Where* are we?"[3]

On Katahdin, Thoreau not only reached for the summit, but he reached for himself. Now, others can do so here as well, for today the mountain is public conservation land to be "forever wild," thanks to one man, Percival P. Baxter.

41

CHESUNCOOK

The 1853 Trip

Seven years after his trip to Katahdin, the wilderness of Maine drew Thoreau back. In the late afternoon of September 5, 1853, he boarded a steamer in Boston and after a restless night arrived in Bangor, Maine, around noon. His companion on this trip was once again his Bangor relative George Thatcher, who obtained the services of a Penobscot guide, Joe Aitteon. Thoreau and Thatcher traveled from Bangor to Greenville in an open wagon, meeting Aitteon there. A steamer took them to Northeast Carry where they launched their canoe in the upper West Branch of the Penobscot River and paddled some twenty miles downriver to Chesuncook Lake. On the way, Thatcher and Aitteon hunted moose. At the lake, the party stayed a night at Ansel Smith's place, now known as Chesuncook Village, still a tiny, remote settlement. The next day they traveled back upriver to Northeast Carry. All in all, Thoreau's trip from Greenville to Chesuncook and return to Greenville took less than five days, but in that time he had seen a good part of the upper West Branch of the Penobscot; had experienced a wild country, little logged and relatively unsettled; and had met face to face with what he had hoped to see—"a moose near at hand."[1]

The trip sharpened his view of the dichotomy between wilderness and civilization. He said near the end of his chronicle of this trip that "it was a relief to get back to our smooth, but varied landscape. For a permanent residence, it seemed to me that there could be no comparison between this and the wilderness, necessary as the latter is for a resource and a background, the raw material of all our civilization."[2] From his perspective, he wrote: "not only for strength but for beauty, the poet must from time to time travel the logger's path and the Indian's trail . . . far in the recesses of the wilderness."[3]

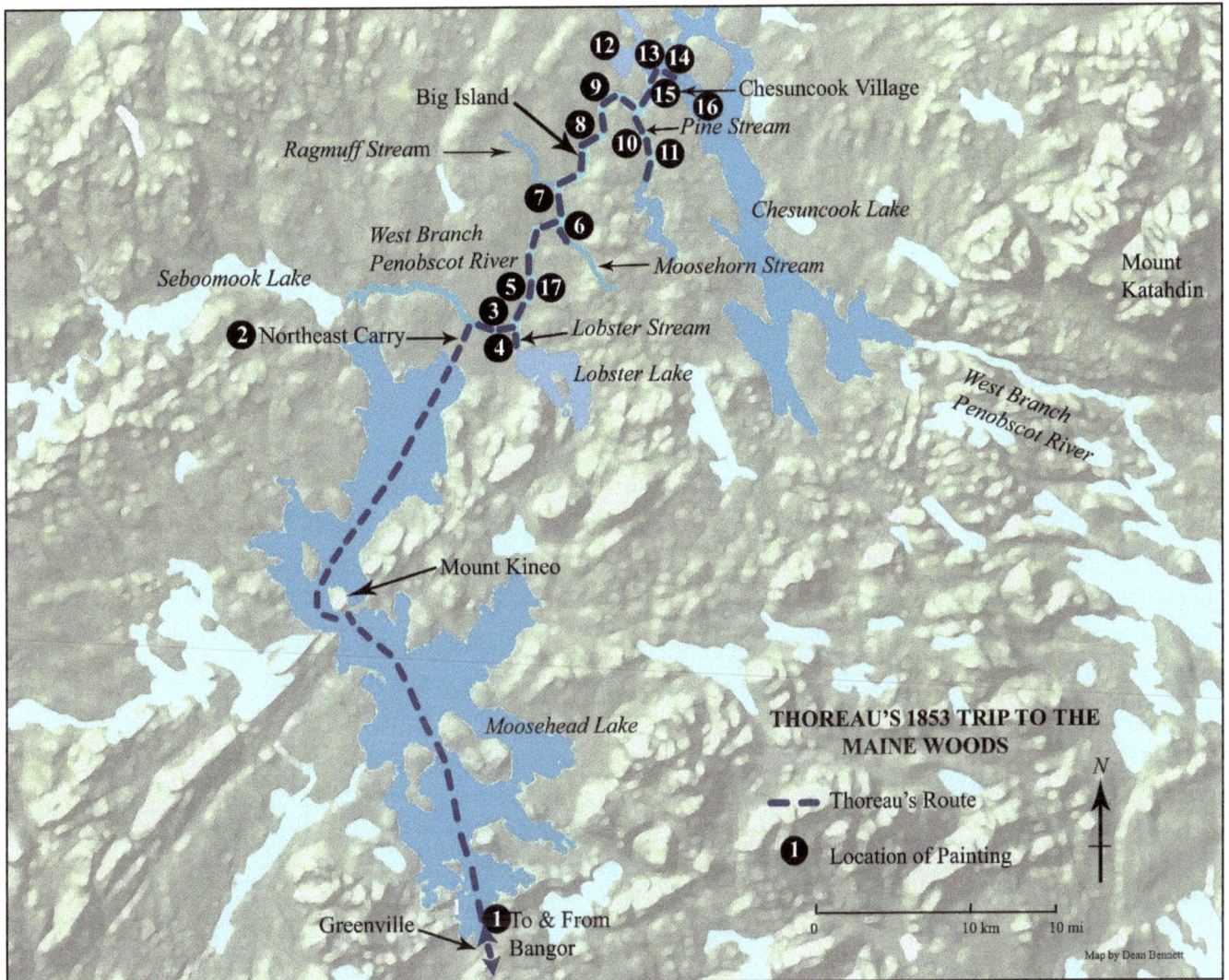

THOREAU'S 1853 TRIP TO THE MAINE WOODS

- - - Thoreau's Route

1 Location of Painting

0   10 km   10 mi

N

Map by Dean Bennett

Big Island

Ragmuff Stream →

West Branch
Penobscot River

Seboomook Lake

2 Northeast Carry

← Lobster Stream

Lobster Lake

Chesuncook Village

Pine Stream

← Moosehorn Stream

Chesuncook Lake

Mount
Katahdin

West Branch
Penobscot River

Mount Kineo

Moosehead Lake

Greenville

1 To & From
Bangor

1. MOOSEHEAD LAKE

"suitably wild-looking sheet of water, sprinkled with
small low islands . . . covered with shaggy spruce and
other wild wood"
September 16, 1853

On the morning of September 15, 1853, Thoreau, his relative and companion George Thatcher, and Penobscot guide Joe Aitteon boarded a stage in Bangor for their ride to Greenville on Moosehead Lake, some sixty miles to the north. They arrived at their destination early the next morning after spending the night in Monson. The Greenville that Thoreau saw that morning was a small village on the edge of the lake. It had been incorporated as a town in 1836, only about a decade and a half earlier and given its name for its surroundings of green forests.

Thoreau wrote that "it was not till we were within a mile or two of its south end that we got our first view of it,--a suitably wild-looking sheet of water, sprinkled with small, low islands, which were covered with shaggy spruce and other wild wood—seen over the infant port of Greenville, with mountains on each side and far in the north . . . ."[1] Later, as the party progressed up the lake in a steamer, Thoreau remarked that the "scenery is not merely wild, but varied and interesting; mountains were seen, farther or nearer, on all sides but the northwest, their summits now lost in clouds, but Mount Kineo is the principal feature . . . ."[2]

Years later, Thoreau contemplated the characteristics that make a town attractive to live in: "What are the natural features," he wrote, "which make a township handsome and worth going far to dwell in? A river with its waterfalls, meadows, lakes, hills, cliffs, or individual rocks, a forest and single ancient trees. Such things are beautiful. They have a high use which dollars and cents never represent. If the inhabitants of a town were wise, they would seek to preserve these things, though at a considerable expense."[3]

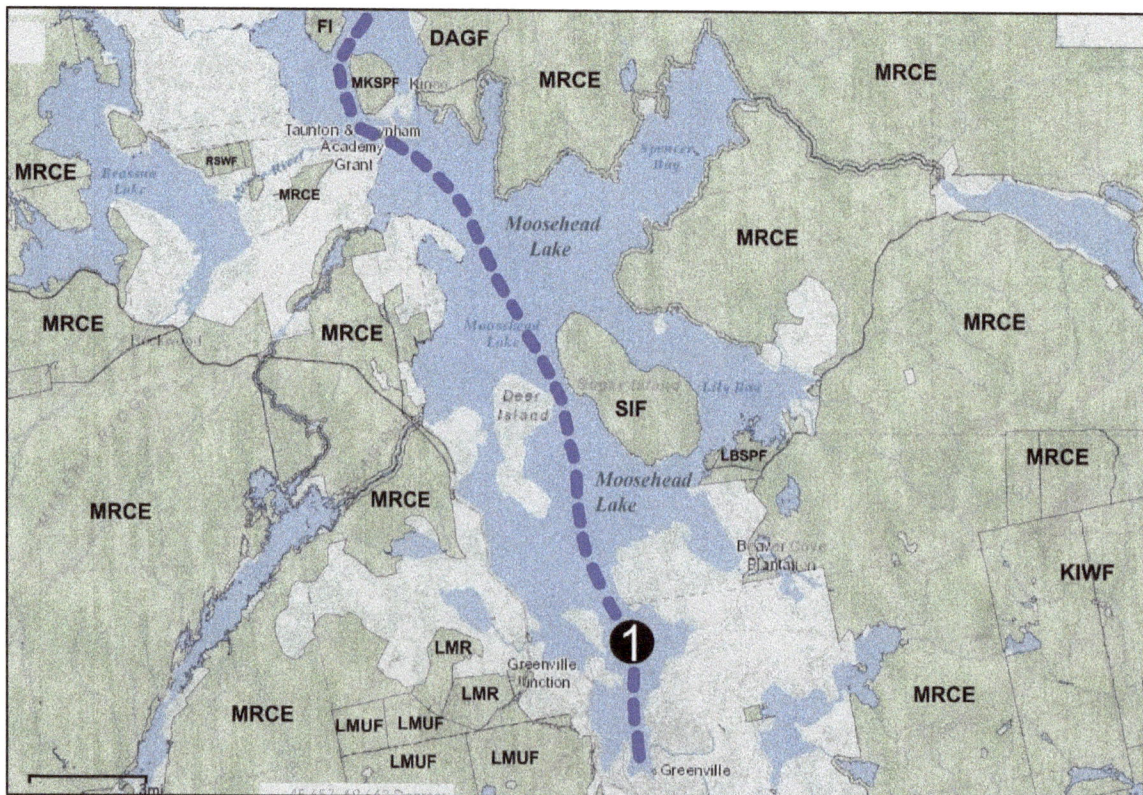

Today, as the accompanying map shows, a great amount of land surrounding Greenville and Moosehead Lake is protected by a conservation easement of 363,000 acres to offset a massive land development proposal for house lots and resorts by the Plum Creek Company in 2005. With so large a development and so much easement land being proposed by the company, a long and bitter conflict ensued, in which the conservation community was also divided. In the end the company's plan was approved with significant conservation measures in place.[4] "The easement will ensure . . . sustainable forestry . . . , protect wildlife habitat, prohibit residential development, and forever guarantee the right of the public to access the lands for traditional recreational pursuits."[5] Additionally, the easement acreage is near to twenty existing state-owned conservation properties. Altogether this is one of the largest areas set aside as recreational lands in the nation.[6] Today, the former Plum Creek land is owned by the Weyerhaeuser Company.

To what extent this easement-protected land meets Thoreau's idea of preserving the beauty and handsomeness, as well as the wildness he sought in the north woods, only he could say.

2. NORTHEAST CARRY

"this railway from the lake to the river . . .
was an interesting botanical locality"
September 16, 1953

"We reached the head of the lake about noon. . . The steamer here approached a long pier projecting from the northern wilderness, and built of some logs,--and whistled, where not a cabin nor a mortal was to be seen. . . . At length a Mr. Hinckley, who has a camp at the other end of the "carry," appeared with a truck drawn by an ox and a horse over a rude log-railway through the woods. The next thing was to get our canoe and effects over the carry from this lake, one of the heads of the Kennebec, into the Penobscot River. This railway from the lake to the river occupied the middle of a clearing two or three rods wide and perfectly straight through the forest. We walked across while our baggage was drawn behind. My companion went ahead to be ready for partridges, while I followed, looking for plants."

Thoreau continued: "This was an interesting botanical locality . . . for many plants which are rather rare, and one or two which are not found at all, in the eastern part of Massachusetts, grew abundantly between the rails,-- . . .Clintonia, . . . creeping snowberry, ... I fancied that the Aster radula [rough wood aster], . . . red trumpet-weed [joe-pye weed], and many others which were conspicuously in bloom on the shore of the lake and on the carry, had a peculiarly wild and primitive look there. (Note: These four plants are pictured here along with a deer mouse, not mentioned by Thoreau.) The spruce and fir trees crowded to the track on each side to welcome us . . . . Through such a front-yard did we enter that wilderness."[1]

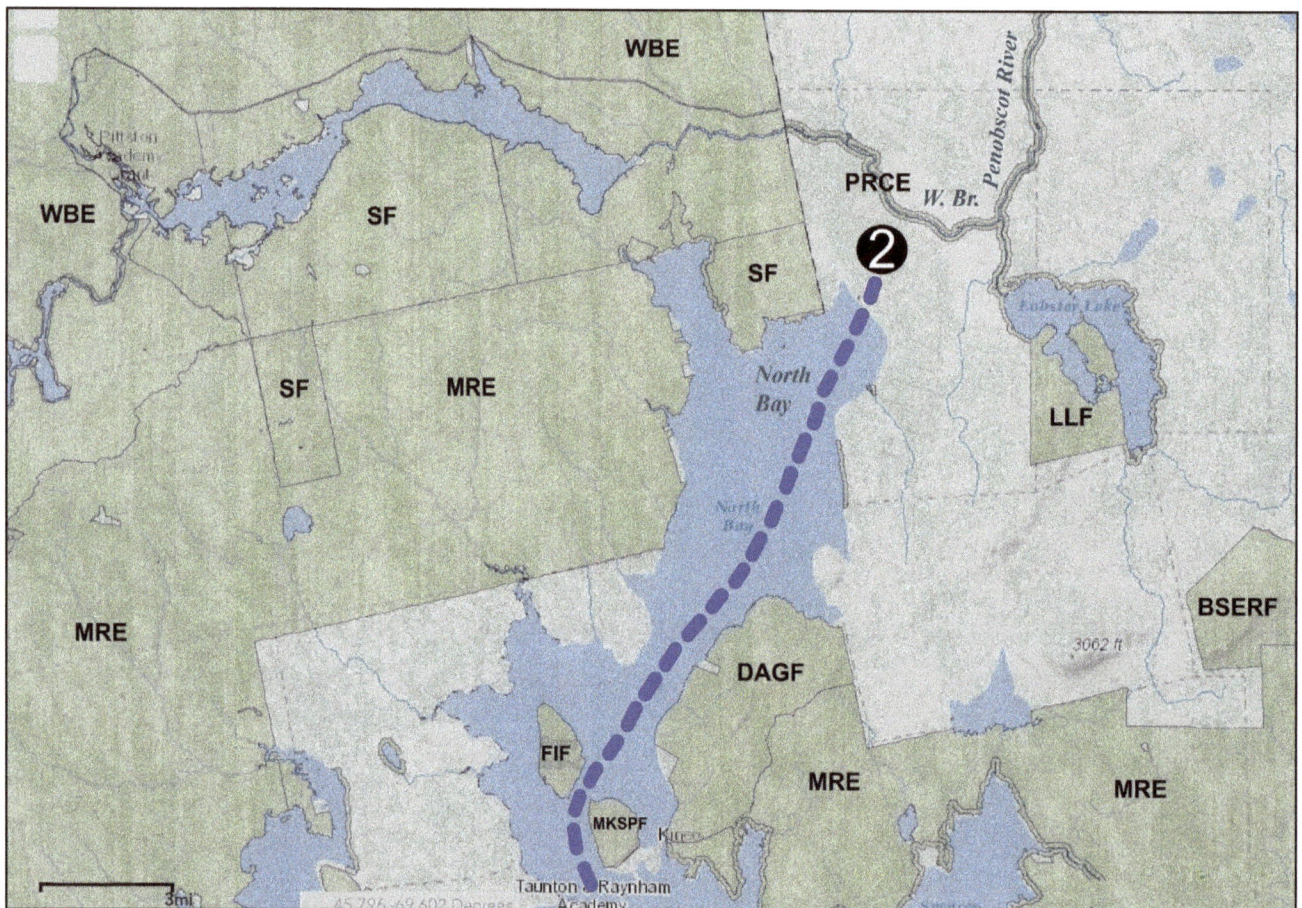

Dean B. Bennett

Thoreau's interest in wildflowers was and still is common in people everywhere. The author's grandmother, who studied botany in college in 1909, kept her reference book *How to Know the Wild Flowers* her whole life—a book that told her "that even a bowing acquaintance with flowers repays generously . . . It invests each boggy meadow and bit of rocky woodland with almost irresistible charm."[2]

Today, in the late spring of each year, our nation celebrates National Wildflower Week, sponsored by the U. S. Forest Service, Bureau of Land Management, Fish and Wildlife Service, and National Park Service, to "emphasize the importance of conservation and management of native plants and plant habitats and to highlight the aesthetic, recreational, biological, medicinal, and economic values of wildflowers."[3]

If Thoreau were to visit Katahdin and portions of the East Branch of the Penobscot River in Baxter State Park now, he could avail himself of a beautiful, comprehensive field guide, *The Plants of Baxter State Park*, indispensable for his botanizing interests there. And because preserved wilderness areas tend to have fewer invasive species, only seven of the 857 species found in the park are non-native.[4]

3. RED MAPLES
"a few red maples along the
stream [West Branch]"
September 16, 1853

Crossing Northeast Carry, Thoreau wrote: "There was a very slight rise above the lake,--the country appearing like, and perhaps being, partly a swamp,--and at length a gradual descent to the Penobscot, which I was surprised to find here a large stream, from twelve to fifteen rods wide, flowing from west to east, or at right angles with the lake, and not more than two and a half miles from it."[1]

By the time his party had had dinner and packed up, it was mid-afternoon before they embarked on the river. Thoreau wrote that "it was dead water for a couple of miles. The river had been raised about two feet by the rain . . . Its banks were seven to eight feet high, and densely covered with white and black spruce . . ." Among the several kinds of other trees that Thoreau noted were "a few red maples." Continuing their paddle down river, "We had not gone far," he wrote, "before I was startled by seeing what I thought was an Indian encampment, covered with a red flag, on the bank, and exclaimed, 'Camp!' to my comrades. I was slow to discover that it was a red maple changed by the frost."[2]

Compared to Thoreau's Concord, fall and cooler weather comes earlier in northern Maine, and the maples, especially, were turning yellow and red when he was there. The colorful foliage he saw on his 1853 trip is known to be therapeutic and mood elevating and to create scientific interest in nature. Scientific explanations of leaf color changes, however, do not change the tendency of people to marvel at the brilliant, autumn spectacle of foliage color.[3]

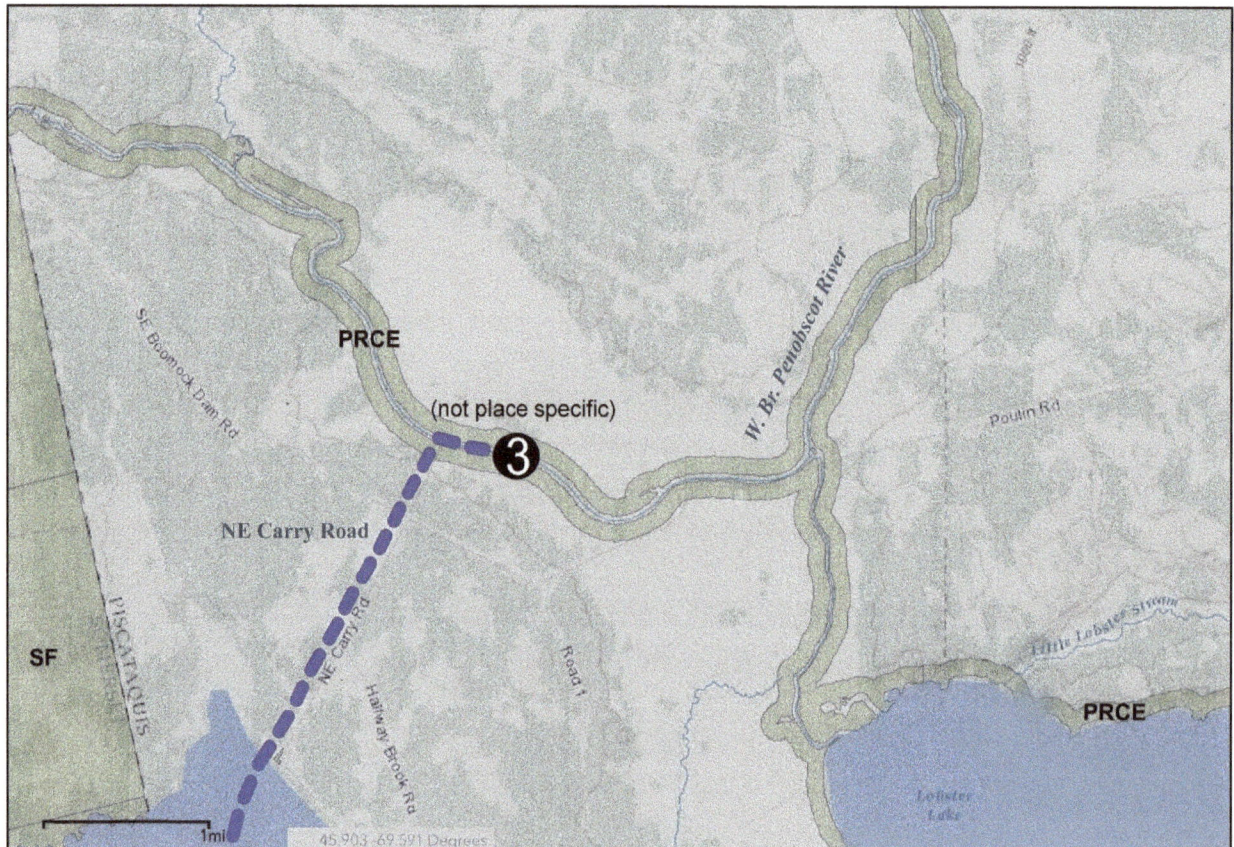

Dean B. Bennett

If Thoreau were alive today, he undoubtedly would not be surprised to learn that the fall foliage change generates "billions of dollars in tourism and remains a key way for people to connect with nature." But climate change, with its effects on temperature and precipitation, could have an impact on the color intensity of fall foliage and, in time, even cause colorful trees to move to more suitable habitat.[4]

One of the ways that humans can respond to climate change is by adapting to it. The U. S. Forest Service suggests in an article prepared by David Cole and Steven Boutcher in 2012 that federally-designated wilderness areas and other types of protected areas "can often serve as a component of a comprehensive response to climate change. In particular, wilderness contributes to climate change adaptation through understanding ecological systems, sustaining biodiversity, connecting landscapes, providing ecosystem services, and fostering human-nature relationships."[5]

In 1862, the year of his death and a century and a half before climate change had become an issue, Thoreau wrote in an article that "October is the month of painted leaves, their rich glow now flashes round the world. As fruits and leaves and the day itself acquire a bright tint just before they fall, so the year near its setting. October is its sunset sky."[6]

4. LOBSTER STREAM

"we turned up Lobster Stream . . .
the kingfisher flew before us"
September 16, 1853

"After paddling about two miles, we . . . turned up Lobster Stream, which comes in on the right, from the southeast. This was six or eight rods wide . . . Joe said that it was so called from the fresh-water lobsters [crayfish] found in it. My companion wished to look for moose signs, and intended, if it proved worth the while, to camp up that way, since the Indian advised it. On account of the rise of the Penobscot the water ran up this stream quite to the pond of the same name, one or two miles. The Spencer Mountains, east of the north end of Moosehead Lake, were now in plain sight in front of us. The kingfisher flew before us . . . Moose-tracks were not so fresh along this stream, except in a small creek about a mile up it. . . After ascending about a mile and a half, to within a short distance of Lobster Lake, we returned to the Penobscot."[1]

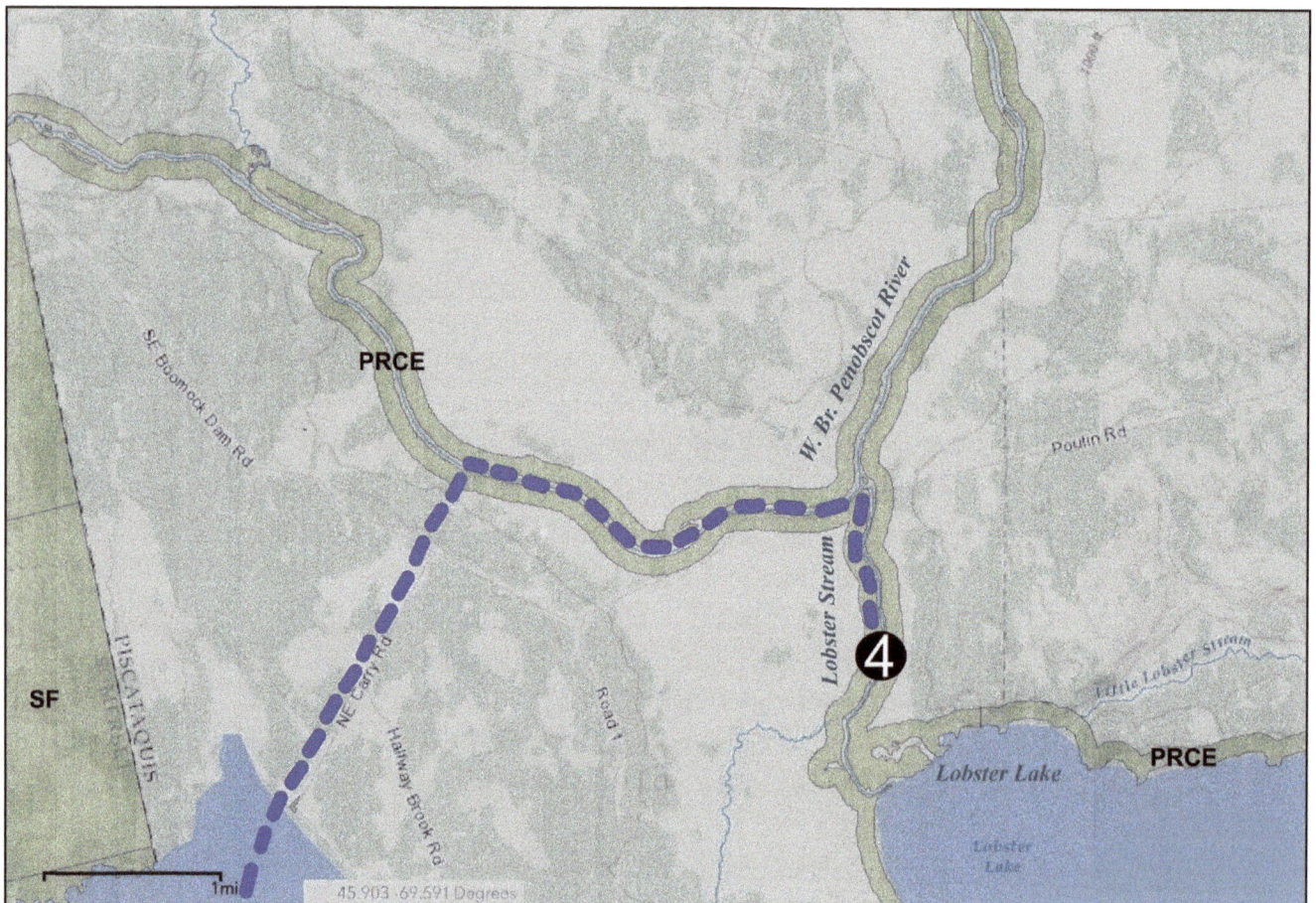

Today, the lake's name is commonly thought to be derived from its lobster-like shape. Indeed, maps call the larger eastern arm Big Claw and the smaller western arm Little Claw.[3] According to the Maine Department of Inland Fisheries and Game [now wildlife], "the view of nearby mountains and white sand beaches make Lobster Lake one of the most beautiful lakes in Maine." Also, it has good conditions for cold-water game fish—land-locked salmon and togue. Brook trout are, unfortunately, suppressed by competition from yellow perch. An unusual condition also occurs when high water in the river causes Lobster Stream to reverse its flow and run into Lobster Lake.[4]

In 1986, Maine recognized Lobster Lake as one of the state's eleven exceptionally outstanding lakes among the many lakes evaluated for their scenic character. The report noted that the lake "has one of the most diverse types of vegetation communities within view. Marshes, hardwoods, super-story trees, and cedars that line sections of the shore combine to make this lake outstanding. It also has many islands, sections of bouldered shore, cliffs, and many beaches. Views of Big Spencer Mountain and other ranges make relief around this lake exceptional." Thus, Lobster Lake will be treated as requiring especially sensitive land use management.[5]

It's too bad that Thoreau turned around before he saw this gem of a lake.

5. SMALL ISLAND
"below the mouth of the Lobster, we reached,
about sundown, a small island"
September 16, 1853

"After proceeding a mile and three quarters below the mouth of the Lobster, we reached, about sundown, a small island at the head of what Joe called the Moosehorn Dead-water (the Moosehorn, in which he was going to hunt that night, coming in about three miles below), and on the upper end of this we decided to camp. On a point at the lower end lay the carcass of a moose killed a month or more before. We concluded merely to prepare our camp, and leave our baggage here, that all might be ready when we returned from moose-hunting. . . . After clearing a small space amid the dense spruce and fir trees, we covered the damp ground with a shingling of fir-twigs, and, while Joe was preparing his birch-horn and pitching his canoe,--for this had to be done whenever we stopped long enough to build a fire, and was the principal labor which he took upon himself at such times,--we collected fuel for the night, large wet and rotting logs, which had lodged at the head of the island, for our hatchet was too small for effective chopping; but we did not kindle a fire, lest the moose should smell it. Joe set up a couple of forked stakes, and prepared half a dozen poles, ready to cast one of our blankets over in case it rained in the night, which precaution, however, was omitted the next night. We also plucked the ducks which had been killed for breakfast.[1]

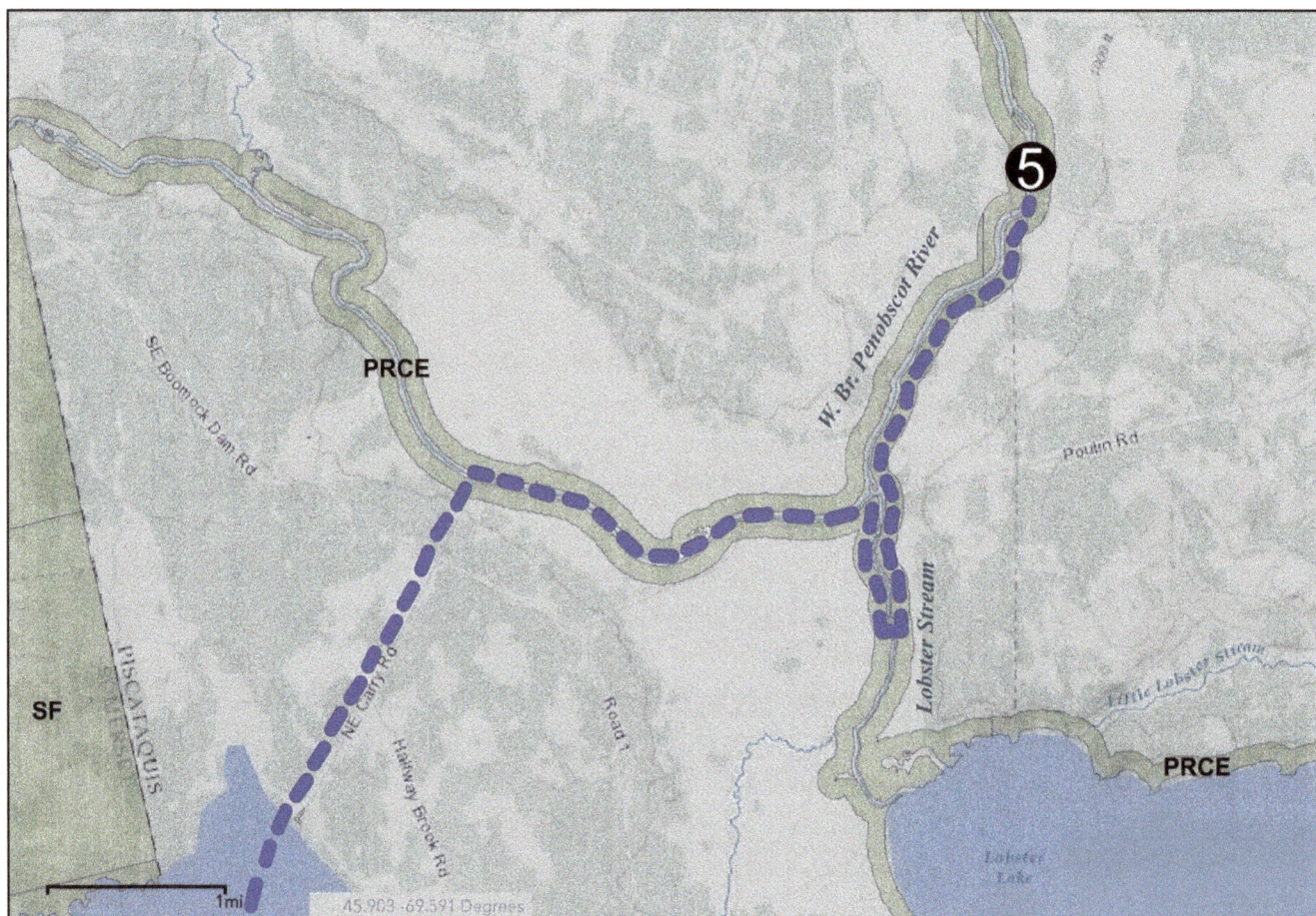

With their preparations for spending the evening moose hunting up Moosehorn Stream, Thoreau admitted that, though he had not made the West Branch to go moose hunting and "felt some compunctions about accompanying the hunters," he did wish "to see a moose near at hand," and would not be sorry "to learn how the Indian managed to kill one." He said that he would go as a "reporter or chaplain to the hunters,--and the chaplain has been known to carry a gun himself."[2]

Before the party had completed their readiness to venture up the Moosehorn, they heard in that direction a faint sound "like two strokes of a woodchopper's axe, echoing dully through the grim solitude." Joe exclaimed that he bet it was a moose. Thoreau wrote that the "sounds affected us strangely, and . . . enhanced the impression of solitude and wildness."[3] Today, one still has an impression of wildness in paddling this country, and the feeling will continue in the future, for 500 feet on each side of the Penobscot here has been protected by easements held by the State which limit development and grants the State the right to manage recreation.[4]

Interestingly, the island is now called Warren Island and also, on at least one map, Thoreau Island. The nearby bridge crossing above the island was also given the name Hannibal's Crossing by a popular weatherman, and the name still remains today.

6. THE MOOSEHORN

"we turned up the moosehorn . . .[seeing] in our
imaginations . . . a gigantic moose"
September 16, 1853

"At starlight we dropped down the stream, which was a dead-water for three miles . . . . At length we turned up the Moosehorn, where the Indians at the carry had told us that they killed a moose the night before. This is a very meandering stream, only a rod or two in width, but comparatively deep, coming in from the right . . . . It was bordered here and there by narrow meadows between the stream and the endless forest, affording favorable places for the moose to feed, and to call them out on. We proceeded half a mile up this, as through a narrow, winding canal, where the tall dark spruce and firs and arbor-vitae towered on both sides in the moonlight, forming a perpendicular forest-edge of great height, like the spires of a Venice in the forest. . . ."[1]

Thoreau watched Joe Aitteon call repeadedly for the moose, but the party "listened in vain to hear one come rushing through the woods, and concluded that they had been hunted too much thereabouts. We saw, many times, what to our imaginations looked like a gigantic moose, with his horns peering from out the forest edge; but we saw the forest only, and not its inhabitants, that night. So at last we turned about. There was now a little fog on the water, though it was a fine, clear night above. There were very few sounds to break the stillness of the forest. . . . Having reached the camp, about ten o'clock, we kindled our fire and went to bed."[2]

The failure of Thoreau's party to call a moose while hunting the Moosehorn and the conclusion that the area had been hunted too much may have been correct. But, there were already changes in the works at that time to better manage the moose population. A law had been passed in 1830 that created a fall open season, but without a bag limit. In 1850 out-of-state hunters were banned from Maine. In 1889, a bag limit was put into effect. Still, by the turn of the century, the moose population had dropped to an estimated 2,000. During the 1900s to the present, however, the moose population rebounded to more than 70,000 due to protective laws and improved habitat.[3]

Today, the Moosehorn is in one of twenty-nine Wildlife Management Districts. The districts are geographical sections with similarities in biological, physical, and other characteristics. This arrangement provides better opportunities for the Department of Inland Fisheries and Wildlife to research and manage populations of species, such as moose. At this writing the Moosehorn district's goal for moose is to "maximize hunting and viewing opportunities while maintaining the availability of mature bulls" and to manage the moose population at 55% to 65% of carrying capacity with 17% mature bulls. The management also sets hunting seasons by district and controls, by lottery, the number of permits to take moose, which in 2016 was set at 2,140 permits.[4]

7. RAGMUFF STREAM

"we stopped to fish for trout at the mouth
of a small stream called Ragmuff"
September 17, 1853

Looking upriver from the bank at the entrance of Ragmuff Stream into the West Branch, you see a large pool where the stream comes in from the right just below you. Here, you may see an osprey doing its fishing hover, for Ragmuff is known for its brook trout. This was Thoreau's experience, too. On September 17, 1853, he noted that "we stopped to fish for trout at the mouth of a small stream called Ragmuff, which comes in from the west, about two miles below the Moosehorn. Here were the ruins of an old lumbering-camp, and a small space, which had formerly been cleared and burned over, was now densely overgrown with the red cherry and raspberries. While we were trying for trout, Joe, Indian-like, wandered off up the Ragmuff on his own errands, and when we were to start was far beyond call. So we were compelled to make a fire and get our dinner here, not to lose time. . . . Joe at length returned, after an hour and a half, and said that he had been two miles up the stream exploring, and had seen a moose, but, not having the gun, he did not get him."[1]

In the late 1970s, the forest that Joe Aitteon saw when he wandered up Ragmuff Stream two miles had changed considerably. It was the time when the spruce budworm had killed millions of acres of spruce trees in northern Maine, including around Ragmuff Stream. To make use of the dead wood, it was harvested by loggers working for large companies. One result was a big clearcut in the Ragmuff Stream watershed.

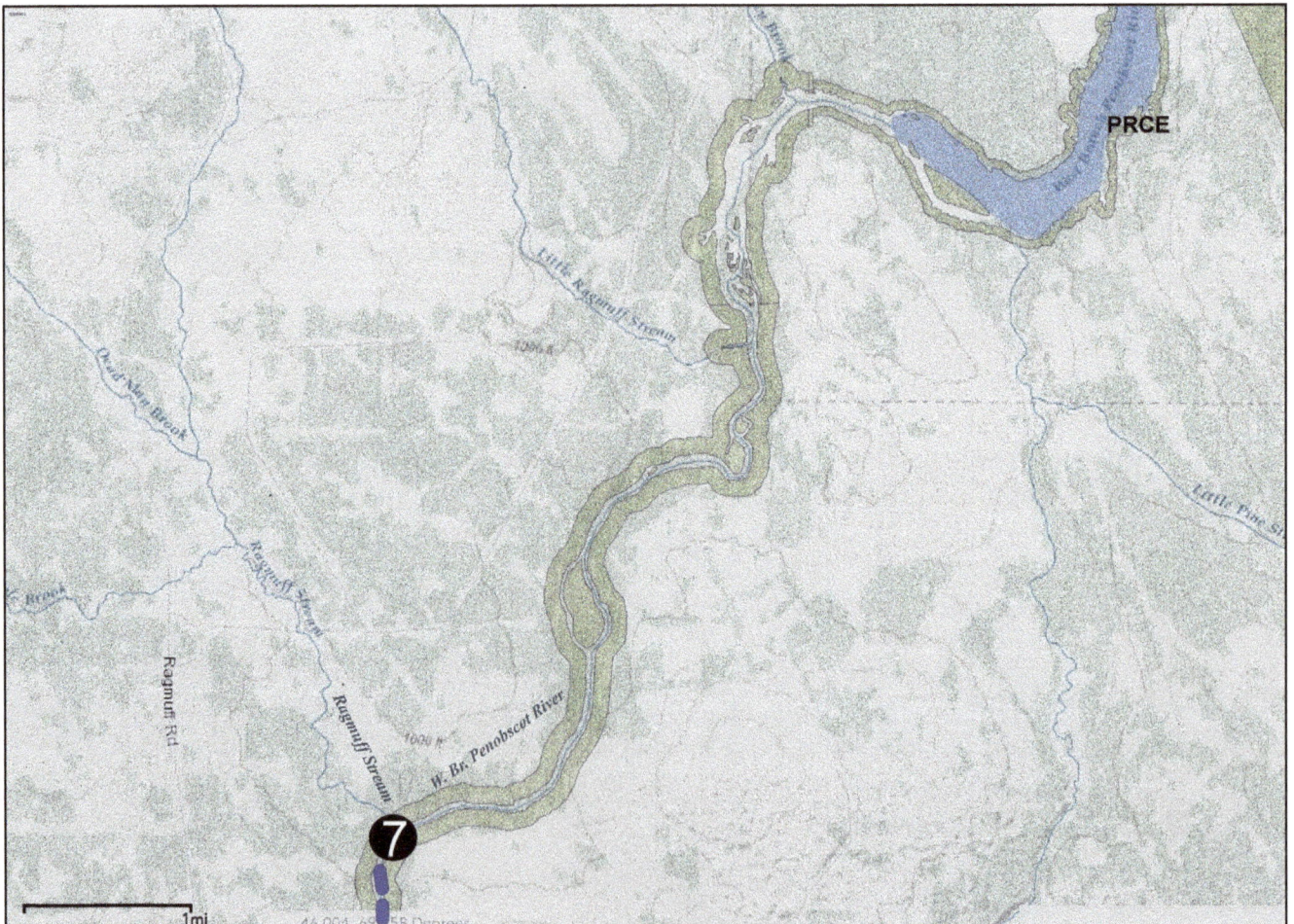

Following the clearcutting, a study was initiated in the late 1970s and published in 1981 to study the environmental effects of clearcutting. The streams in the Ragmuff area were among many streams draining clearcuts in New England that were selected for study. A major objective of the study was "to quantify the magnitude of the differences in stream chemistry between uncut and clearcut areas over a broad spectrum of vegetative cover, soil and geologic types, and harvesting practices . . ." The focus on water chemistry was important because of its role in the amount, diversity, and health of aquatic life in a stream. The study found that clearcutting altered the stream chemistry very little in the selected areas, but with a major exception: "At Ragmuff, in the coniferous forest of northwestern Maine, streams from clearcuts were more acidic than those from references [uncut areas], often by a whole pH unit [10 times more acid]." It put the stream near the tolerance level of brook trout, one of our prized game fish common to Ragmuff Stream.[2]

Today, forest practices and laws continue to benefit from such studies and influence the health and sustainability of our environment. Certainly one could imagine that Thoreau would appreciate the conservation efforts that have been carried out along the routes of his Maine woods' trips since he first traveled them.

8. BIG ISLAND

"passing through some long rips, and by a large island"
September 17, 1853

Thoreau passed by Big Island three times—twice, going downstream and upstream in September of 1853, on his trip to Chesuncook, and once, going downstream in July of 1857, on his Allagash-East Branch trip. Of his approach to Big Island he wrote: "You paddle along a narrow canal through an endless forest . . . of the small, dark, and sharp tops of tall fir and spruce trees, and pagoda-like arbor-vitaes, crowded together on each side, with various hardwoods, intermixed."[1] A short time later, he and his party canoed "through some long rips, and by a large island [Big Island]."[2] On his return trip from Chesuncook two days later, he passed Big Island without comment. When Thoreau returned to the West Branch in 1857, he stopped above the island and bathed in Ragmuff Stream. Afterwards, "as we were pushing away again," he wrote, "a white-beaked eagle sailed over our heads."[3]

In 1888, some thirty years after Thoreau's two trips down the West Branch, a young college-educated woman, Fannie Hardy, in the company of her father, Manly Hardy, and a guide, retraced Thoreau's Allagash-East Branch trip. Manly was a well-known trapper, furrier, ornithologist, and outdoor writer. Fannie, a naturalist and writer herself, left a diary of her trip. Like Thoreau, she saw evidence of the region's attraction to loggers and recreationalists alike, but their presence had increased. She wrote that her party camped near a "deserted lumber camp . . . just above Big Island," and the next day they passed the island where some people she knew "had a camp and killed their big moose."[4]

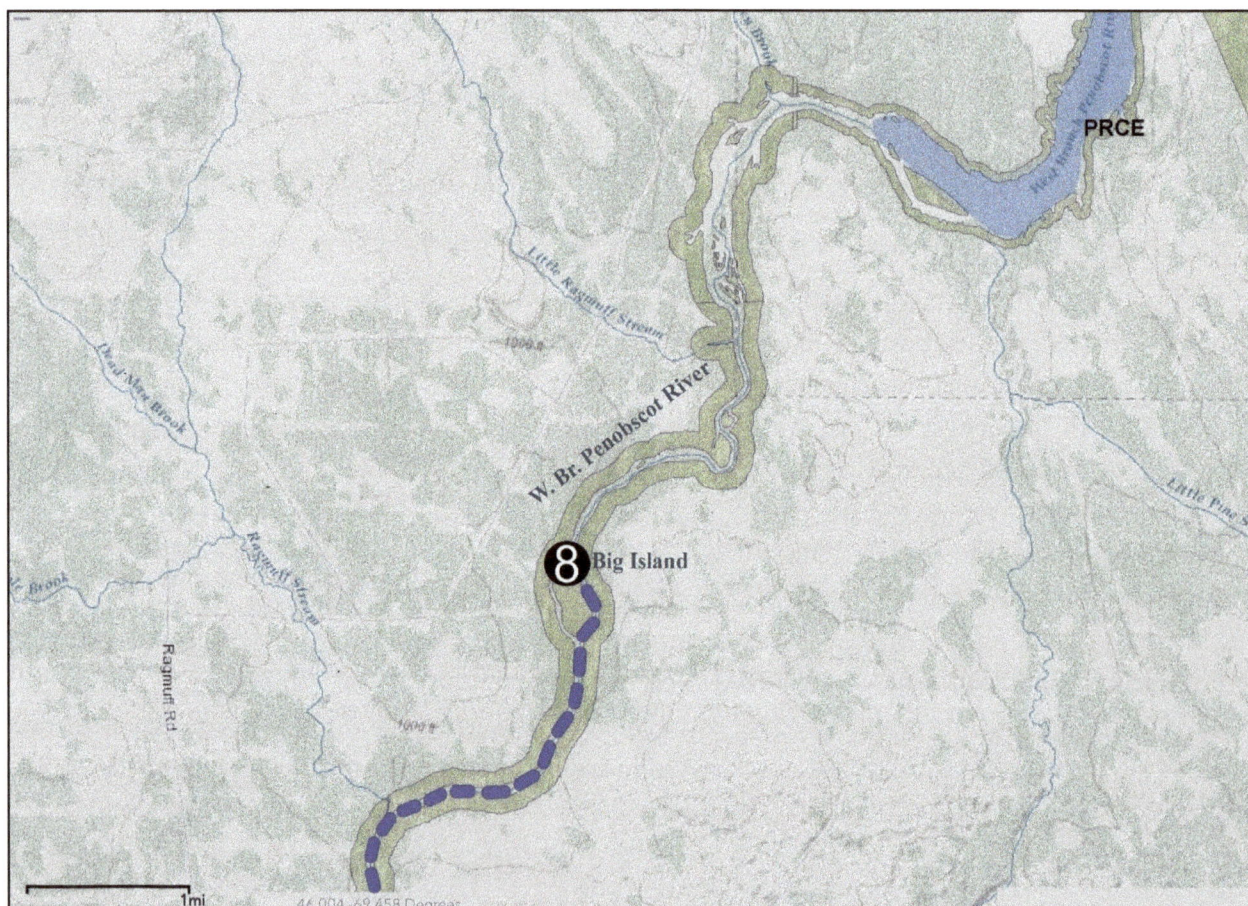

By 1920, the presence of loggers and visitors along the West Branch had grown considerably. The land was feeding paper machines in Millinocket and the river had become a great conveyor belt to meet the voracious appetite of the mills for spruce and fir while, at the same time, the region was accommodating "some 5,000 canoeists yearly [who] made the portage across North East Carry . . . gateway to the Penobscot and Allagash headwaters."[5]

As the intensity of use increased during the century and threatened the loss of those values that had drawn Thoreau to the area, public concern grew, but it was not until early in the next century that circumstances allowed political will to emerge and take action. In 2004, 329,000 acres of this West Branch forestland were protected by conservation easement on private land and the purchase and management of publicly owned land to protect outdoor recreation, sustainable forestry, and ecological values. That year, nearly 12,000 visitors camped in the West Branch corridor, and 232,000 visitor days were logged in the region.[6]

Today, Big Island, the largest island in the upper section of the West Branch, is protected by a big parcel of conserved forestland. In fact, it "is the largest contiguous tract of land ever brought under conservation in Maine," which includes a 500-foot protected zone on each side of the river.[7]

9. THOREAU'S PINE

"strange that so few come to the woods to
see how the pine lives and grows and spires"
September 17, 1853

Sitting before a campfire on his trip down the West Branch of the Penobscot, Thoreau's thoughts turned to the cutting of pine trees. "Strange," he thought, "that so few ever come to the woods to see how the pine lives and grows and spires, lifting its evergreen arms to the light,--to see its perfect success; but most are content to behold it in the shape of many broad boards brought to market, and deem *that* its true success! But the pine is no more lumber than man is, and to be made into boards and houses is no more its true and highest use than the truest use of a man is to be cut down and made into manure. There is a higher law affecting our relation to pines as well as to men. A pine cut down, a dead pine, is no more a pine than a dead human carcass is a man . . . Every creature is better alive than dead, men and moose and pine-trees, and he who understands it aright will rather preserve its life than destroy it."[1]

On his trips to the Maine woods, he found mature white pine to be scarce. On his Katahdin excursion, the woods "abounded in beech and yellow birch . . . also spruce, cedar, fir and hemlock, but," he observed, "we saw only the stumps of the white pine here . . . ."[2] On his Chesuncook trip, he saw "at one place . . . a small grove of slender sapling white pines, the only collection of pines I saw on this voyage."[3] I found it a scarce tree," he wrote, and learned that, in addition to its legal cutting, "much has been stolen from the public lands."[4] And on his Allagash trip at Mud Pond Carry, where he had heard that there was a great abundance of pine twenty years before, the pine was "an uncommon tree."[5]

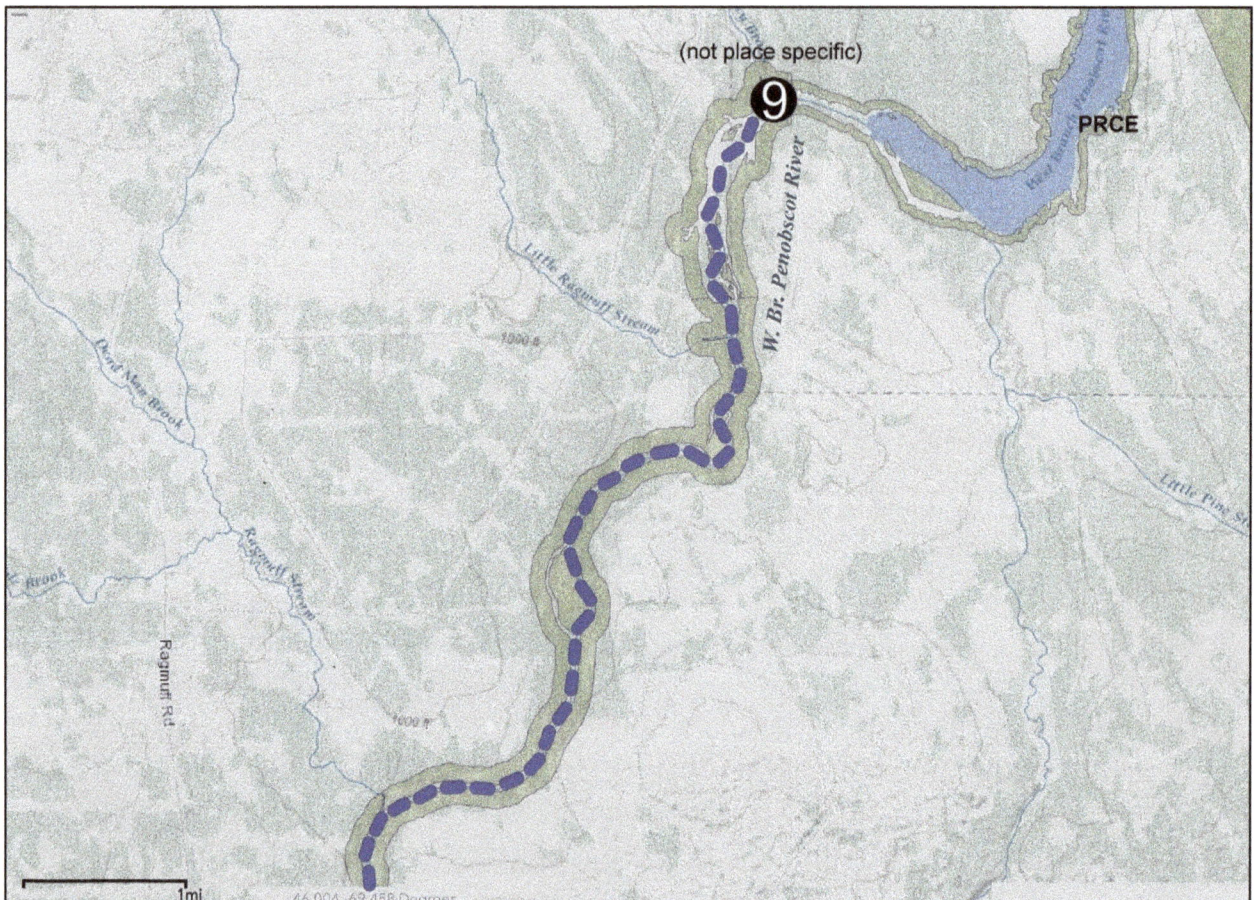

Today, in Maine, the mature white pine still remains a prized tree due to heavy demand, and its conservation is an important goal. It is recommended that, to conserve particular stands, surrounding lands should be maintained as forest.[6] Regeneration of white pine stands can also be accomplished but can be challenging, and attention should be given to timing of harvesting and cone production, providing adequate soil disturbance, and managing sunlight for growing trees.[7] Control of the white pine weevil should also be undertaken if it is evident in stands. The most serious disease of white pine in Maine is white pine blister rust, and methods are also available to control this as well.[8]

In Thoreau's day, forestry had not become the science it is today, and the concept of sustainability was not in the language. It was the time of "cut and move on." In fact the concept of conservation was not coined until the end of the nineteenth century.

10. PINE STREAM

"we turned up a small branch three or four rods wide . . .
called Pine-Stream, to look for moose signs"
September 17, 1853

After passing by Big Island, Thoreau wrote that "we reached an interesting part of the river called the Pine-Stream Dead-Water . . . Here, about two o'clock, we turned up a small branch three or four rods wide… called Pine-Stream, to look for moose signs. We had gone but a few rods before we saw very recent signs along the water's edge, the mud lifted up by their feet being quite fresh, and Joe declared that they had gone along there but a short time before. We soon reached a small meadow . . . As we were advancing along the edge of this . . . I heard a slight cracking of twigs, deep in the alders, and turned Joe's attention to it; whereupon he began to push the canoe back rapidly; and we had receded thus half a dozen rods, when we suddenly spied two moose standing just on the edge of the open part of the meadow which we had just passed, not more than six or seven rods distant, looking round the alders at us."[1]

Thoreau was about to get his wish to see a moose close at hand—a wish that many have to this day. In Maine and elsewhere, wildlife watching has become a popular pastime. In 2011, a national survey of fishing, hunting, and wildlife-associated recreation was conducted, which included 1.1 million Maine residents and nonresidents 16 years old and older. The survey showed that 838 thousand of the respondents watched or photographed wildlife in Maine. Nearly half, or 48 percent, enjoyed these activities close to home and 64 percent participated in away-from-home activities (at least one mile from home). That year state residents and nonresidents spent $799 million on wildlife recreation in Maine.[2]

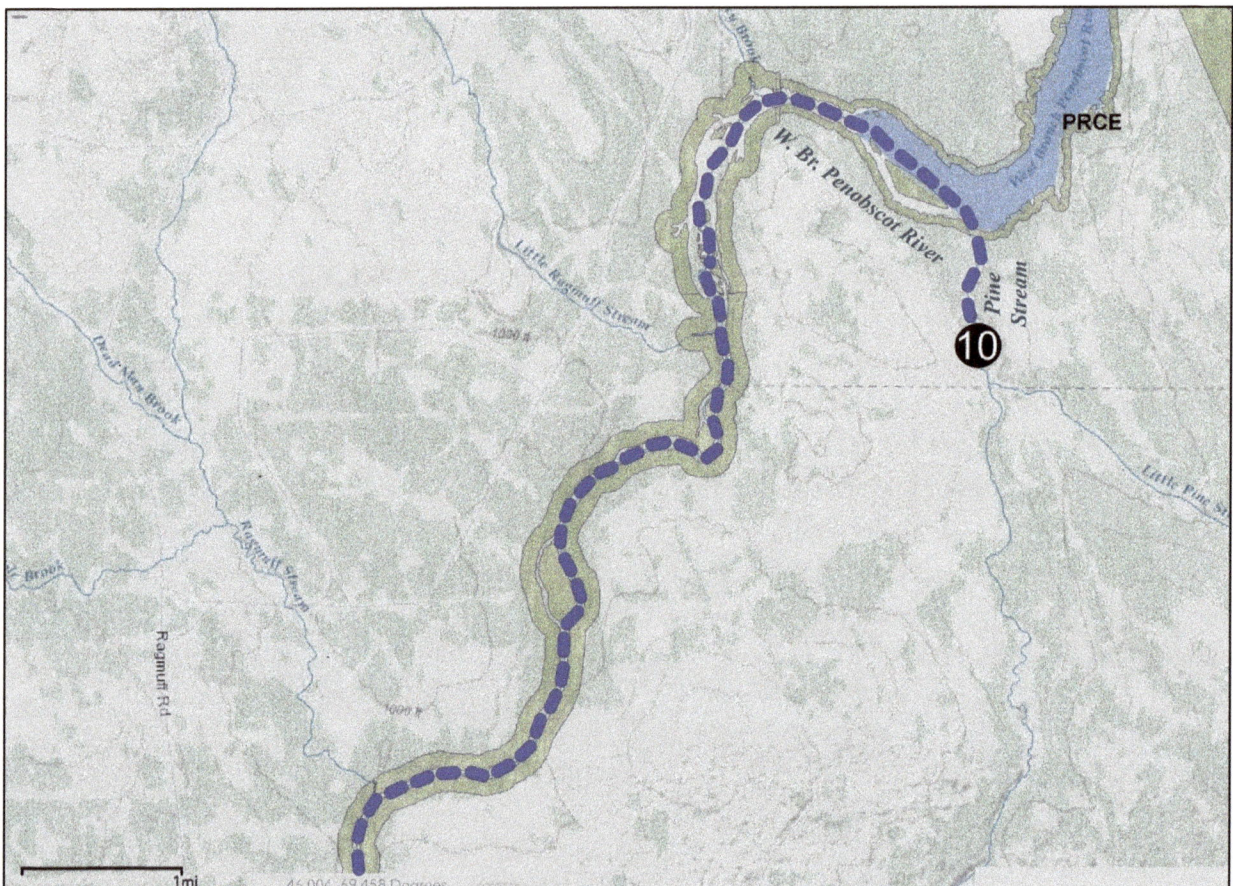

Dean B. Bennett

Thoreau was not only a wildlife watcher on Pine Stream when he saw the moose; he was also an observer of a moose hunt. In the national survey referred to above, only 181 thousand hunted out of the 1.1 million residents and nonresidents surveyed, or less than 17 percent.[3] In 2016, 48,865 Maine residents and 13,803 nonresidents entered the Maine lottery for moose hunting permits. A total of 2,140 permits were drawn that year. Each year the Maine Department of Inland Fisheries and Wildlife also auctions off ten moose hunting permits to send children to conservation camps in the state. It was reported in 2017 that $133,000 was raised to send more than 600 boys and girls ages 8 through 17 to the camps for outdoor and classroom experiences. Students are taught "the importance of conservation, respect for the environment, and a working knowledge of a variety of outdoor skills. Subjects taught at camp include wildlife identification, fishing, boating safety, archery, firearms handling, hunter safety, forest conservation, map and compass work, and much more."[4] Certainly Thoreau's own skills in some of these areas were augmented by what he learned during his weeks in the Maine woods.

11. MOOSE

"they were a cow and her calf,--a yearling"
September 17, 1853

The moose Thoreau had startled in Pine Stream made him "think of great frightened rabbits with their long ears and half-inquisitive, half-frightened looks . . . . The Indian said that they were a cow and her calf,-- a yearling, or perhaps two years old . . . ."[1] Both Thoreau's relative, George A. Thatcher, and his native guide, Joe Aitteon, shot at the two moose who ran out of sight. Later, after continuing upstream they "found the cow-moose lying dead, but quite warm, in the middle of the stream . . . ."[2] After Aitteon had skun the moose and cut off some meat, the party prepared a camp a mile or more upstream at the foot of a waterfall and ate a supper of moose meat. Afterwards, the party proceeded to hunt upstream in the moonlight, and on the way back, Thoreau decided that he "had had enough of moose-hunting . . . . and had not come to the woods for this purpose . . . . this hunting of the moose . . . . is too much like going out by night to some wood-side pasture and shooting your neighbor's horses . . . ."[3]

Of this experience, Thoreau wrote: "As I sat before the fire on my fir-twig seat, without walls above or around me, I remembered how far on every hand that wilderness stretched, before you came to cleared or cultivated fields, and wondered if any bear or moose was watching the light of my fire; for Nature looks sternly upon me on account of the murder of the moose."[4]

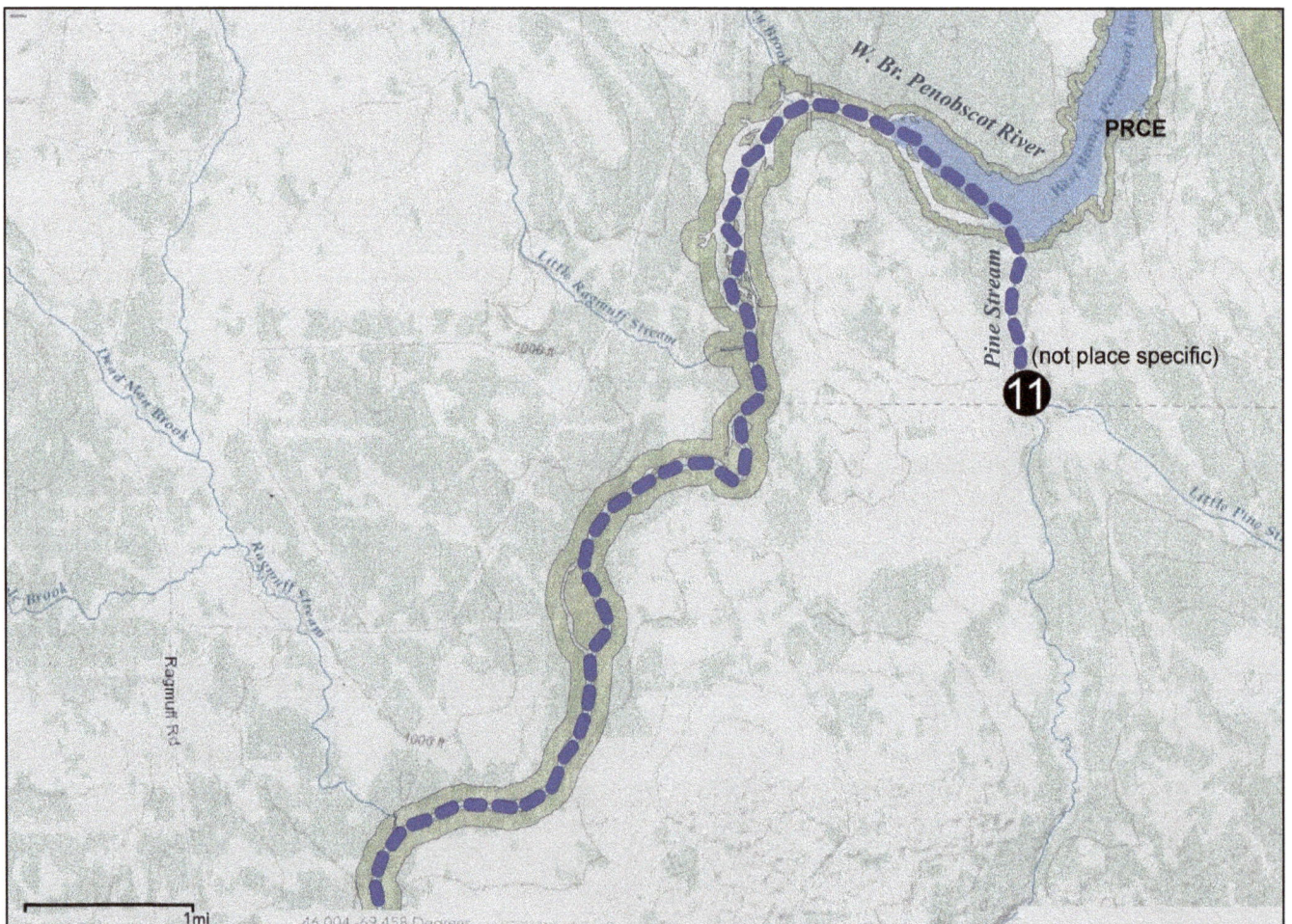

Dean B. Bennett

The ethics of hunting, including moose hunting, is a subject of importance and is still a subject of wide opinion today. The *2016 Maine Moose Hunter's Guide*, published by the Maine Department of Inland Fisheries and Wildlife (IF&W), contains a special section titled "Hunter Ethics." It noted that "while hunting is considered a respectable activity in Maine, it is frowned upon in many areas by an increasing number of people." The agency believes that the primary reason for this disapproval is the conduct of some irresponsible hunters. There appears to be much agreement on this point, and most of those who hunt and public agencies and private organizations that support hunting have now established standards of ethical conduct based on desirable attitudes and criteria in determining behavior. "A hunter's conduct," the IF&W states, "is determined by his or her: Philosophy on harvesting game, Preparation, Commitment to the sport of hunting above any personal accomplishments, Use of traditional skills and methods of fair chase, Regard for the feelings of others, Willingness to obey the unwritten laws, Attitude toward wildlife, and Respect for the law."[5]

While moose hunting has changed considerably from the moose hunt Thoreau experienced, the attitudes and criteria outlined above still applied then, though to different degrees and in practice may have been expressed differently.

12. WHITE-TAILED DEER
"there were none of the small deer up there"
September 19, 1853

Seeing the beauty of a white-tailed deer escaped Thoreau on his trips in the Maine north woods, and he concluded that "there were none of the small deer up there; they are more common about the settlements."[1] While deer did exist in the region, several reasons why they were scarce can be found in reports from the Maine Department of Inland Fisheries and Wildlife (DIF&W). First, it is known that "habitat quality and winter climate interact to determine the distribution of white-tailed deer in Maine. Deer are not well adapted to foraging or eluding predators in deep snow, non-supporting crusts, and glare ice . . . . Maine is near the northernmost limit of deer distribution in the East . . . . Consequently, there are winters during which the duration and depth of snow cover exceeds the physiological ability of deer to survive. Both climate and vegetative cover are continually changing in Maine. Some changes are clearly man-induced; others are completely beyond our control."[2]

Clues to the status of deer in Thoreau's time can be found DIF&W's book *A History of the White-tailed Deer in Maine* by Don Stanton. When Maine became a state in 1820, the virgin forests of northern Maine "were largely devoid of good deer habitat . . . . The cutting of these forests initiated the growth of prime deer range . . . ." Stanton noted that "the only serious check on the deer was the wolf which still persisted in the wilder areas."[3] Thoreau and other adventurers also mentioned encountering evidence of wolves in middle 1800s. Stanton also wrote that great forest fires, like the one in 1837 that burned 150,000 acres, including the

Dean B. Bennett

area Thoreau encountered along the upper East Branch in 1857, "were probably as disastrous for deer as they were for everything else in their path."[4] In the 1850s, market and hide hunters also took a toll on the deer. For example, in 1859, four men hunting on the East Branch killed 45 deer in about five weeks. Deer hunting was legal from 1853 to 1870 from September 1 to January 15, however, and there was no bag limit.[5]

Since Thoreau's time, the white-tailed deer population in northern Maine has had its ups and downs, but in recent years it has become scarce in places. A number of factors are cited for this, such as: the coyote, which has replaced the wolf; changes in forest harvesting practices; and the problem of deer survival in winter, including the cutting of deer wintering areas. Today, we know much more about the mortality of deer in winter and the importance of deer wintering areas, their characteristics, and why we need to protect and manage them to help deer survive severe winters.[6] We now have guidelines and research on the effectiveness of state regulations aimed at protecting the wintering deer herd.[7] In the long run, however, climate change might help ease the wintering problems of the deer and push their natural range northward.[8]

13. MOUNTAIN ASH

"The mountain-ash was now very handsome"
September 15, 1853

On his way by stage from Bangor to Greenville and Moosehead Lake at the beginning of his Chesuncook trip, Thoreau commented on the landscape he passed, including the mountain ash, which he said "was now very handsome, as also the wayfarer's tree or hobble-bush, with its ripe purple berries mixed with red."[1] He had seen the small tree on his first trip to the Maine woods in 1846 when his party had bushwhacked through the woods toward Katahdin. They had just "reached an elevation sufficiently bare to afford a view of the summit . . . . But this glimpse at our whereabouts was soon lost, and we were buried in the woods again. The wood was chiefly yellow birch, spruce, fir, mountain-ash, or round-wood, as the Maine people call it, and moose-wood."[2]

Thoreau saw the tree several times on his 1853 trip. Soon after his party began canoeing on the Upper West Branch of the Penobscot River at the beginning of their trip, Thoreau wrote that "it was dead water for a couple of miles . . . . [and the river's] banks were seven or eight feet high, and densely covered with white and black spruce . . . and a few red maples, beech, black and mountain ash" as well as other trees. On Lobster Stream, where Thoreau called the mountain ash by its Native American name, *Upahsis*, he noted that it was "very abundant and beautiful." While paddling by the mouth of the Moosehorn to Ragmuff Stream, he reported that the conspicuous berry-bearing bushes and trees along the shore were the red osier, with its whitish fruit, hobble-bush, mountain ash, tree-cranberry, choke-cherry, now ripe, alternate cornel, and naked viburnum."[3]

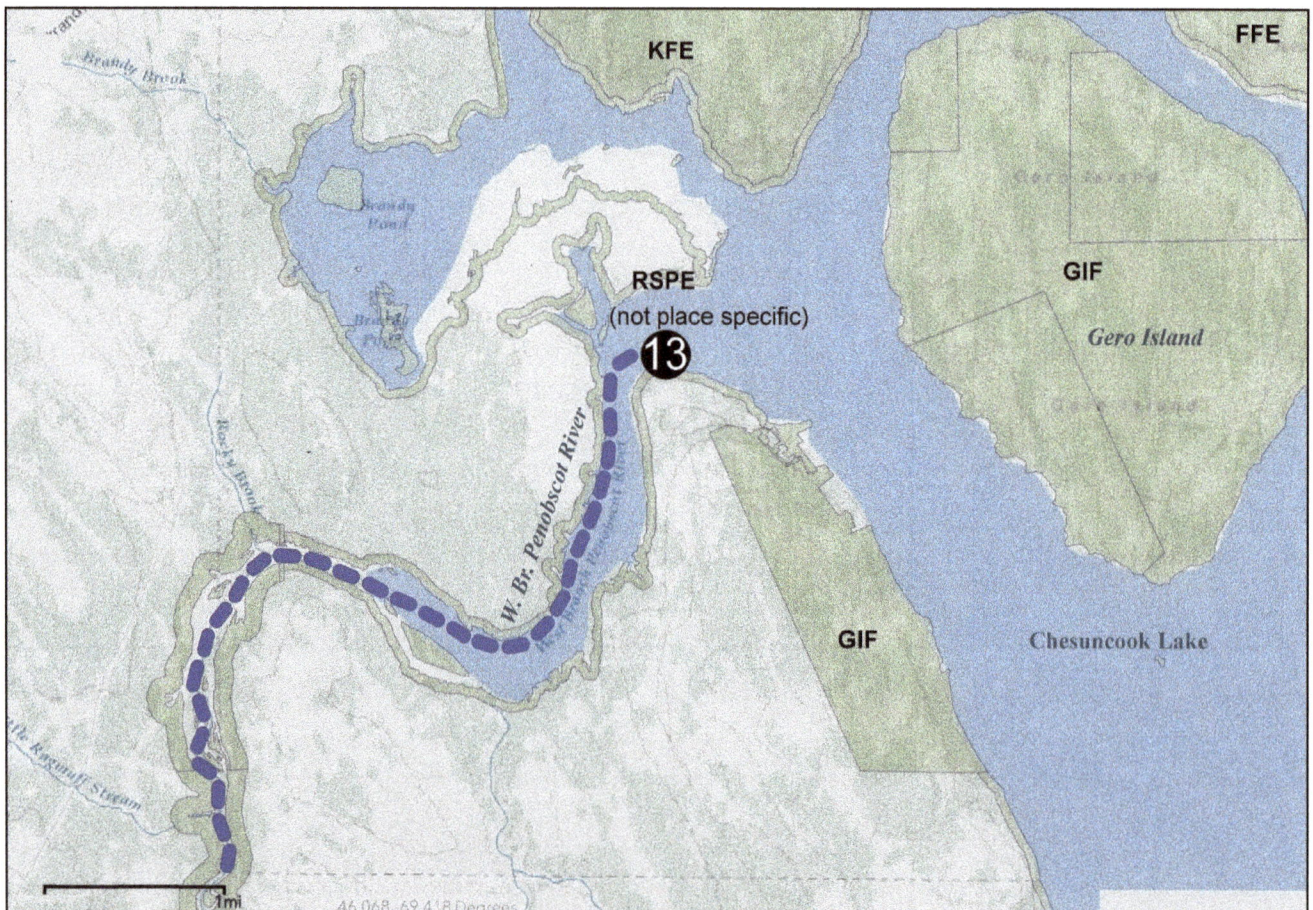

The mountain ash is a small tree, usually fifteen to twenty feet tall, but it may grow as high as thirty feet in favorable places. In higher elevations, such as where Thoreau saw it on his trip to Katahdin, it may be reduced to shrub size. With its small white flowers in showy, flat-topped clusters; colorful fall leaves; and five-inch-wide clusters of bright, shining, red berries, it is used as an ornamental tree in parks and gardens. Because it tolerates air pollution, it is also used sometimes along city streets. The tree's fleshy fruit ripens in late August and September and is sought after by a variety of birds, including ruffed grouse, American robins, cedar waxwings, and jays, among others and is particularly valued by some birds in winter. Its foliage is a favorite of deer and moose.

For humans, another of its many values might also be found in a thought expressed by Thoreau about a decade before his Chesuncook trip: "When I detect a beauty in any of the resources of nature, I am reminded by the serene and retired spirit in which it requires to be contemplated, of the inseparable privacy of a life, how silent and unambitious it is."[4]

14. CHESUNCOOK LAKE

"on entering the lake [Chesuncook] . . . we had
a view of the mountains about Ktaadn"
September 18, 1853

"On entering the lake [Chesuncook], where the stream runs southeasterly, and for some time before, we had a view of the mountains about Ktaadn, (*Katahdinauquoh* one says they are called,) like a cluster of blue fungi of rank growth, apparently twenty-five or thirty miles distant, in a southeast direction, their summits concealed by clouds. Joe called some of them the *Souadneunk* mountains. This is the name of a stream there, which another Indian told us meant 'Running between mountains.' Though some lower summits were afterward uncovered, we got no more complete view of Ktaadn while we were in the woods. The clearing to which we were bound was on the right of the mouth of the river, and was reached by going round a low point, where the water was shallow to a great distance from the shore. Chesuncook Lake extends northwest and southeast, and is called eighteen miles long and three miles wide, without an island. We had entered the northwest corner of it, and when near the shore could see only part way down it."[1]

According to the list of Indian names in Thoreau's appendix for *The Maine Woods*, the name *Chesuncook* has different meanings. One interpretation is "Big Lake." Another refers to the formation of the name from *Chesunk*, or *Schunk* (a goose), and *Auke* (a place), and means "The Goose Place."[2]

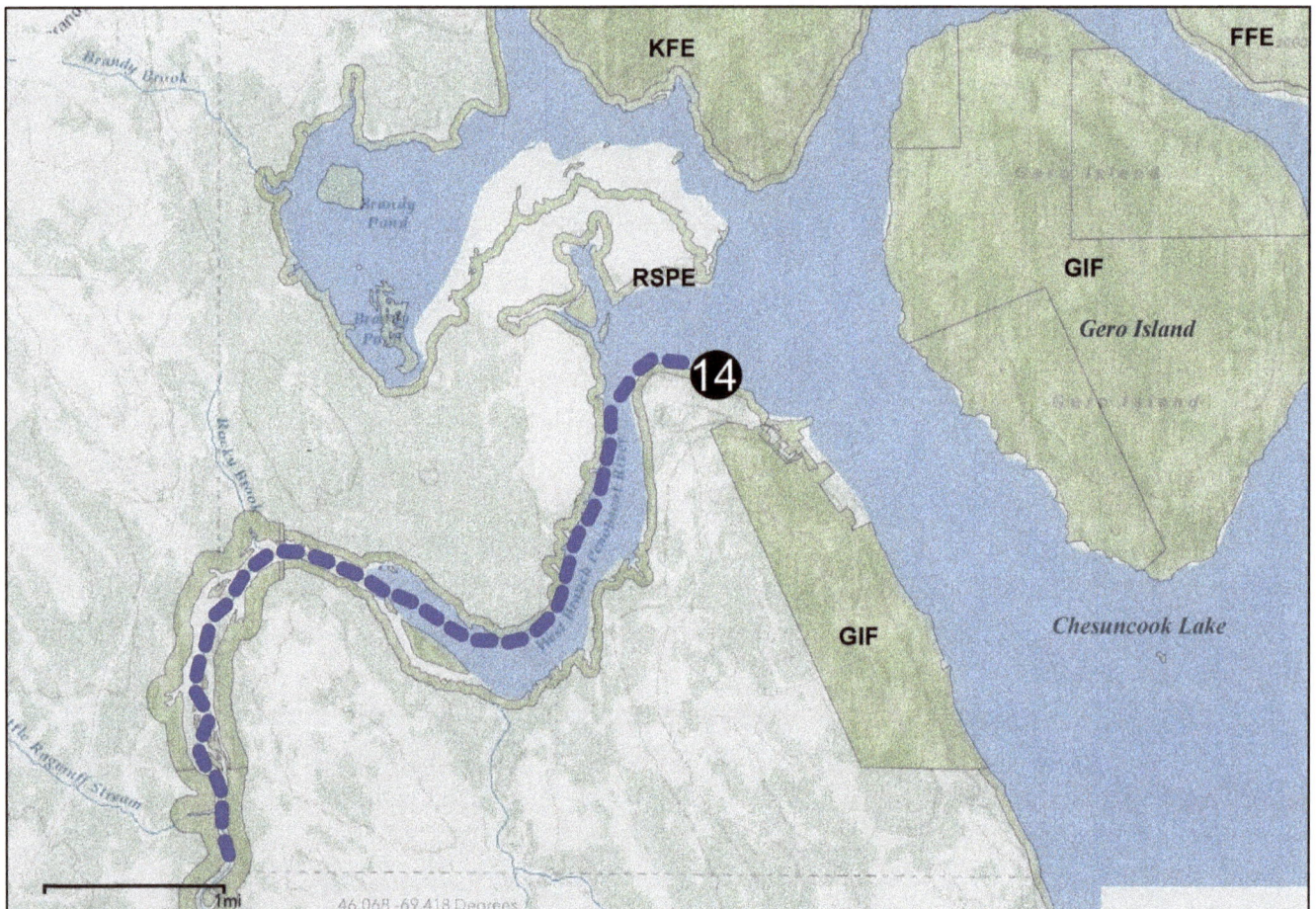

When Thoreau saw the lake, it was not its natural size; a dam for log driving had already been built at its outlet in 1835. Another dam was built in 1903, and in 1916, the present dam, the 92-foot Ripogenus Dam, was constructed, which greatly enlarged the lake. Today, the lake is the third largest lake in Maine. It is 22 miles long, 1 to 4 miles wide, and covers 26,200 acres at a maximum depth of 150 feet. Ripogenus Dam originally facilitated the driving of pulpwood down the Penobscot to the paper mills below. In 1953, the McKay hydroelectric station was completed, and the dam provided electric power to the mills downstream. Today, the lake is primarily used for water storage, hydroelectric power, and recreation, including boating and fishing. The lake is managed for salmon and trout, with emphasis on salmon. Brook trout are held back by competition with other fish and lake trout reproduction is influenced by the lake's fluctuating water levels.[3]

If Thoreau were to enter the lake today as he did in 1853, the scene would still appear much the same as it did then. A large part of the opposite shore is in conservation land and relatively undeveloped. Katahdin and its attendant mountains in Baxter State Park are predominantly natural. Their summits and slopes are free of wind turbines and lights, cleared swaths of forest cut for power lines, service roads, and other facilities. No communications towers, buildings, and equipment intrude on the natural setting of the landscape.

15. CHESUNCOOK VILLAGE

"Ansell Smith's, the oldest and principal clearing,
about this lake appeared to be quite a harbor . . . ."
September 18, 1853

When Thoreau and his party came out of the mouth of the Upper West Branch into Chesuncook Lake, they were headed to a clearing on the right. "Ansell Smith's," Thoreau reported, "the oldest and principal clearing about this lake, appeared to be quite a harbor for *bateaux* and canoes; seven or eight of the former were lying about, and there was a small scow for hay, and a capstan on a platform, now high and dry, ready to be floated and anchored to tow rafts with. It was a very primitive kind of harbor, where boats were drawn up amid the stumps . . . . As we approached the log-house, a dozen rods from the lake, and considerably elevated above it, the projecting ends of the logs lapping over each other irregularly several feet at the corners gave it a very rich and picturesque look, far removed from the meanness of weather-boards. It was a very spacious, low building, about eighty feet long, with many large apartments. . . . The cellar was a separate building, like an ice-house, and it answered for a refrigerator at this season, our moose-meat being kept there. . . . There was a large, and what farmers would call handsome, barn . . . . There was a blacksmith's shop, where plainly a good deal of work was done. . . . Smith owned two miles down the lake by half a mile width.

There were about one hundred acres cleared here. . . . There was a large garden full of roots, turnips, beets, carrots, potatoes, etc., all of great size. . . . Twenty or thirty lumberers, Yankee and Canadian, were coming and going . . . . The white-pine-tree was at the bottom or farther end of all this. It is a war against the pines, the only real Aroostook or Penobscot war. . . . Such were the first rude beginnings of a town.[1]

The village was settled in 1849, four years before Thoreau arrived on the scene, by Ansell A. Smith, a logger. Today, two different conservation protections apply to the settlement. Most of the historic village site is owned by the State of Maine as part of Gero Island Public Reserved Land, and in 1973, seven historic properties in the village were listed on the National Register of Historic Places. The village's oldest house is the Chesuncook Lake House, which was built in 1864 and is still in operation for lodging. There are a few summer houses, a cemetery, a combined church and school, a few other buildings, and a public boat launch. A handful of year-round residents endure the long winters here. The village is a recreational destination for those who come here to fish, hunt, snowmobile, boat, canoe, camp, and engage in other outdoor activities. The community remains isolated as it was when Thoreau visited.[2]

16. CHESUNCOOK SHORE

"after dinner . . . I walked across the clearing . . .
Southward, returning along the shore"
September 18, 1853

Thoreau and his party stayed at Ansell Smith's the night of September 18, 1853, and he said that "after dinner . . .I walked across the clearing into the forest, southward, returning along the shore. For my desert, I helped myself to a large slice of the Chesuncook woods, and took a hearty draught of its waters with all my senses. The woods were as fresh and full of vegetable life as a lichen in wet weather, and contained many interesting plants; but unless they are of white pine, they are treated with as little respect here as a mildew, and in the other case they are only the more quickly cut down. The shore was of course, flat, slate rocks, often in slabs, with the surf beating on it. The rocks and bleached drift-logs, extending some way into the shaggy woods, showed a rise and fall of six or eight feet, caused partly by the dam at the outlet. They said that in winter the snow was three feet deep on a level here, and sometimes four or five,--that the lee on the lake was two feet thick, clear, and four feet including the snow-ice. Ice had already formed in vessels."[1]

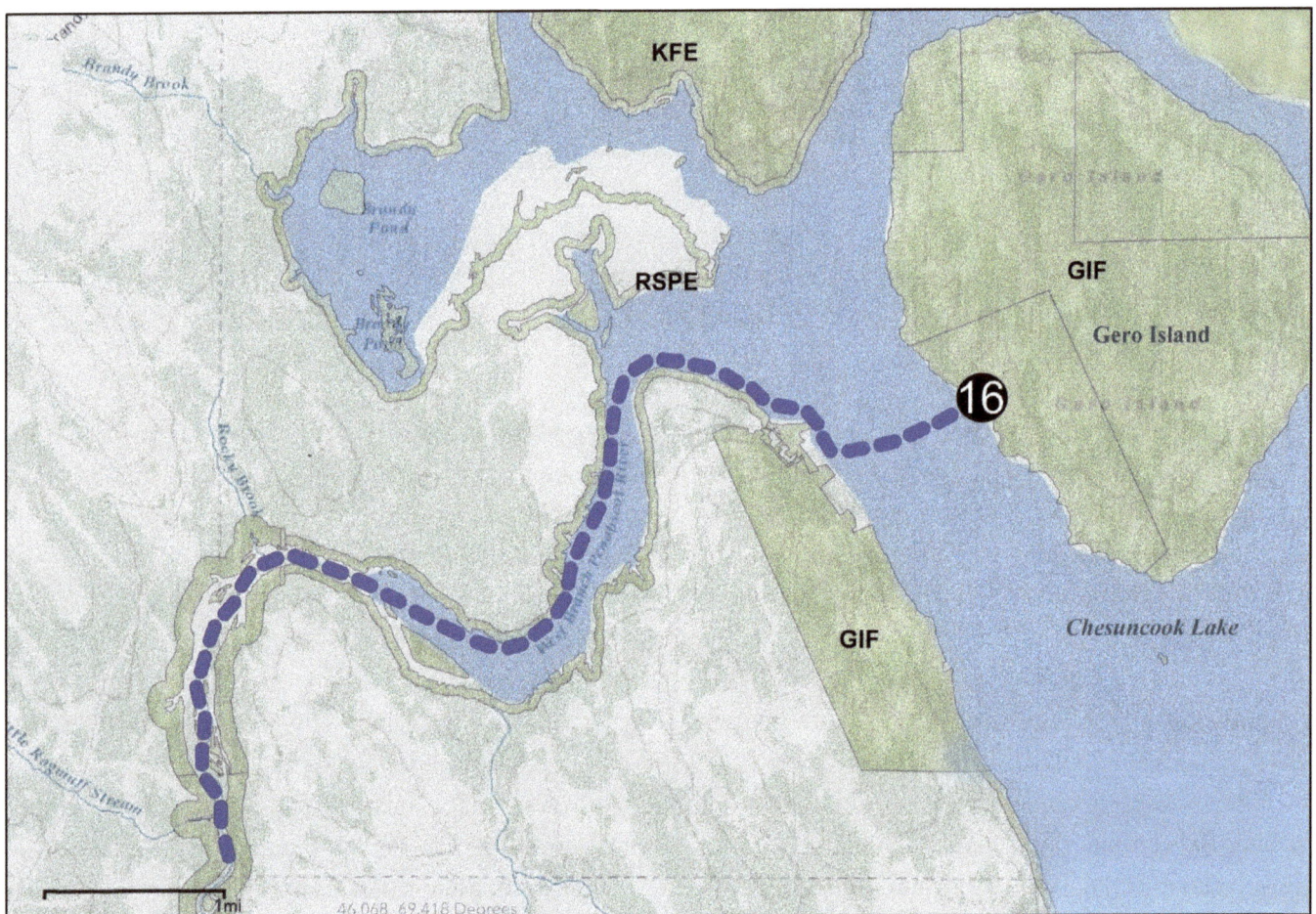

Dean B. Bennett

Gero Island lies directly across Chesuncook Lake from Chesuncook Village. The state of Maine acquired the island by fee purchase in 1984 and conserved it as public reserved land. The island is 3,175 acres in size. Much of the timber on the island was cut in the 1920s and again in the 1980s as a result of a spruce-budworm infestation. The budworm had a severe effect on the island's forest. The island is now an ecological reserve. Two exemplary natural communities have been identified on the island. One is a lower elevation spruce-fir forest on poorly drained soils in the south-central portion of the island. The other is a mixed white pine/red spruce stand in the northeastern part of the island. The pine trees in this stand average a little more than three feet in diameter. A rare plant has also been identified as a resident of the island, the slender rush, *Juncus subtilis*, also known as the greater creeping rush. It is a grass-like plant and rare in Maine because it is at the southern limit of its range here. Among the New England states, it is present only in Maine.[2]

From the shore of Gero Island, looking back across the lake to the village of Chesuncook, Thoreau could have seen the sunset he missed on his after-dinner walk—a sweet topping to his "desert." Gero Island is uninhabited land with four campsites along the shore that afford boaters and canoeists an opportunity to view and contemplate in silence the breadth and beauty of the north woods.

17. OSPREY

"we also heard the note of one fish-hawk . . . and
saw him perched near the top of a dead white-pine"
September 19, 1853

On Thoreau's return trip from Chesuncook Lake up the West Branch of the Penobscot, he reported: "We also heard the note of one fish-hawk [osprey], somewhat like that of a pigeon-woodpecker, and soon after saw him perched near the top of a dead white-pine against the island where we had first camped, while a company of peetweets were twittering and teetering about over the carcass of a moose on a low sandy spit just beneath. We drove the fish-hawk from perch to perch, each time eliciting a scream or whistle, for many miles before us."[1]

The osprey and other hawks are protected today, but when the author was a boy growing up in rural Maine, it was not uncommon to see some resident in my town shooting at what were commonly called hen hawks. A century earlier, Thoreau wrote of the same practice in his journal: "I would rather save one of these hawks than have a hundred hens and chickens. It is worth more to see them soar, especially now that they are so rare in the landscape. It is easy to buy eggs, but not to buy hen-hawks. My neighbors would not hesitate to shoot the last pair of hen-hawks in the town to save a few chickens! But such economy is narrow and groveling. It is unnecessarily to sacrifice the greater value to the less. I would rather never taste chickens' meat nor hens' eggs than never see a hawk sailing through the upper air again. This sight is worth incomparably more than a chicken soup or a boiled egg. So we exterminate the deer and substitute the hog."[2]

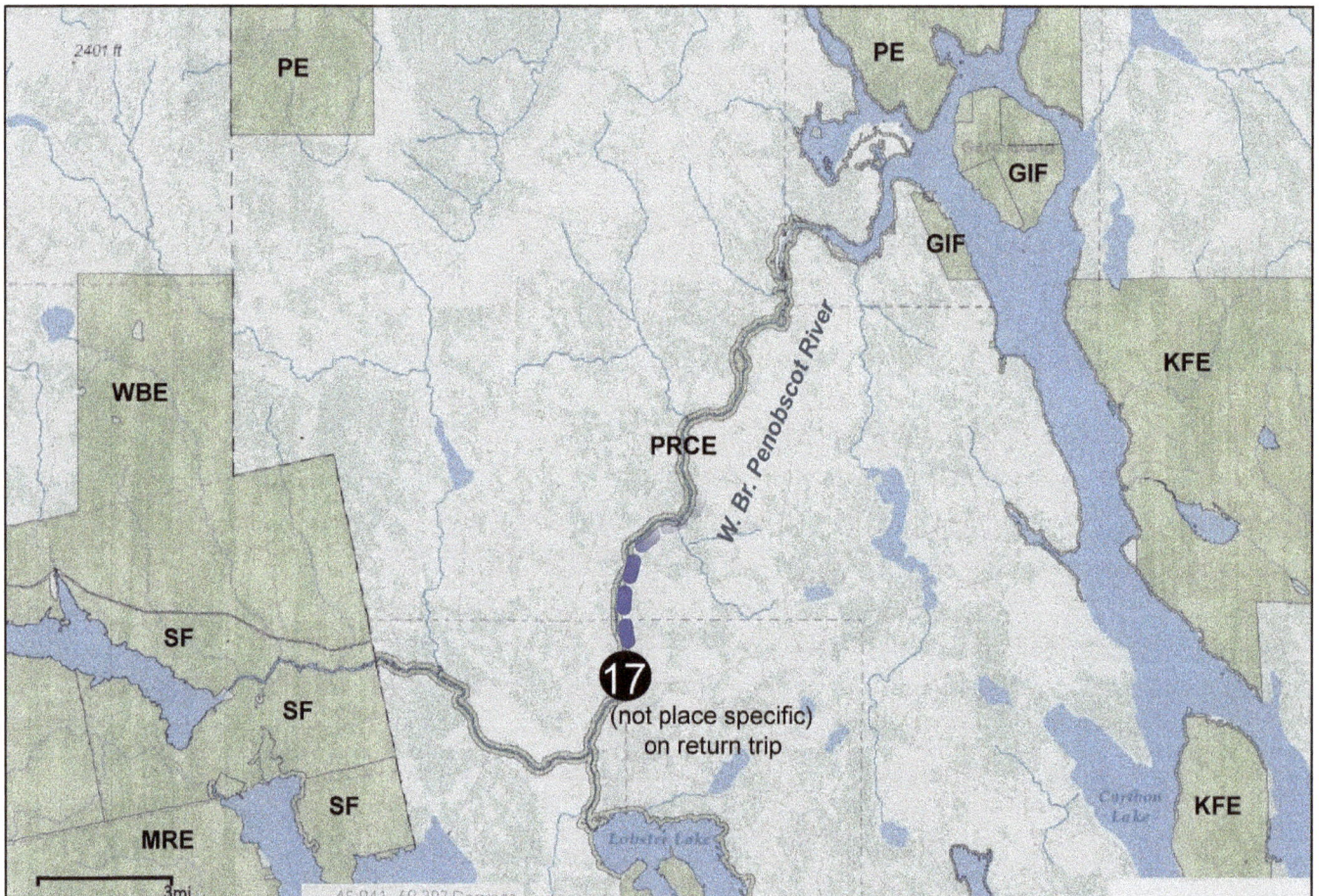

Feeding almost exclusively on fish, the osprey is designed for fishing. It has long, curved talons and its legs have strong, heavy shanks. The pads of the toes are covered with spicules, small, sharp-pointed bodies, for holding slippery fishes. Its outer toe is reversible, enabling it to grasp a fish with two toes in front and two toes in back. Compact plumage helps reduce the impact and wetting down when it dives into the water after a fish. It has keen eyesight and a relatively large beak for tearing flesh. The osprey is a large bird with a wingspread of 54-72 inches, nearly eagle size. The sexes look alike. It flies with slow and powerful wingbeats, alternating with glides. Ospreys often perch near water and fly 30 to 100 feet above the surface of the water it is hunting. It hovers when it spots a fish and dives at great speed.[3]

The species experienced a large decline from the 1950s to the 1970s as a result of pesticides. With the banning of pesticides, especially DDT, and the construction of artificial nest sites, the population rebounded. Ospreys have never been listed as endangered or threatened in Maine.[4]

THE ALLEGASH AND EAST BRANCH

The 1857 Trip

Thoreau began his last trip to the Maine woods on Monday, July 20, 1857, again leaving Concord, Massachusetts, by train and taking a steamer from Boston to Bangor. This time he took his lawyer-botanist friend Edward Hoar with him. George Thatcher did not go on this trip, but he did assist Thoreau in fortuitously obtaining Joseph Polis as his Penobscot guide. On the 24th, the party of three left Greenville in a canoe. For the next eleven days, they paddled and portaged in the watersheds of the Kennebec River (Moosehead Lake), Penobscot River (West and East Branches), and the Allagash River (headwater lakes). Here, Thoreau found his "wildest country." Here, he learned from Polis about the Wabanaki, the People of the Dawn—their sense of humor, names for plants and animals, lore, beliefs, stories, medicines, and their keen awareness and understanding of nature. Here, he learned about these wild lands of the Maine woods: their beauty—of "a very beautiful lake" on a bright morning, "perfectly still and serene . . . smooth as glass . . . . dark mountains about it . . . seen through a glaucous mist, and the brilliant white stems of canoe-birches mingled with the other woods around it"[1]; their vastness—of "the traveler in the forest" coming out into the big lakes from some stream or river and looking down a wooded shore for miles and seeing the forested mountains revealed, giving "ample scope and range" to one's thought[2]; their mysteriousness—of "making your camp just at sundown" where "you may penetrate half a dozen rods farther into that twilight wilderness, after some dry bark to kindle your fire with, and wonder what mysteries lie hidden still deeper in it"[3]; their overwhelming silence—of finding that "at night the general stillness is more impressive than any sound"[4]; their potential to cause one to become lost—of "those dense spruce and fir woods there is hardly room for the smoke to go up" and if you saunter off "ten or fifteen rods . . . from your companions [at a camp site] . . . you come back with the air of a much traveled man, as from a long journey, with adventures to relate, though you may have heard the crackling of the fire all the while—and at a hundred rods you might be lost beyond recovery, and have to camp out"[5]; their vulnerability and fragility—of burnt land where the moon sets over "bare rocky hills, garnished with tall, charred, and hollow stumps or shells of trees"[6] or the effect of dams on Chamberlain Lake where a "belt of dead trees stood all around the lake"[7] or the clearing at Chamberlain Farm "extending back from the lake to a hill-top."[8] Thus, with these thoughts and experiences, Thoreau eased back into civilization as the party canoed down the Penobscot to Old Town, passing homes and farms, hearing cowbells, and smelling the sweet fragrance of hay from mowed fields.

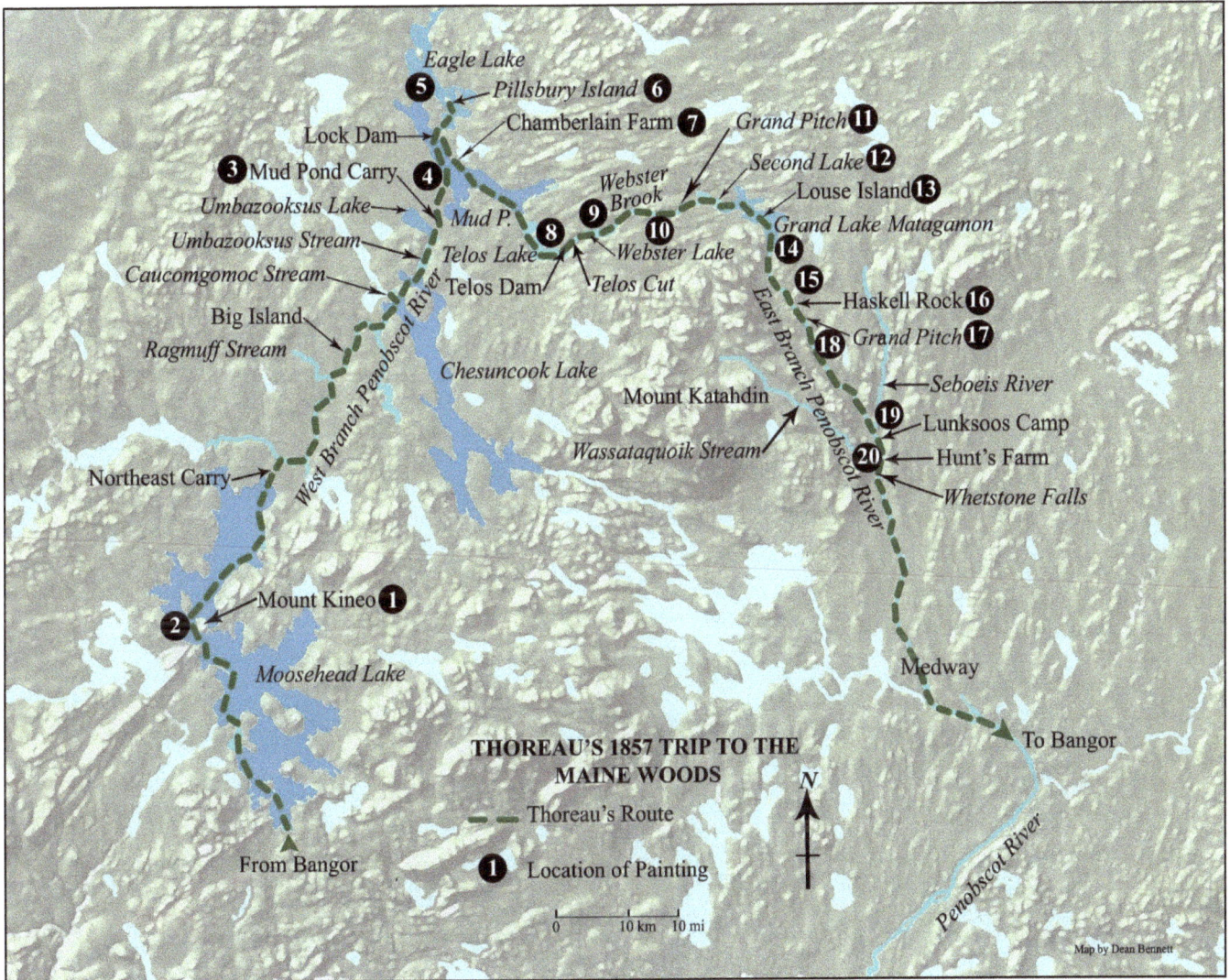

Eagle Lake

5 ← *Pillsbury Island* **6**

Lock Dam → Chamberlain Farm **7** *Grand Pitch* **11**

3 Mud Pond Carry **4** *Second Lake* **12**

Webster Brook Louse Island **13**

Umbazooksus Lake → *Mud P.* **9** *Grand Lake Matagamon*

Umbazooksus Stream → **8** **10** **14**

Caucomgomoc Stream → *Telos Lake* → *Webster Lake* **15**

Big Island → *Telos Dam* *Telos Cut* Haskell Rock **16**

Ragmuff Stream **18** *Grand Pitch* **17**

Chesuncook Lake ← *Seboeis River*

Mount Katahdin Lunksoos Camp

Northeast Carry *Wassataquoik Stream* **19**

20 ← Hunt's Farm

Whetstone Falls

Mount Kineo **1**

2

Moosehead Lake

Medway

THOREAU'S 1857 TRIP TO THE MAINE WOODS

N

─ ─ Thoreau's Route To Bangor

From Bangor **1** Location of Painting

Penobscot River

0   10 km   10 mi

Map by Dean Bennett

83

1. MOUNT KINEO

"Mt. Kineo, which was generally visible . . .
a level bar of cloud concealing its summit"
July 24, 1857

"About four o'clock the next morning (July 24th), though it was quite cloudy . . . in twilight, we launched our canoe from a rock on Moosehead Lake. . . . Mt. Kineo, which was generally visible, though occasionally concealed by islands or the mainland in front, had a level bar of cloud concealing its summit, and all the mountain-tops about the lake were cut off at the same height. . . . While we were crossing the bay, where Mount Kineo rose dark before us, within two or three miles, the Indian repeated the tradition respecting this mountain's having anciently been a cow moose . . . . this mountain had still the form of the moose in a reclining posture, its precipitous side presenting the outline of her head."[1]

"After dinner we . . . began to ascend the mountain along the edge of the precipice. . . . The clouds breaking away a little, we had a glorious wild view, as we ascended, of the broad lake with its fluctuating surface and numerous forest-clad islands, extending beyond our sight both north and south, and the boundless forest undulating away from its shores on every side . . . . It was a perfect lake of the woods. . . . From the summit of the precipice . . . its most remarkable feature, being described as five or six hundred feet high, we looked . . . down to the water . . . . It is a dangerous place to try the steadiness of your nerves. . . . Having explored the wonders of the mountain, and the weather being now entirely cleared up, we commenced the descent."[2]

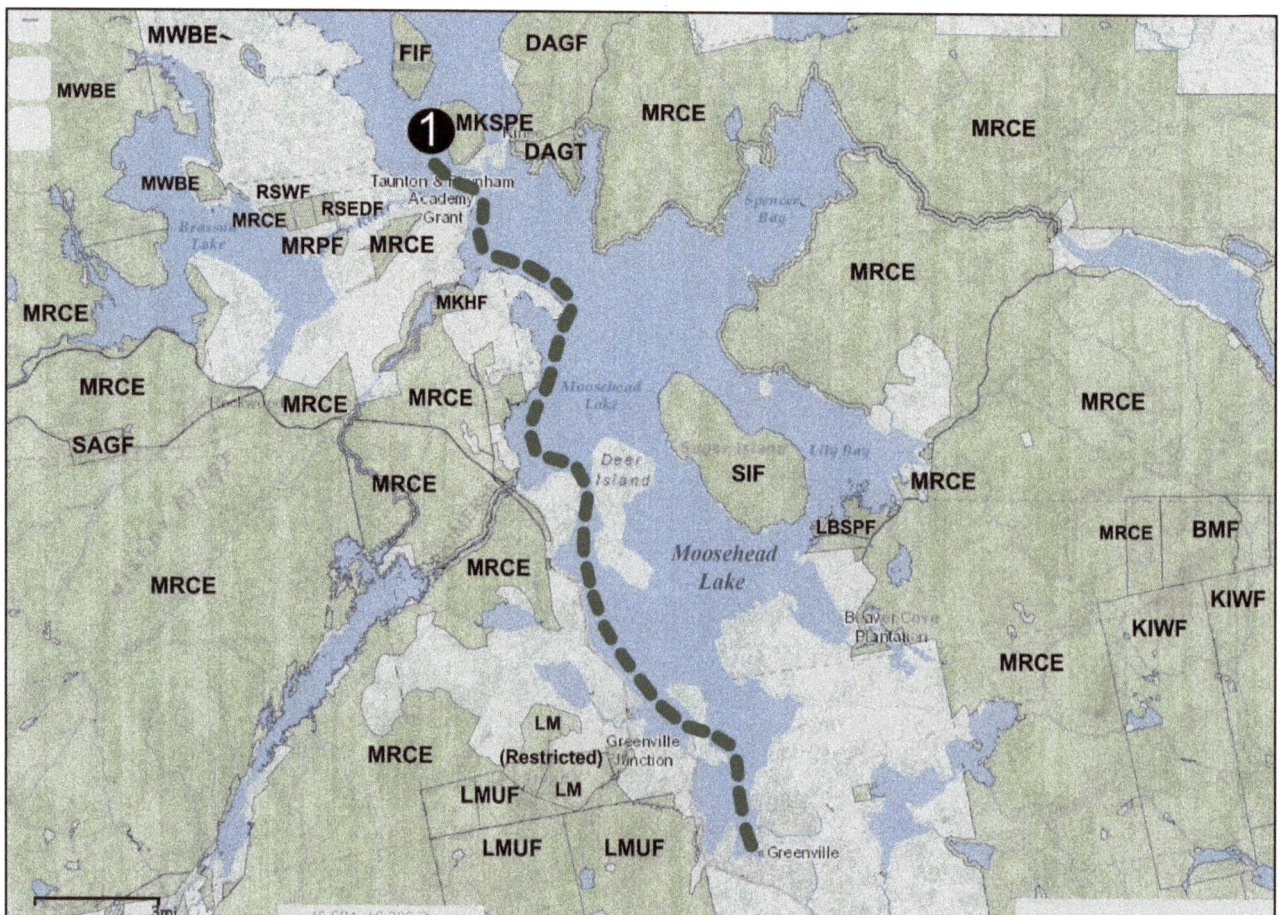

Mount Kineo is a peninsula of 1,150 acres in size. It has a long human history beginning with Native Americans who, for centuries, traveled great distances for its rhyolite rock, perhaps one of the largest formations of this rock in the world. From the flint-like rock, they fashioned arrowheads, spear points, and many kinds of tools and implements, which, through trading, have been found throughout New England and in more distant places.[3]

Beginning in 1848, the first of several Mount Kineo Houses were built on the peninsula. Their presence symbolized a changing view of the north woods as people sought to escape the conditions of urban life, many of which were unhealthy, and sought a respite from the increasing pace and pressure of professional and managerial occupations and as they began to see nature as a source for recreation, better health, and spiritual renewal. The last Kineo House burned in the late 1930s. Only a golf course remains, which is still maintained and used.[4]

In 1990, 800 acres of Mount Kineo were purchased by the State of Maine and designated as the Mount Kineo State Park and, thus, became conservation land to be enjoyed by the public.

2. PHOSPHORESCENT WOOD
"a light shining in the darkness
of the wilderness"
July 24, 1857

Thoreau had one of the strangest experiences in all his trips to the Maine woods while camping at Mount Kineo. Picture in your mind the dark, moonlit woods in which he awakened in the middle of the night. A light glowing from a rotting stump among the deep, damp beds of moss on the forest floor draws your eye, as it did Thoreau's who "little thought that there was such a light shining in the darkness of the wilderness for me."[1]

The discovery for Thoreau, when he crawled out of his tent in the middle of the night, was both surprising and entrancing. For among the warm, dull-red coals of the languishing campfire, was a "perfectly regular elliptical ring of light . . . . white and slumbering . . . , like the glowworm's. . . . I saw at once," he wrote, "that it must be phosphorescent wood, which I had so often heard of, but never chanced to see." [2]

Thoreau was not the first to see this phenomenon. Aristotle, the Greek philosopher who lived between 384 and 322 BC, recorded observations of it. But it was not until the very decade that Thoreau was marveling at it on Mount Kineo that the Austrian physician and chemist Johann Florian Heller confirmed that this luminescence from decayed wood has its origin in fungi.[3] Today, we call it bioluminescence, where light is created within a living organism, as opposed to phosphorescence, where light is absorbed from an external source and released at a different wavelength.

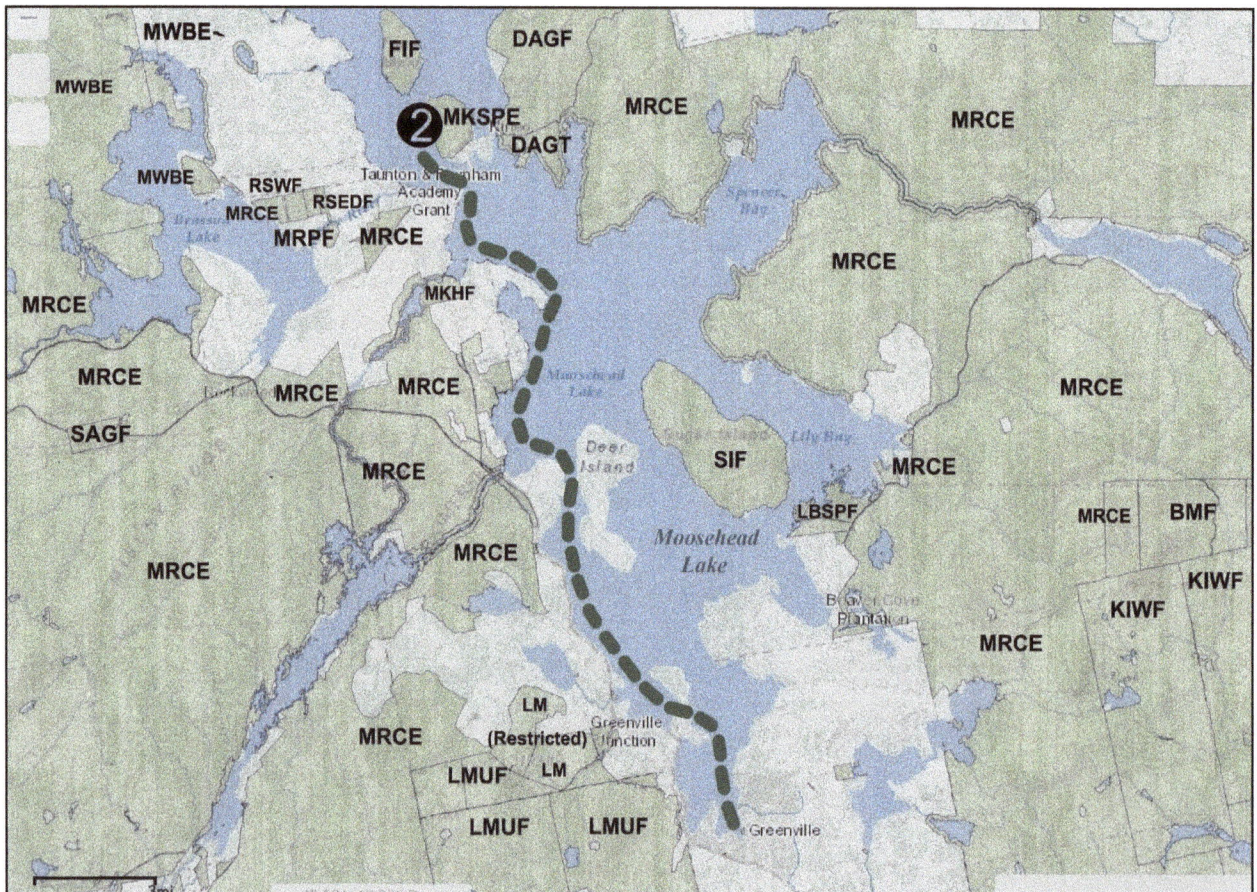

Dean B. Bennett

"I was exceedingly interested by this phenomenon," Thoreau wrote, "and already felt paid for my journey. It could have hardly thrilled me more . . . ."[4] His encounter with the "phosphorescent wood" and subsequent discussion with Polis put Thoreau in the mood to take in and accept the mysteries of the woods that are unexplained by science. "I was in just the frame of mind to see something wonderful, and this was a phenomenon adequate to my circumstances and expectation, and it put me on the alert to see more like it. . . . A scientific *explanation*, as it is called, would have been altogether out of place there. . . . It suggested to me that there was something to be seen if one had eyes. It made a believer of me more than before. I believed that the woods were not tenantless, but choke-full of honest spirits . . . . [and] . . . I was glad to make acquaintance with the light that dwells in rotten wood."[5]

It is in nature, raw and undisturbed, that we can have encounters that bring us closer to the natural world, of which we are a part. The conservation of wild places, such as Mount Kineo State Park, helps ensure that we will continue to have encounters that humble us with the realization that we know so little about the mysteries of nature.

3. MUD POND CARRY

"we entered on a level and very wet and
rocky path . . . a loosely paved gutter"
July 27, 1857

In 1857, after following his 1853 route down the West Branch from Moosehead Lake, Thoreau and his party continued beyond Chesuncook Lake to Mud Pond Carry, which would lead them into the Allagash watershed. Thoreau wrote that Polis, his guide, "said that this was the wettest carry in the State, and as the season was a very wet one, we anticipated an unpleasant walk." They soon realized that this was a correct assumption, for Thoreau reported that "after a light assent from the lake [Umbazooksus] . . . we entered on a level and very wet and rocky path through the universal dense evergreen forest, a loosely paved gutter merely, where we went leaping from rock to rock and from side to side, in the vain attempt to keep out of the water and mud. . . . The Indian with his canoe soon disappeared before us; but erelong he came back and told us to take a path which turned westward . . . and agreed to leave a bough in the regular carry at that place, that we might not pass it by mistake."[1]

Thoreau did not have much faith in the plan, and all too soon he and his companion, Edward Hoar, became lost. "It was impossible," he wrote, "for us to discern the Indian's trail in the elastic moss . . . ." But the two kept going, even as the walking grew worse and the land became increasingly swampy. "We sank a foot deep in water and mud at every step, and sometimes up to our knees, and the trail was almost obliterated."

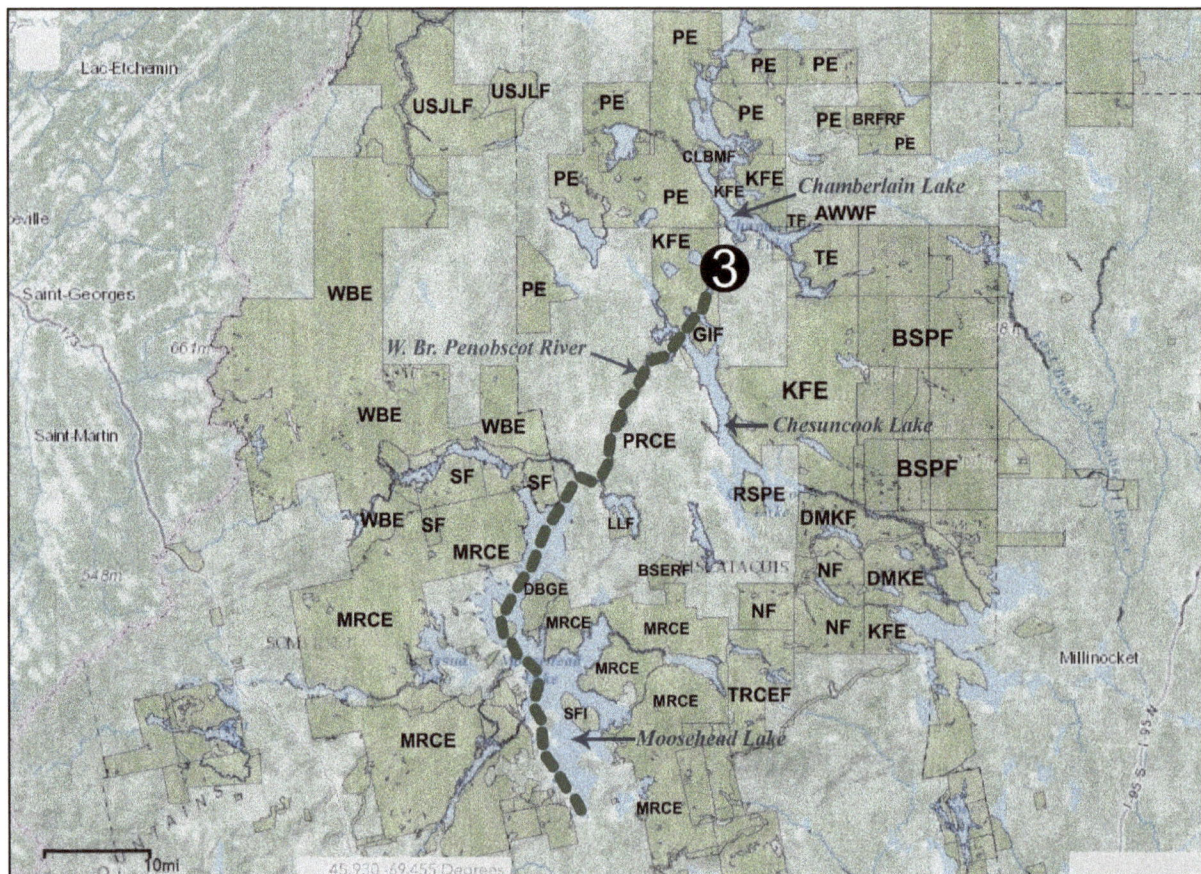

Dean B. Bennett

Eventually, Polis found them after he had discovered their disappearance. They reconnoitered, and Polis decided to go back and continue with the canoe while Thoreau and Hoar continued "through alternate mud and water" to Chamberlain lake. They joined up with Polis on the lake's shore, had a late supper, and slept that night under the stars. Reminiscing about the experience, Thoreau said, "I would not have missed that walk for a good deal."[2]

In July of 1999, 142 years later, the author made the trip down the West Branch and across Mud Pond Carry into Chamberlain Lake with family members. Each evening Thoreau's account of the area just traveled was read. Except for three bridges and a road that crosses Mud Pond Carry trail, the canoeist, traveling between protected corridors of uncut trees that screen from sight the logging beyond, is still able to capture the feeling of remoteness and wildness Thoreau expressed on his trip. And the carry itself lived up to its reputation, as the author, like Thoreau, had to wade knee high into the lake to wash off footwear and clothing after the carry. There are no conservation measures in place to protect the carry except the last 500 feet before entering Chamberlain Lake, as it lies in land purchased by the state for the Allagash Wilderness Waterway.

4. CHAMBERLAIN LAKE

"we had come out on a point extending into
Apmoojenegamook or Chamberlain Lake"
July 27, 1857

After spending the night on the shore, Thoreau said that "when we awoke we found a heavy dew on our blankets. . . . It was a pleasant sunrise, and we had a view of the mountains in the southeast. Ktaadn appeared about southeast by south. . . . [after breakfast] we crossed the lake early . . . to the outlet . . . .The Indian name, Apmoojenegamook, means lake that is crossed, because the usual course lies across, and not along it. This is the largest of the Allagash lakes. . . ."[1]

"A belt of dead trees stood all around the lake, some far out in the water, with others prostrate behind them, and they made the shore, for the most part, almost inaccessible. This is the effect of the dam at the outlet. Thus the natural sandy or rocky shore, with its green fringe, was concealed and destroyed. We reached the outlet in about an hour, and carried over the dam there, which is quite a solid structure, and about one quarter of a mile farther there was a second dam. . . . the result of this . . . damming . . . is that the head-waters of the St. John are made to flow by Bangor. They have thus dammed all the larger lakes, raising their broad surfaces many feet . . . that they might float their spoils out of the country. They rapidly run out of these immense forests all the finer, and more accessible pine timber, and then leave the bears to watch the decaying dams . . . ."[2]

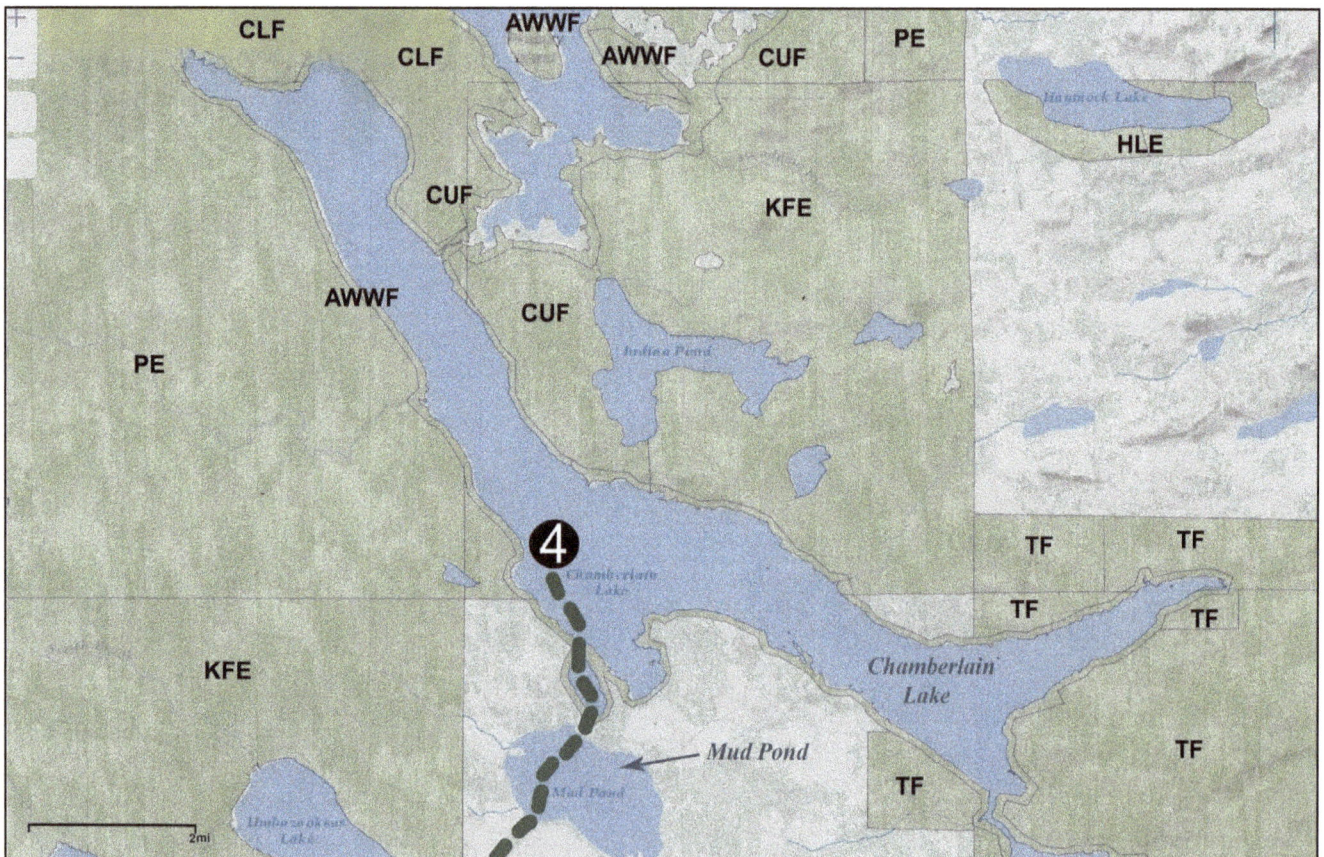

Dean B. Bennett

"Below the last dam, the river being swift and shallow, though broad enough, we two walked about half a mile to lighten the canoe. . . . We were now fairly on the Allagash River, which name our Indian said meant hemlock bark. These waters flow northward . . . ."[3]

Today, the Allagash waters Thoreau entered are within the state-owned Allagash Wilderness Waterway, where one may paddle nearly a hundred miles from one end to the other. The waterway was created in 1966 by the State of Maine and supported by the vote of a bond issue by the citizens. With both state and federal funding, Maine purchased an average of 500 feet around all the headwaters lakes and the river—a total length of perhaps 250 miles of frontage. This land is called a restricted zone and must, by law, be "developed for its maximum wilderness character." The state owns about 23,000 acres in the restricted zone, including three dams and two grandfathered sporting camps. Beyond this zone, is a one-quarter mile area where any new construction requires approval. Beyond a "mile zone" provides further protections as a buffer. If Thoreau were to return today, he would still see some dri ki remnants of the dead trees that once littered the shores of the lakes and that most of the waterway's shoreland is still undeveloped, and he could take comfort in knowing that it never will be.

5. EAGLE LAKE

"after perhaps two miles . . . we entered
Heron Lake [now Eagle Lake]"
July 28, 1857

Having left the dam between Chamberlain and Eagle Lakes, Thoreau related that he and his party went on, and "after perhaps two miles of river, we entered Heron Lake [now Eagle Lake]. This is the fourth great lake, lying northwest and southeast, like Chesuncook and most of the long lakes in the neighborhood, and, judging from the map, it is about ten miles long. We had entered it on the southwest side, and saw a dark mountain northeast over the lake, not very far off nor high, which the Indian said was called *Peaked Mountain*, and used by explorers to look for timber from. . . . The shores were in the same ragged and unsightly condition, encumbered with dead timber, both fallen and standing, as in the last lake, owing to the dam on the Allegash below. Some low points of islands were almost drowned. I saw something white a mile off on the water, which turned out to be a great gull on a rock in the middle . . . ."[1]

Today, one must still carry over a dam between Chamberlain and Eagle Lakes to follow Thoreau's route to Eagle Lake. In 1857, there were two dams providing a "lock" so that logs could be floated from Eagle Lake through a gate behind the lower dam and then the water level raised between the two dams to the higher level of Chamberlain Lake to allow the logs to be floated into that lake down through the Telos Lake dam into the Penobscot River and on to the Bangor mills. The name Lock Dam is still used, but only one dam remains— an earthen dam with a large culvert allowing water into a small stream flowing into Eagle Lake. The stream opens into a broad marsh with a widening channel where in summer feeding moose are sometimes seen mingling among the dead trunks and bleached limbs of long-drowned trees. In the distance the southern end of Eagle Lake is visible—the most remote of the large Allagash lakes. The lake, with a maximum depth of 124 feet, consists of two deep basins with a large volume of cold, well oxygenated water offering an ideal home for brook and lake trout, whitefish, and others. The irregular shoreline conceals inlets of brooks and streams and sporting beautiful sand beaches and rocky bluffs. Islands and juts of land provide a haven for wildlife and old-growth trees.[2]

Those following Thoreau's canoe today, nearing Pillsbury Island, would pass by the same forest of white pines that he did, trees that may have started their lives in the 1700s. The old-growth forest contains pines more than three feet in diameter and up to 130 feet tall—among the tallest in Maine. With a life span of up to 450 years, some may exist here for another two centuries provided that wind-throw, fire, or some other natural catastrophe doesn't occur. A spectacular, occasional inhabitant of this forest is the bald eagle. Today, the forest is in a State Ecological Reserve.[3]

6. PILLSBURY ISLAND

"the grandest thunder. . . and the lightning . . . .
all for the moose and us"
July 28, 1857

You see it coming—the storm—and paddle harder toward the island you know as Pillsbury. The wind is rising and so are the waves, drumming their determined high-hat rhythm against the rumbling beat of thunder. You steer into a shallow channel between low ledges closest to the mainland side, brushing reeds and sedges that swish and tremble in the gusting wind. Beneath the wildly waving limbs of an overhanging maple, you find some protection behind a barrier of shrubs, already bent in submission to the growing weight of the storm. The approaching shower looks heavy. The sky darkens and lowers, squeezing light to the horizon—a sunset mirage. Overhead, the maple's leaves ignite and mingle chameleon-like with flashes of lightning that slash the sky. A moose on the point decides it's time to leave. It has more sense than you thought.

It was nearly a century and a half before that Thoreau recorded: "Rounding a point, we stood across a bay for a mile and a half or two miles, toward a large island three or four miles down the lake. . . . We landed on . . . a rocky shore . . . ." It was here that Thoreau was "tempted" to continue down the Allagash and St. John Rivers to reach the Penobscot River and Bangor by way of the Mattawamkeag River. When he asked Polis which way would take them "through the wildest country," Polis said "the route by the East Branch [of the Penobscot River]." That was the route chosen.[1]

It was close to noon when the party landed on the island. After having their dinner, the wind came up, and all too soon they found themselves windbound. As the day wore on, they saw an approaching "thunder-shower" and hastily pitched their tent, huddling under it as the storm passed. Thoreau said that "we listened to some of the grandest thunder which I ever heard . . . and the lightning was proportionally brilliant. The Indian said 'It must be good powder.' All for the benefit of the moose and us, echoing far over the connected lakes."[2]

It was late afternoon when the storm let up, and despite the distant rumbles of thunder, the party packed up and paddled rapidly back toward the dams and Chamberlain Lake. Thoreau was headed for the "wildest country" where he hoped to find a primeval nature remote from human habitation, where he could experience the raw, powerful forces with which humans must contend, and where he could obtain a clearer view of a more direct human relationship with the natural world.

Today, many come to places in the Allagash for the same reasons, and the island he just left, Pillsbury Island, is one of those places—a place managed for its maximum wilderness character as a part of Maine's Allagash Wilderness Waterway.

7. CHAMBERLAIN FARM

"we were glad to reach . . . in the dusk,
the cleared shore of the Chamberlain Farm"
July 28, 1857

Chased by thunderstorms and shoved and pommeled by violent waves down the north side of Chamberlain Lake, Thoreau and his companions were relieved and "glad to reach . . . the cleared shore of the Chamberlain Farm." Landing "on a low and thinly wooded point," they saw "a clearing extending back from the lake to a hill-top, with some dark-colored log buildings and a storehouse in it."[1]

While his companions were making camp, Thoreau, mindful that this was a supply depot, "ran up to the house to get some sugar," for their six pounds were gone. "Polis had a sweet tooth. He would first fill his dipper nearly a third full of sugar, and then add the coffee to it." For the remainder of the trip, however, Polis had to ration his sugar, as the supply-keeper at the farm was "unwilling to spare more than four pounds of brown sugar,--unlocking the storehouse to get it."[2]

When Thoreau returned to the shore in the dark, he found "a rousing fire to warm and dry . . . by, and a snug apartment behind it." After "cutting spruce and arbor-vitae twigs for a bed," he rolled himself in his blanket, stretched out on his six- by two-foot bed under a thin sheet of cotton for a roof, and felt "snug as a meadow-mouse in a nest."[3]

Of his encounter with the farm, Thoreau would later write: "The Chamberlain Farm is no doubt a cheerful opening in the woods, but such was the lateness of the hour that it has left but a dusky impression in my mind."[4] Thoreau would never know that the farm would become the largest farm and logging depot in the Maine woods. At the time of his brief visit, the farm consisted of six buildings: a farmhouse, a storehouse, and four barns. Ten years later, it had grown to ten buildings.[5] The small clearing that he saw would eventually expand to 600 acres of cleared farmland.[6]

Today, more than a century and a half later, one can visit the old site of Chamberlain Farm and still experience its quiet peacefulness and enjoy its view of the lake, its wooded shoreline, and the majestic Katahdin range, almost unchanged from that experienced by Thoreau. There is still no road to it, nor will there ever be for it sits in the restricted zone of the Allagash Wilderness Waterway. By law, this narrow band of land surrounding the Allagash River and its headwater lakes and streams, must be developed for its "maximum wilderness character." This act of conservation was not easy. It took a long, contentious political battle to bring it about, and, notably, many who fought it were inspired by Thoreau and his account of his trip through these woods.[7]

97

8. RED PINES AND FOSSILS

"we landed on a rocky point . . . to look at some
Red Pines (*Pinus resinosa*), the first we had noticed"
July 29, 1857

"When we awoke [at Chamberlain Farm], . . . We decided to cross the lake at once, before breakfast, or while we could . . . . It was well enough that we crossed early, for the waves now ran quite high . . . . Leaving a spacious bay . . . on our left [Chamberlain Arm], we entered through a short strait into a small lake a couple of miles over, called on the map *Telasinis* . . . and thence into *Telos* Lake . . . . We landed on a rocky point on the northeast side to look at some Red Pines (*Pinus resinosa*), the first we had noticed, and got some cones, for our few which grow in Concord do not bear any."[1]

Red pine, also called Norway pine, undoubtedly grows along this shore because it is sunny and the land is dry and rocky. It usually grows in groves or stands, as it does here, and in a forest where other species dominate, it often is noticeable, and, in this case, it attracted Thoreau's attention. The tree may grow to 100 feet high with a straight trunk up to three feet in diameter. It is a beautiful, dark evergreen tree with reddish-brown bark having shallow fissures and flat plates or ridges. It is valued as an ornamental tree and for construction. Here along the Allagash shore, this stand is protected by the waterway's restricted zone.

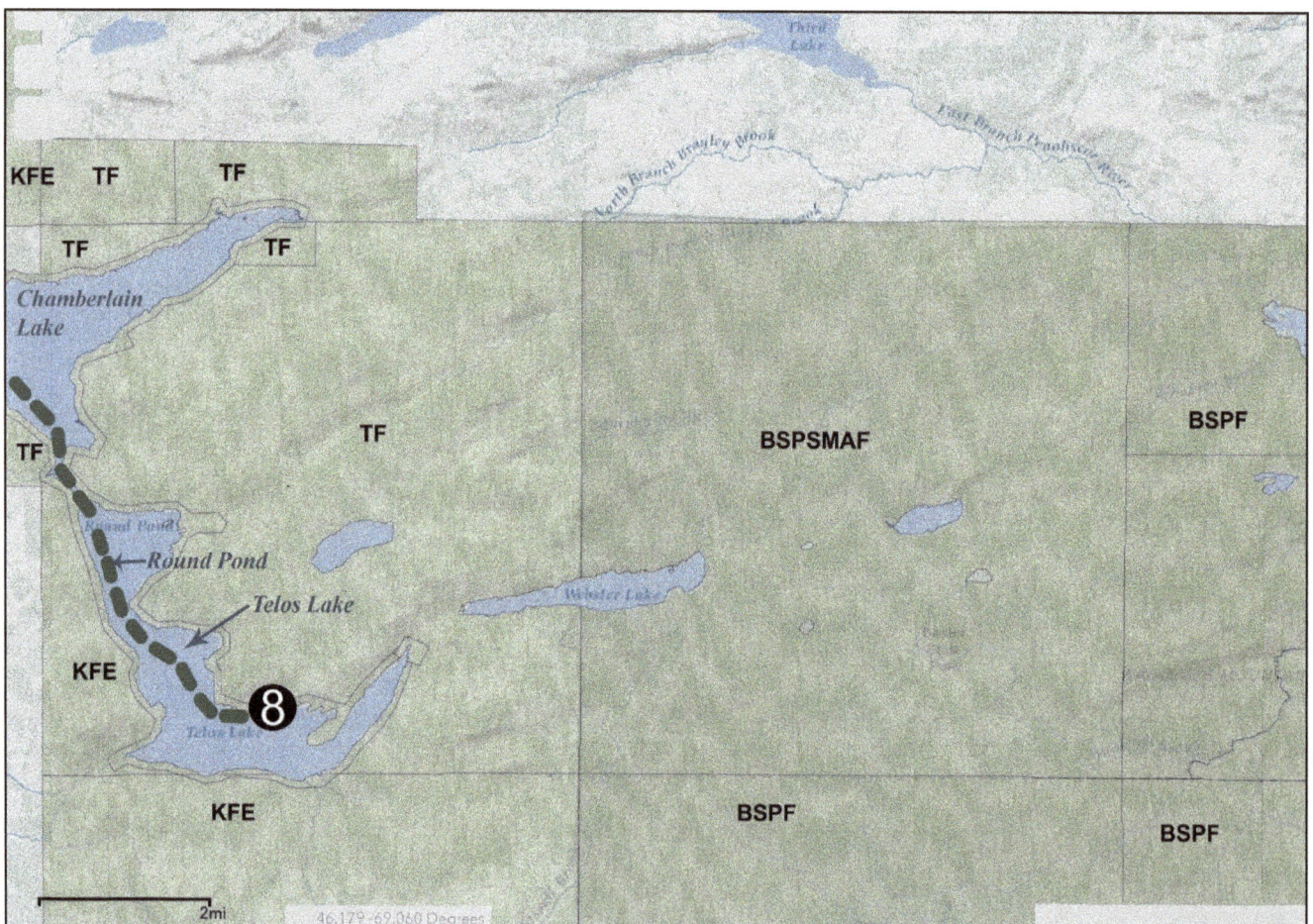

Within sight of the red pine stand, about which Thoreau did not comment and probably did not notice, are striking outcrops of Seboomook slate containing fossils of bi-valved organisms called brachiopods that lived hundreds of millions of years ago. These were discovered four years after Thoreau's 1857 trip by the Massachusetts geologist Charles H. Hitchcock, one of two appointees to head up the 1861 Maine Scientific Survey. The other appointed head was Ezekiel Holmes, who taught chemistry and natural history at Waterville College [now Colby College] in Maine. While the scientific party stayed at Chamberlain Farm, Hitchcock spent a day studying the fossils near the red pines that he had discovered on the trip to the farm. When Hitchcock returned from his study and collecting, Holmes said that Hitchcock "had found a large harvest of fossils, and some of them he exhibited triumphantly as 'not being in the books,' and therefore new to science. In these days of fratricidal warfare and bloody victories [a reference to the Civil War currently being fought] . . . but after all, there are no victories so really and lastingly beneficial to the world, and so productive of good to the great brotherhood of man as the sinless and noiseless triumphs of mind over matter, as manifested in the scientific developments of the mysteries of nature."[2]

9. SHELDRAKES

"a long string of sheldrakes,
which something scared"
July 29, 1857

Thoreau called them sheldrakes, the customary name used until the late nineteenth century to identify the common merganser, a species of old-world waterfowl, which was also called goosander, among other names. This variegated, web-footed bird is one of the largest of inland ducks in North America. To become airborne, it must beat its wings wildly and literally run over the water for some distance. Its forte, however, is diving and fishing, for which it is superbly designed and smoothly coordinated. One distinguished authority on nature said that it is the "possibly worst enemy of fish in the whole duck family," although he went on to say that this "has not been definitely established."[1] But being a top predator in a food chain, the bird has become an environmental-health indicator of the presence of contaminants and acidification in lakes and streams.[2]

Thoreau made numerous observations of sheldrakes in the Maine woods. On July 9, 1857, as he sat on the shore of Webster Brook, he saw "a long string of sheldrakes, which something scared . . . ."[3] He saw them on all three trips, noting that they are "very abundant on all the streams and lakes which we visited, and every two or three hours they would rush away in a long string over the water before us, twenty to fifty of them at once, rarely ever flying, but running with great rapidity up or down the stream, even in the midst of the most violent rapids, and apparently as fast up as down, or else crossing diagonally, the old, as it appeared, behind, and driving them, and flying to the front from time to time, as if to direct them.[4]

Sheldrakes generally nest in hollow trees but also will nest on the ground or in crevices. It will also nest in artificial nesting boxes. The availability of nesting sites seems to be a factor in its populations, and it has experienced loss of habitat because of development and urbanization. However, populations in North America are stable and not considered to be threatened at this time. The common merganser is protected by the U. S. Migratory Bird Act.[5]

As abundant as this duck was, Thoreau never mentioned it being taken for food on his Maine woods trips. One well known naturalist has said that the common merganser might be edible in emergencies "if entrails are removed immediately after [the] bird is killed."[6] But another was more blunt about its fitness to be eaten: "Its flesh as ordinarily cooked is so rank and strong that its flavor is not much superior to that of an old kerosene lamp-wick but some of the hardy gunners of the Atlantic coast know how to prepare it for the table in a way to make it quite palatable."[7]

Fortunately, for the Sheldrake, palatable has more than one meaning. For those who, like Thoreau, venture into this north woods country to savor a taste of its wildness, an unexpected encounter with a family of sheldrakes is palatable, indeed.

10. BURNT LAND

"this burnt land was an exceedingly
wild and desolate region"
July 29, 1857

It was when Polis took the canoe by himself down a difficult place in Webster Brook, that Thoreau and Hoar, while walking along through the woods, came "at the edge of some burnt land, which extended three or four miles above Second Lake . . . . This burnt region was still more rocky than before, but, though comparatively open, we could not yet see the lake. . . . This burnt land was an exceedingly wild and desolate region. Judging by the weeds and sprouts, it appeared to have been burnt about two years before. It was covered with charred trunks, either prostrate or standing, which crocked our clothes and hands, and we could not easily have distinguished a bear there by his color. Great shells of trees, sometimes unburnt without, or burnt on one side only, but black within, stood twenty or forty feet high. The fire had run up inside, as in a chimney, leaving the sap-wood. Sometimes we crossed a rocky ravine fifty feet wide, on a fallen trunk; and there were great fields of fire-weed (*Epilobium angustifolium*) on all sides, the most extensive that I ever saw, which presented great masses of pink. Intermixed with these were blueberry and raspberry bushes."[1]

At one point while following along on foot as Polis was taking the canoe down the rapids, Thoreau and Hoar climbed a high rocky ridge near the brook to see if they could glimpse Second Lake toward where the party was headed. "There was a remarkable series of these great rock-waves revealed by the burning; breakers, as it were," Thoreau wrote. "No wonder that the river that found its way through them was rapid and obstructed by falls. No doubt the absence of soil on these rocks, or its dryness where there was any, caused

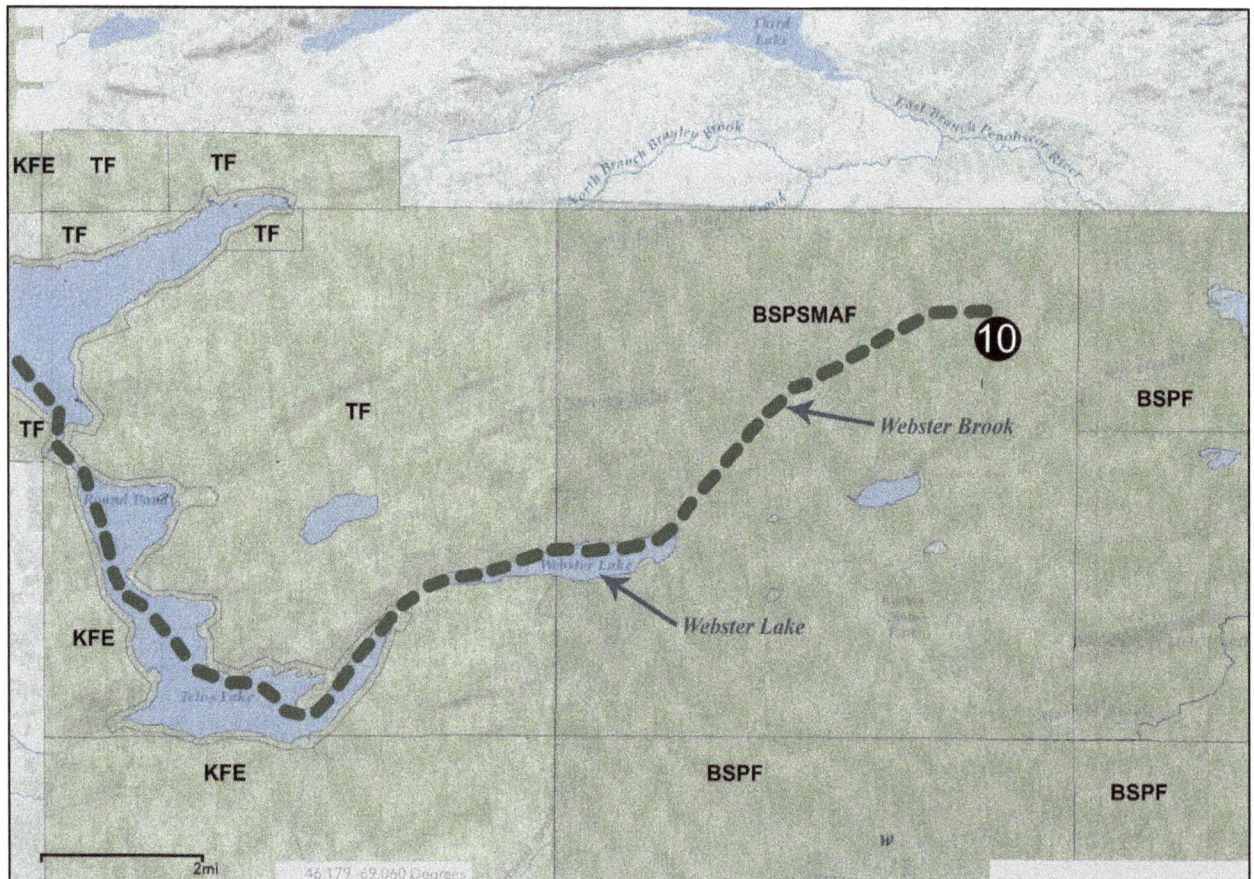

this to be a very thorough burning. We could see the lake over the woods, two or three miles ahead . . . ." It was not long afterward that Thoreau and Hoar became separated, and it was not until after a worrisome night that Thoreau found Hoar the next morning.[2]

Large forest fires occurred throughout the Maine north woods in the centuries before Thoreau's journeys into the region. It was not until the 1890s, well after his trips, that Maine created the Maine Forest Commission and the position of forest commissioner. Preventing and fighting forest fires was a major concern of the commission, attested by forest fire lookout towers on many tall mountains throughout the state. Studies show that 90 percent of all wildfires in Maine are caused by people and are preventable. Only lightning-caused fires cannot be prevented. Today, under the Maine Forest Service, many programs and services are in place to prevent and extinguish forest fires. These include holding membership in the Northeastern Forest Fire Protection Commission and training and recruitment of forest rangers in detecting, preventing, and suppressing forest fires, as well as enforcing forestry, environmental, and conservation laws.[3]

11. GRAND PITCH WEBSTER BROOK

"the fall close by was the principal one on this stream,
and it shook the earth under us"
July 29, 1857

With Hoar separated from them and missing and darkness descending on them, Thoreau and Polis decided the best thing to do would be to set up camp where they were. Thoreau said that with the side of the river they were on "being so encumbered with rocks, we crossed to the eastern or smoother shore, and proceeded to camp there, within two or three rods of the Falls. We pitched no tent, but lay on the sand, putting a few handfuls of grass and twigs under us, there being no evergreen at hand. For fuel we had some of the charred stumps. Our various bags of provisions had got quite wet in the rapids, and I arranged them about the fire to dry. The fall close by was the principal one on this stream, and it shook the earth under us. It was a cool, because dewy night; the more so, probably, owing to the nearness of the falls." Thoreau did not sleep well, anxious as he was about his companion.[1]

In 1977, the State of Maine, through its Critical Areas Program, initiated a study to identify and evaluate the waterfalls of the state and to recommend those for designation as critical areas. The waterfalls were evaluated for their geologic, historic, economic, and ecological significance and for their scenic and recreational value. The program encouraged the conservation of designated waterfalls by working with landowners, planning agencies, state and federal agencies, and private organizations. The program recognized that one of

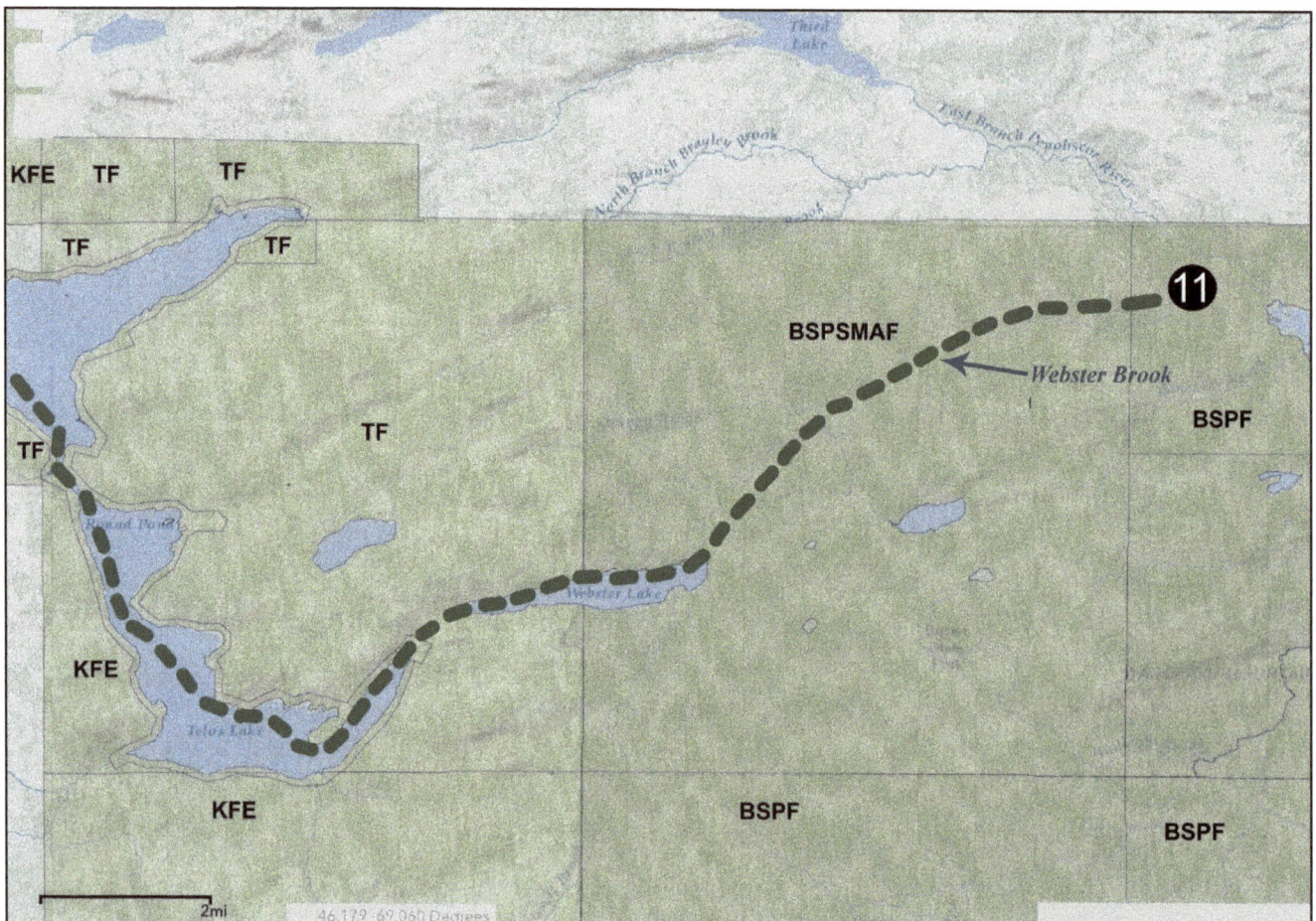

the greatest threats to the preservation of waterfalls is the damaging effect that increasing numbers of visitors can have on locations that have fragile environments. One of the waterfalls designated as having state signif-icance was the waterfall that Thoreau and Polis slept near on Webster Brook during the night of July 29, 1857. This is known as Grand Pitch on Webster Brook.[2]

Grand Pitch was field checked in 1984, and was found to have a 20 to 25 foot pitch in two stages, occurring in immediate succession. A short break of about three feet interrupts the two portions at about midpoint. Each stage is about vertical. The location is still remote, as it is about a five-mile hike along a foot path from the Baxter State Park perimeter road. Both the waterfalls and the woodland along the trail beside the falls are highly natural and are also protected by being within the park. Above Grand Pitch, Webster Brook has additional, smaller pitches, including one known as Indian Pitch. Sections of Webster Brook above and below Grand Pitch have also been identified as critical whitewater areas. Grand Pitch is seen as one of the most beautiful falls in the state. Potholes also occur in the bedrock near the falls. Those who see the falls when sunlight conditions are right will see a small rainbow near the top of the falls.[3]

12. SECOND LAKE

"we glided swiftly down the winding stream
Toward Second Lake . . . . a very beautiful lake"
July 30, 1857

Soon after leaving Grand Pitch on the morning of July 30th, Polis and Thoreau found Hoar on a point below their campsite. Feeling relieved, Thoreau wrote that "we all had good appetites for breakfast which we made haste to cook here, and then, having partially dried our clothes, we glided swiftly down the winding stream toward Second Lake. . . . This was a very beautiful lake, two or three miles long, with high mountains on the southwest side . . . . The morning was a bright one, and perfectly still and serene, the lake as smooth as glass, we making the only ripple as we paddled into it. The dark mountains about it were seen through a glaucous mist, and the brilliant white stems of canoe-birches mingled with the other woods around it. The beauty of the scene may have been enhanced to our eyes by the fact that we had just come together again after a night of some anxiety. . . . A white (or whitish) gull sat on a rock which rose above the surface in mid-lake not far off, quite in harmony with the scene; and as we rested there in the warm sun . . . ."[1]

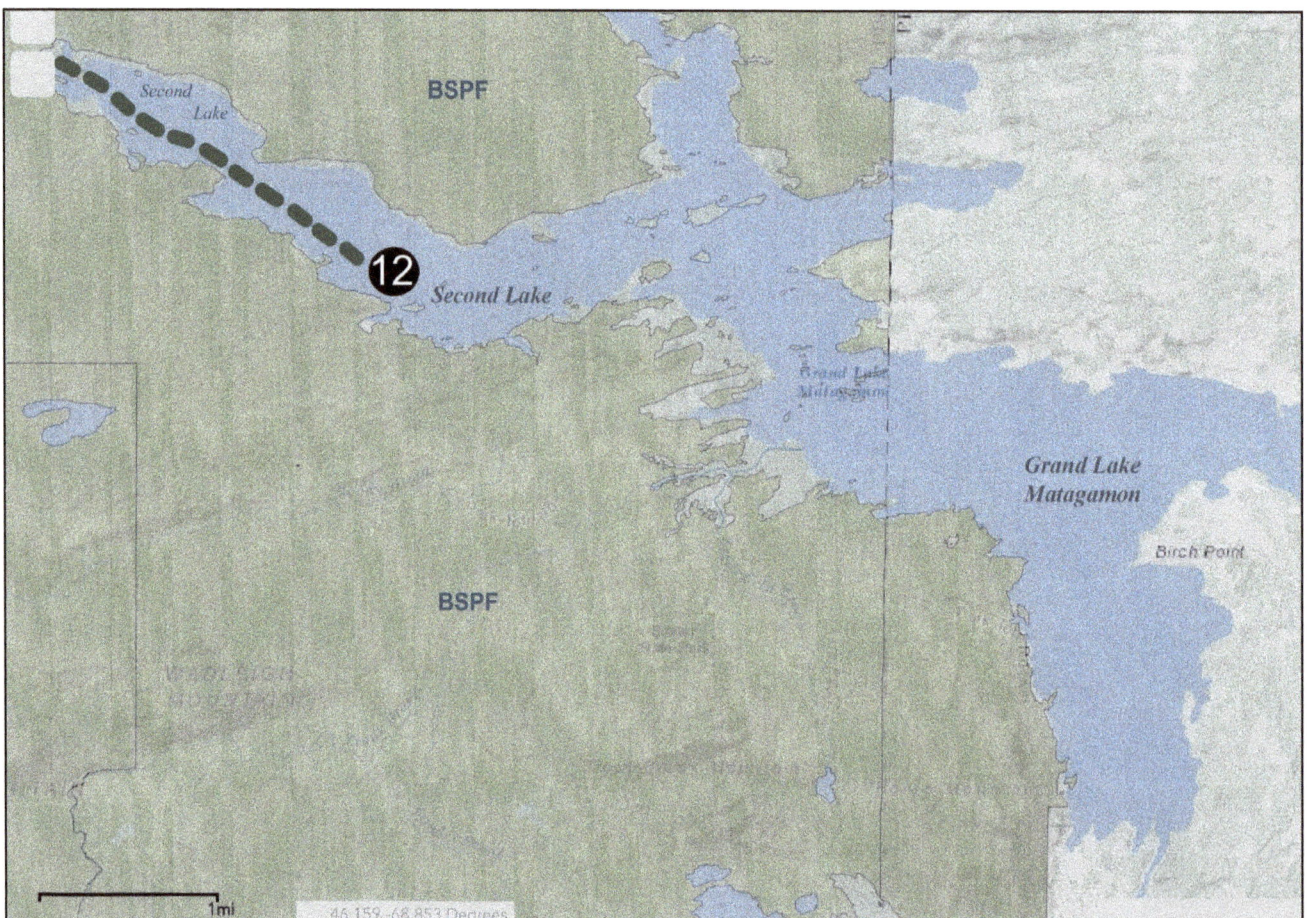

Dean B. Bennett

"As we were approaching the outlet, it being still early in the forenoon, he [Polis] suddenly exclaimed, 'Moose! Moose!' and told us to be still. He put a cap on his gun, and standing up in the stern, rapidly pushed the canoe straight toward the shore and the moose [a cow moose]. . . . the canoe soon grounded in the mud eight or ten rods distant from the moose, and the Indian seized his gun and prepared to fire. After standing still a moment, she turned slowly as usual, so as to expose her side, and he improved this moment to fire, over our heads. . . . we approached the place where the moose had stood, when he exclaimed, 'She is a goner'."[2] Polis proceeded to skin the moose and save what meat and parts he desired. After all was loaded into the canoe, Thoreau wrote that "we continued along the outlet toward Grand Lake, through a swampy region, by a long, winding, and narrow dead water, very much choked up by wood, where we were obliged to land sometimes in order to get the canoe over a log. At length we reached Grand Lake . . . ."[3]

The author has on several occasions camped on Second Lake and watched the beautiful sunsets over the lake. The campsite has a small beach nestled between rocky outcrops where gulls can be watched. The site, itself, is among red pines and beyond is a small wetland through which a stream meanders and an occasional moose may be seen. All of this is within the protective boundaries of Baxter State Park.

13. JACK PINE

"A peculiar evergreen hung over our fire"
July 30, 1857

You land on the island in a little cove out of the wind—a quiet, rocky place. You climb the high ridge running the length of the island where Thoreau saw "a fine view hence over the sparkling lake, which looked pure and deep, and had two or three rocky islands in it."[1] Your view is equally as fine and still retains a degree of wildness, framed as it is by the jack pine with their seemingly unkempt limbs in disarray and irregular clumps of needles.

Around noon of July 30, 1857, Thoreau recorded, "We stopped to dine on an interesting high rocky island, soon after entering Matungamook Lake . . . ."[2] The island is now identified on maps as Louse Island in Grand Lake Matagamon, reportedly named in historic records for its use as a place where lumbermen were deloused after spending a winter in the woods. Thoreau continued his narrative: "We proceeded to make a fire and cook our dinner amid some pines . . . . A peculiar evergreen overhung our fire . . . . We found it to be Pinus Banksiana—Banks or the Labrador Pine, also called Scrub Pine, Gray Pine, &c., a new tree to us. These must have been good specimens, for several were thirty or thirty-five feet high."[3]

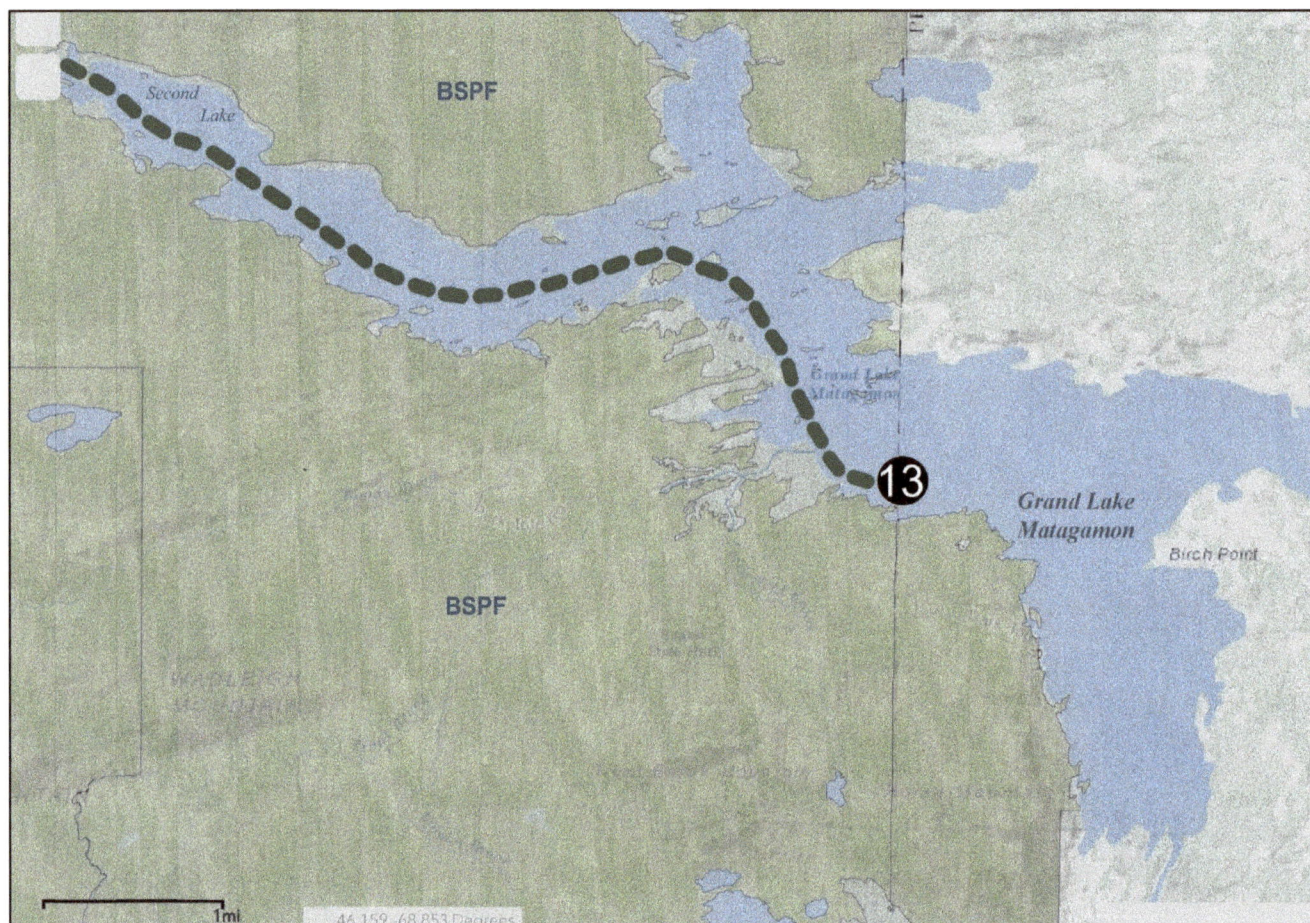

The tree, named in honor of the botanical scientist, Sir Joseph Banks, currently goes by the accepted common name of jack pine. While the name "jack" is somewhat of a mystery, it is associated with the idea of being generally useful, such as a "jack-of-all-trades." The wood has construction and pulp value, and the tree is the hardiest of the pines when it comes to withstanding cold.[4]

Four years after Thoreau and his party visited the island, George L. Goodale, the botanist with the Maine Scientific Expedition, also arrived there and reported finding the jack pine: "Here I found it was abundant, and was informed by an experienced lumberman attached to our party, that this 'Shore pine' or 'Rock pine' occurs very rarely in the forests of the State . . . ."[5] While Goodale confirmed the existence of jack pine on the island, the credit for its first identification goes to Thoreau and Hoar. According to a report prepared by Maine's Critical Areas Program in the early 1980s, Thoreau and Hoar's discovery of jack pine on the island "represents the earliest historical record for the species" in Maine.[6] Hoar deposited a specimen in the New England Botanical Club's herbarium. [7]

So it was that a small, tough, scraggly pine, sporting tufted clumps of short, twisted needles, contorted cones, and scaly bark, living on an island with the unusual name of "Louse," captured the attention of two botanists while they dined on moose meat provided by a Penobscot Native on an island that is now Penobscot National Trust land.

14. EAST BRANCH

"I could not distinguish the outlet
till we were almost in it."
July30, 1857

"There was a fine view hence over the sparkling lake, which looked pure and deep, and had two or three, in all, rocky islands in it. Our blankets being dry, we set out again . . . .We paddled southward down this handsome lake, which appeared to extend nearly as far east as south, keeping near the western shore. . . . It was three or four miles across it. . . . I could not distinguish the outlet till we were almost in it, and heard the water falling over the dam there. Here was a considerable fall, and a very substantial dam, but no sign of a cabin or camp.[1]

Having carried over the dam, he [Polis] darted down the rapids, leaving us to walk for a mile of more, where for the most part there was no path, but very thick and difficult traveling near the stream. . . . At length, climbing over the willows and fallen trees, when this was easier than to go round or under them, we overtook the canoe, and glided down the stream in smooth but swift water for several miles. . . . We decided to camp early to-night, that we might have ample time before dark; so we stopped at the first favorable shore, where there was a narrow gravelly beach on the western side, some five miles below the outlet of the lake. . . . the last of the peculiar moose-faced . . . mountains not far southwest of Grand Lake rose dark in the northwest a short distance behind, displaying its gray precipitous southeast side, but we could not see this without coming out upon the shore."[2]

Dean B. Bennett

In 1941, eighty-four years after Thoreau's party came to the dam at the outlet of Grand Matagamon Lake, the existing dam was constructed. It is a concrete structure, 218 feet long and 30 feet high. It replaced a timber crib structure, which was built in the 1880s and, in turn, replaced the one Thoreau described. The 1941 dam backs up waters that include Second Lake and First Lake, which combined to become Grand Matagamon Lake with a total impoundment of 4,200 acres and a total drainage area of 496 square miles. It was owned and operated by the East Branch Improvement Company and managed for hydroelectric storage in the Penobscot River System. In January 2001, the ownership of Matagamon Dam was transferred to Matagamon Lake Association for the "expressed purpose of maintaining the structure for the benefit of fisheries, wildlife, recreational values, and downstream safety (flood control). The operation of Matagamon Dam is essential to the cold-water ecosystem: supporting a high quality sport fishery in the East Branch system; regulating the flows . . . [that are] critical to the rehabilitation of the wild brook trout, landlocked and Atlantic salmon. . . .[and] water levels . . . for lake trout . . . and waterfowl nursery."[3]

15. EAST BRANCH COUNTRY

"it was an interesting spot, where the river
began to make a great bend to the east"
July 30, 1857

If Thoreau could have made his way nine miles directly east of the East Branch from below the dam, he would have come to Sugarloaf Mountain. At 1,862 feet in elevation, it would have given him a spectacular view of the country he was about to pass through. He would have been high above the East Branch in the distance and the "interesting spot [he had camped at], where the river began to make a great bend to the east . . . ."[1] He would have seen Katahdin in the distance where he had hoped to climb, the Seboeis River below, the course of the Wassataquoik Stream, the mountains along the East Branch, and the Katahdin Woods and Waters National Monument.

On August 24, 2016, President Barack Obama issued a proclamation that 87,563 acres of land in the East Branch country of the Penobscot River become the Katahdin Woods and Waters National Monument. It is within a larger landscape of lands already conserved by public and private efforts. The Monument, the words of the President's proclamation, "contains a significant piece of this extraordinary natural and cultural landscape: the mountains, woods, and waters east of Baxter State Park (home of Mount Katahdin, the northern terminus of the Appalachian Trail), where the East Branch of the Penobscot River and its tributaries, including the Wassataquoik Stream and the Seboeis River, run freely. Since the glaciers retreated 12,000 years ago these waterways and associated resources—the scenery, geology, flora and fauna, night skies, and more—have attracted people to this area. Native Americans still cherish these resources. Lumberjacks, river drivers, and timber owners have earned their livings here. Artists, authors, scientists, conservationists, recreationalists, and others have drawn knowledge and inspiration from this landscape."[2]

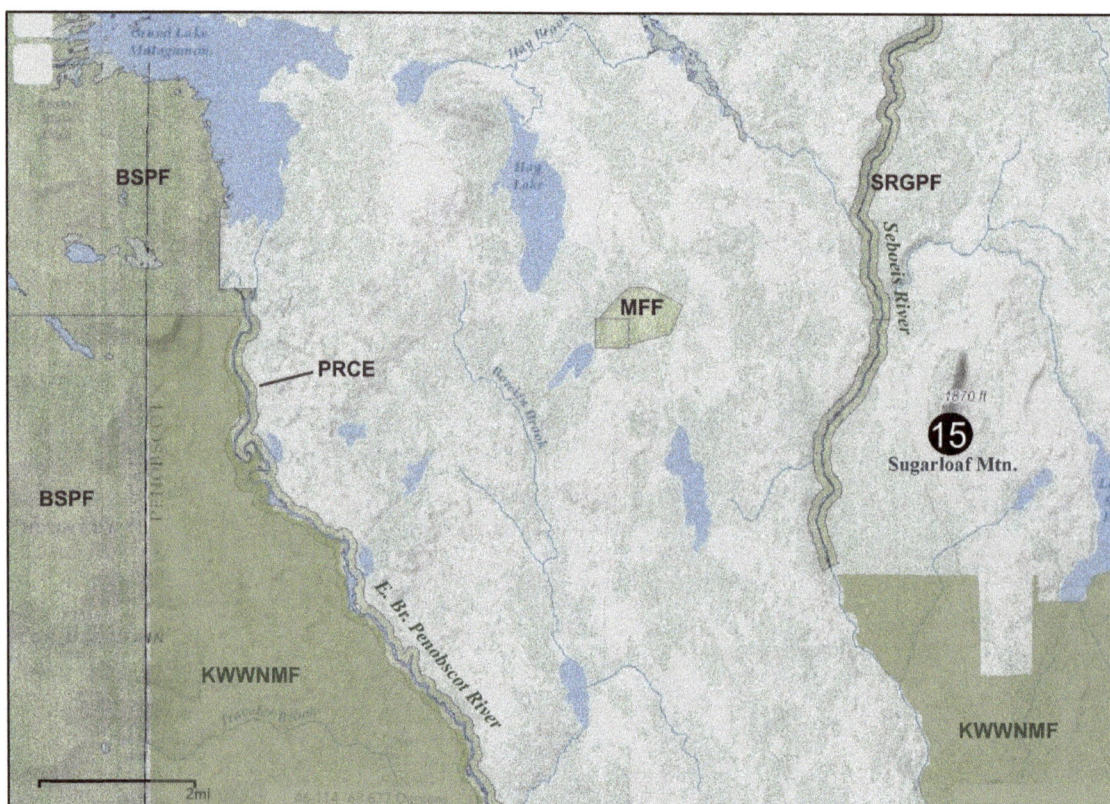

112

Dean B. Bennett

The area has attracted well-known people throughout its history including: Henry David Thoreau, President Theodore Roosevelt, Percival P. Baxter who purchased and gave the nearby 200,000 acre-plus woods (Baxter State Park) to the people of Maine, the artist and naturalist John James Audubon, the artist Frederick Edwin Church, and others.[3]

"The extraordinary significance of the Penobscot East Branch River system has long been recognized. A 1977 Department of Interior study determined that the East Branch of the Penobscot River, including the Wassataquoik Stream, qualifies for inclusion in the National Wild and Scenic Rivers System based on its outstandingly remarkable values, and a 1982 Federal-State study of rivers in Maine determined that the Penobscot East Branch River System, including both the Wassataquoik Stream and the Seboeis River, ranks in the highest category of natural and recreational rivers and possesses nationally significant resource values."[4]

The Katahdin Woods and Waters National Monument represents another of America's great acts of conservation. The land was purchased by Roxanne Quimby and donated by her organization, Elliotsville Plantation, Inc., to the Federal Government of the United States along with a substantial endowment to the National Park Foundation to support its administration.[5]

16. HASKELL ROCK

"we were obliged to carry around
some rapids and falls"
July 31, 1857

On Friday morning, July 31, 1857, about five miles below the dam at the outlet of Grand Lake Mataga-mon, a party of three launched a canoe. In Thoreau's words, "we glided rapidly along, scaring up ducks and kingfishers. But as usual, our smooth progress erelong came to an end, and we were obliged to carry canoe and all about half a mile down the right bank, around some rapids and falls."[1]

This carry, the first of three, took them around a set of rapids known as Haskell Rock Pitch. Here in the river is the rock Thoreau missed, Haskell Rock, named after William M. Haskell, a twenty-five-year-old river driver who drowned on June 19, 1841, while breaking up a log jam.[2] The rock is a curious-looking, river-sculpted outcropping of cemented pebbles and stones once imbedded in sediments of sand or mud and hardened into rock. In a way, the rock is not only a monument to river drivers but to the fascinating geology of a region that was already drawing scientists in Thoreau's day. To the trained eyes of the geologist, this pedestal rising out of the river-scoured bedrock speaks of nearly unfathomable changes in the earth: of continental movement, of land uplifting and tilting, of the creation of ocean basins and building of volcanic islands, of mountains removed mineral grain by mineral grain, of deep water sedimentation, of new rock formation under pressure—all producing a rock outcrop dated to 450 million years ago.[3]

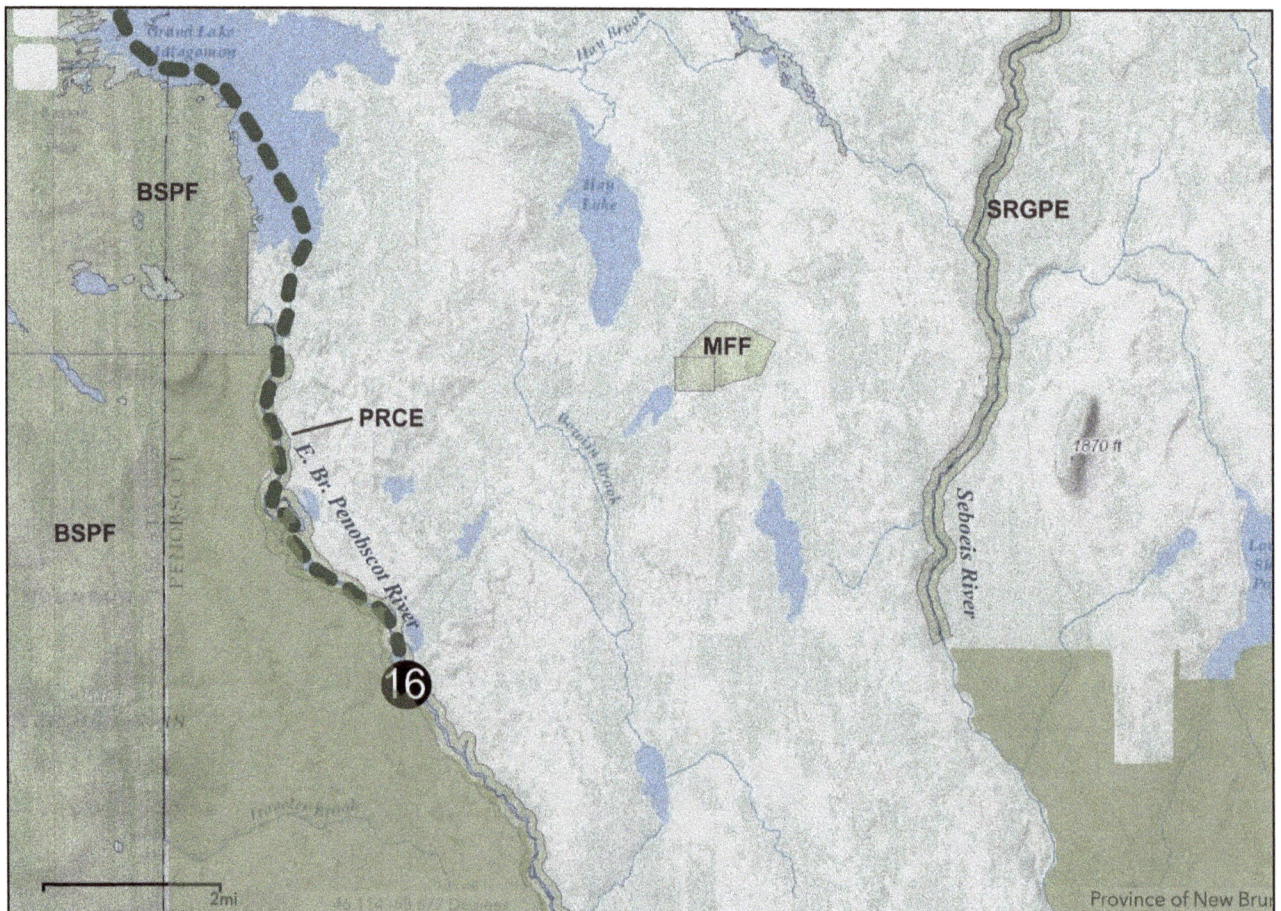

About thirty years after Thoreau passed by the rock, Fannie Hardy, recently graduated from Smith College, was on the East Branch nearing the end of a twenty-four-day trip with her father, Manley Hardy and a guide. Fannie saw the rock on Monday, September 10, 1888. She wrote in her journal that in the morning they broke camp above Stair Falls, where they had been camping for two days, and headed down river. When they reached the falls, she and her father carried their gear and supplies around while their guide dropped the canoe over. "Below Stair Falls," she recorded, "is more quick water and then quite a long space of dead water and logans down to Haskell Rock and Pitch. Here I crawled out on a rock and caught two trout—very small ones . . . . Haskell Rock is a great boulder 15 feet or more above the water, much worn away by water and logs. It stands below the upper pitch. There is here a wing dam to keep logs from striking. Took dinner here and after that lugged our things to the further end of the carry . . . ."[4]

What Thoreau missed, others hadn't, leaving one to wonder what he might have said about this peculiar rock of the Maine woods. But it will be around for a long time for all of us to contemplate, for it is now protected by the Penobscot River Corridor, an easement established in 2005 and held by the Maine Bureau of Parks and Lands.

115

17. GRAND PITCH EAST BRANCH

"we had heard of a Grand Fall on this stream"
July 31, 1857

One of the outstanding features of the East Branch is the section containing numerous difficult but picturesque falls and rapids several miles below the dam. When Thoreau and his party first encountered the rapids and falls and had begun the first of their portages, Thoreau remarked, "We had heard of a Grand Falls on this stream, and thought that each fall we came to must be it, but after christening several in succession with this name, we gave up the search. . . . I can't tell how many times we had to walk on account of falls or rapids. However, the carries were an agreeable variety. So surely as we stepped out of the canoe and stretched our legs we found ourselves in a blueberry and raspberry garden, each side of our rocky trail around the falls being lined with one or both. There was not a carry on the main East Branch where we did not find an abundance of both these berries. . . . In our three journeys over the carries, for we were obliged to go over the ground three times whenever the canoe was taken out, we did full justice to the berries, and they were just what we wanted to correct the effect of our hard bread and pork diet." Before that day was over, the party came to what Thoreau called "the most considerable fall on this stream [Grand Pitch], ..."[1]

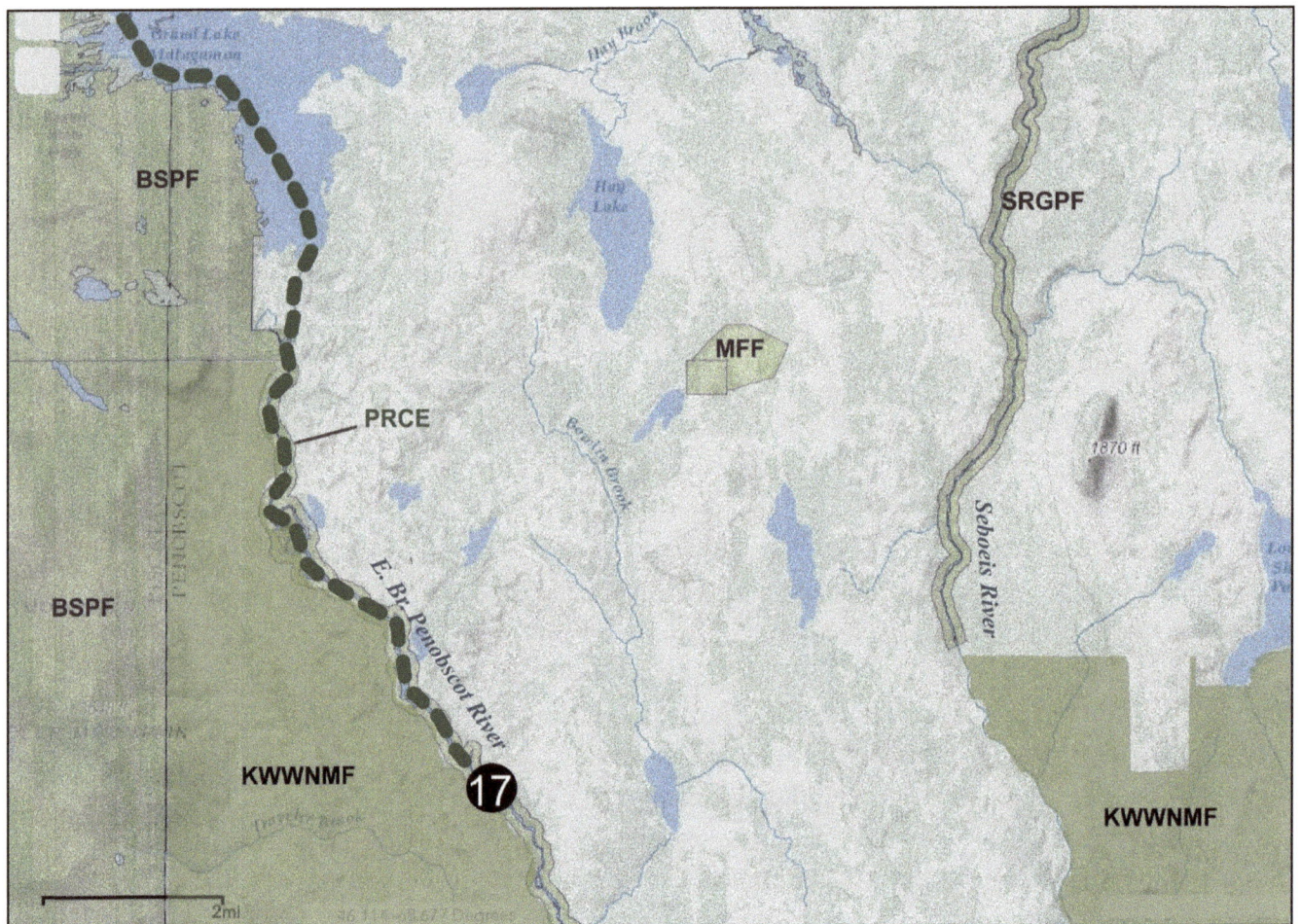

Grand Pitch is one of the outstanding falls investigated by the Maine Critical Areas Program. It was field checked in 1977 and again in 1984 and judged to be of state significance. The general description reported by the researchers is as follows: "Grand Pitch is a spectacular, high-volume, 23-foot drop across the full width of the E. Branch of the Penobscot. The flow is dependent on discharge from Grand Lake Dam, but is typically thousands of ft/sec. There are several good vistas. The site can be reached by . . . a hike. More often it is seen by those taking the popular canoe trip along this section of the river. There is a well-used portage trail around the falls . . . . A large exposure of the Grand Pitch Formation . . . occurs here. Cambrian trace fossils have been reported from this locality . . . . This was a famous site in connection with the log driving history of the State."[2]

Today, the falls can be seen from a trail, the Grand Pitch Trail that follows part of the International Appalachian Trail along the East Branch in the Katahdin Woods and Waters National Monument. However, it would take a long day to complete the trail. The falls also lie within the conservation easement of the Penobscot Corridor. However, all access to significant natural features, including Grand Pitch, places a burden of responsibility on those who visit them—to treat them gently with respect for their integrity and to preserve their natural character not only for itself but for others to enjoy.

18. OLDHAMIA

"we spent at least half the time in walking . . . .
the carry-paths . . . were more than usually indistinct"
July 31, 1857

The Maine woods can be full of surprises, and on their portage around Grand Pitch, Thoreau had a surprise and missed one. Thoreau wrote: "At the most considerable fall on this stream, when I was walking over the carry, close behind the Indian, he observed a track on the rock, which was but slightly covered with soil, and stooping, muttered 'caribou.' When we returned, he observed a much larger track near the same place, where some animal's foot had sunk into a small hollow in the rock, partly filled with grass and earth, and he exclaimed with surprise, 'What that?' 'Well, what is it?' I asked. Stooping and laying his hand in it, he answered with a mysterious air, and in a half whisper, 'Devil [that is, Indian Devil, or cougar) lodges about here—very bad animal . . . .' I had been told that the scream of a cougar was heard about Ktaadn recently, and we were not far from the mountain."[1]

Even Thoreau, Hoar, and Polis, with his sharp eyes, missed another track on that carry, albeit very tiny and faint, and, to them, perhaps surprising, for it was in the rock, itself, rather than on it. It was a fossilized track of a tiny worm-like creature of Early to Middle Cambrian age, around 500 million years ago. It is considered an indicator fossil for that time period. The organism lived in soft sediments and came out of its bur-

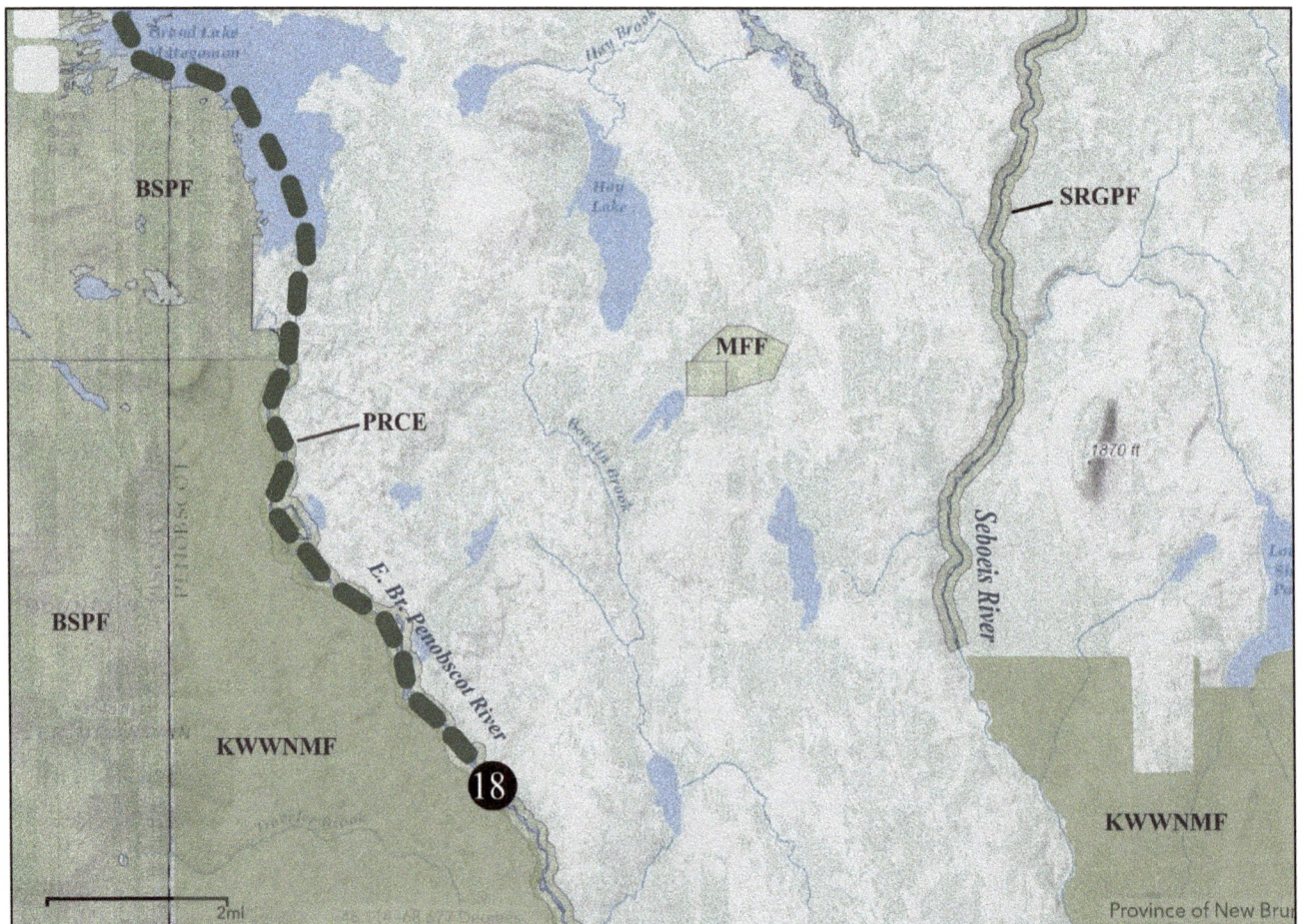

row, perhaps to forage for food, and crawled over the surface, leaving behind a track, trail, or other structure—a trace of its movement, which paleontologists refer to as a trace fossil. This one was named *Oldhamia*, after its discoverer the Anglo-Irish geologist Thomas Oldham (1816-1878). He discovered the radiating, fan-like impressions in 1840. We surmise that the burrows or tracks of the animal, emerging from a hole and moving outward in a line, returning to the hole, and moving outward again in another direction, and returning, on and on, created the appearance of the tiny fan. The individual burrow-like tracks are 0.5 mm in diameter and vary in length from 15 to 30 mm.[2] In 1967, the geologist/paleontologist Robert B. Neuman reported the fossil occurring in "finely laminated micaceous red slate and siltstone" . . . downstream of Grand Pitch along the river bank.[3]

Oldham saw the poetry in fossils and was inspired in 1886 to write the sonnet *Oldhamia antiqua*, of which the following is excerpted: "We—promise of the ages!-Lift thine eyes,/ And gazing on these tendrils intertwined/ For Aeons in the shadows, recognize/ In Hope and Joy, in heaven-seeking Mind,/ In Faith, in Love, in Reason's potent spell/ The visitants that bid the world farewell!"[4]

Today, the fossil remains undisturbed and legally protected inside the Penobscot Corridor.

19. SEBOEIS RIVER

"we passed the mouth of the Seboois on our left"
July 31, 1857

"For seven or eight miles below that succession of 'Grand' falls, the aspect of the banks as well as the character of the stream was changed. After passing a tributary from the northeast, perhaps Bowlin Stream, we had good swift smooth water, with a regular slope. . . . Low, grassy banks and muddy shores began. Many elms, as well as maples, and more ash trees overhung the stream, and supplanted the spruce. . . . Polis detected once or twice what he called a 'tow' road, an indistinct path leading into the forest. In the mean while we passed the mouth of the Seboois on our left. This did not look so large as our stream, which was indeed the main one."[1] The Seboeis, in fact, is a major tributary of the East Branch with its headwaters many miles above in Grand Lake Seboeis, which abuts the Aroostook River watershed.

Grand Lake Seboeis, six miles long, drains to the south into a small body of water called Snowshoe Lake and from there into the Seboeis River. The river soon feeds into White Horse Lake, which is about a mile and a half long, and from there, the Seboeis River continues to its confluence with the East Branch, a total of thirty-six miles from the headwaters of Grand Lake Seboeis, or 28.1 miles from the outlet of the lake.[2]

In a study of Maine's rivers, the most significant value of Seboeis River is its undeveloped character. Other resource values judged to be significant, but which meet a minimum standard of significance, are geologic-hydrologic, scenic, fisheries, whitewater boating, and backcountry excursion.[3]

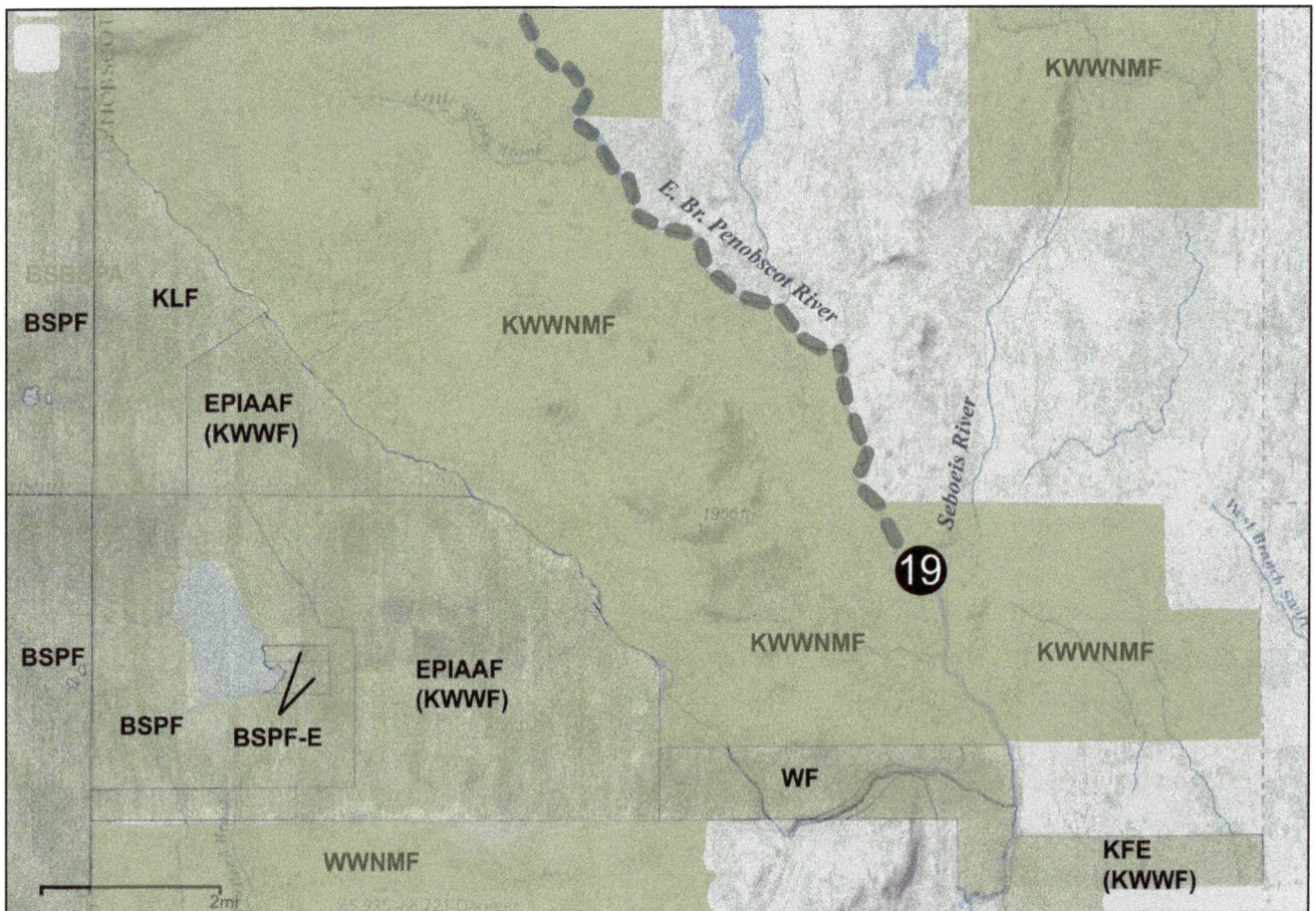

One of the unique natural features of the river is Upper Seboeis River Gorge—a steep, V-shaped gorge, 150 feet deep and six miles long. This is an uninhabited area where no roads reach the river. A waterfall is near the head of the gorge and drops into a large pool. At the foot of the pool, is a small gravel island, and on this, if the season and conditions are right, one may see profuse stands of the beautiful, deep-red cardinal flower.[4]

The mouth of the Seboeis River, where Thoreau passed by, has been identified by the Maine Natural Areas Program as occurring in a focus area of statewide ecological significance. The area "encompasses an ecologically rich confluence of three of Mainc's most intact and scenic waterways [the Seboeis, the Wassataquoik, and the East Branch]. The Focus Area includes significant parts of the rivers, associated floodplain forests and open streamshores, as well as the rugged Hunt, Deasey and Lunksoos Mountains. Local bedrock creates enriched soils here that support an unusual array of rare natural communities and plants, and the backwaters, pools and water quality of the river systems support a diversity of outstanding aquatic features. These are remote, highly scenic, undeveloped rivers with outstanding fishing and recreational opportunities.[5] They are currently protected within the Katahdin Woods and Waters National Monument.

20. THE WASSATAQUOIK

"we had passed the *Wassataquoik*
without perceiving it"
August 1, 1857

After Thoreau and his party had passed the mouth of the Seboeis River, they started looking for a camping place. Thoreau noted that "it was sometime before we found a camping-place, for the shore was either too grassy or muddy, where mosquitoes abounded, or too steep a hillside. . . . We at length found a place to our minds, on the west bank, about a mile below the mouth of the Seboois, where, in a very dense spruce wood above a gravelly shore, there seemed to be but few insects. The trees were so thick that we were obliged to clear a space to build our fire and lie down in, and the young spruce trees that were left were like the wall of an apartment rising around us."[1]

The next day, the party was glad to leave after breakfast, having endured the attack of mosquitoes after all. Thoreau wrote: "We had passed the *Wassataquoik* without perceiving it [on the way to their campsite]. . . . we found that we had camped about a mile above Hunt's [Farm], which is on the east bank, and is the last house for those who ascend Ktaadn on this side."[2] Although Thoreau doesn't mention it, Hunt's was a popular place among visitors who wished to climb Katahdin via the Keep Trail and others exploring up the East Branch and surrounding country.

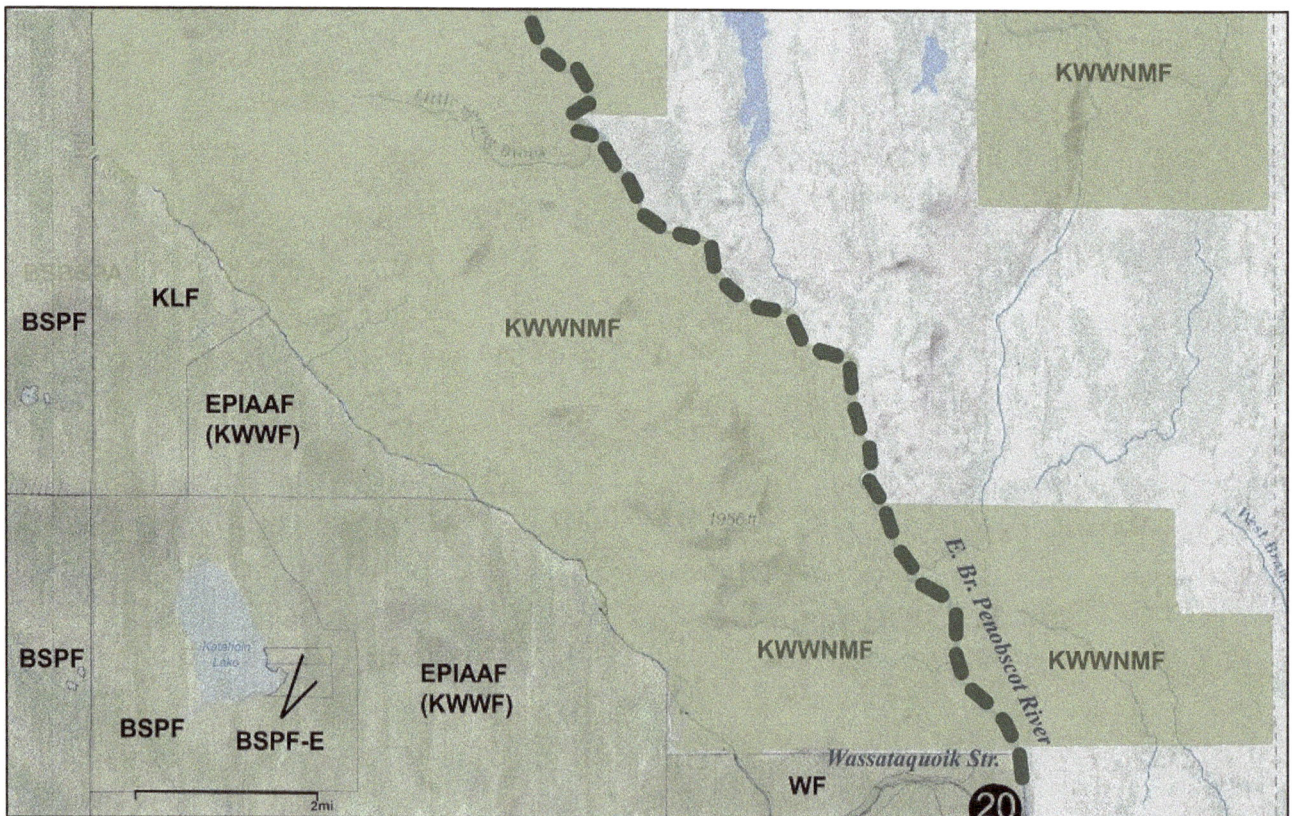

Wassataquoik Stream, from its mouth at the East Branch to its headwaters, is twenty-two miles long. At the confluence of the Wassataquoik with the East Branch is the Wassataquoik Ecological Reserve. According to the Maine Natural Areas Program "the central features are stream bank and river floodplain forests. The steep wooded slopes of Wassataquoik Stream give way at its mouth to a broad floodplain, and the vegetational gradients reflect the effects of topography, hydrology and soils. The mixed forests along the Wassataquoik Stream rise 15-30 meters above the streambed. Both sides of the stream contain scattered older trees, mostly white pine, among a multi-aged mix of hardwood and softwood. On the north bank, large superstory white pine (over 19m tall and over 90cm dbh) emerge over the canopy of hemlock, spruce, pine, and poplar. The south bank lacks these superstory pines but has some large hemlock, sugar maple, poplar and spruce, with some trees over 100 years old. The stumps and traces of logging roads throughout this area are evidence of its past logging history."[3]

This area around the mouth of the Wassataquoik is part of the ecologically rich focus area discussed in the previous Seboeis River writing.[4] The mouth of the stream is public conservation land owned by the Maine Bureau of Public Lands since 1984. The headwaters of the stream are within the boundary of Baxter State Park and managed under a "forever wild" policy. In between, most of the stream flows within the boundary of the Katahdin Woods and Waters National Monument.

Afterword

Henry David Thoreau's trips to the Maine woods were an educational experience for him. The vastness of the north woods, its relatively undeveloped character, and the fascination he found in it all contributed to the opportunities he saw for preservation, a theme that the philosopher-naturalist often wrote and spoke about. Conservation was not a term in general use at that time, and wouldn't be until the end of the eighteenth century, well after his death. So he used the word *preservation*, including in its meaning the major aspects of conservation that we now associate with the term: protection of the natural environment and its wildlife, preservation and restoration of native sites and artifacts, and prevention of the wasteful use of natural resources. For example, he would often relate the waste he saw in terms of its "higher use" as a function of the natural order of things or of aesthetic value rather than the more popular measure of value in dollars and cents. His most sweeping statement on preservation occurred in 1862 after his death and his trips to the Maine woods: "In wildness is the preservation of the world," published in his essay *Walking*.

Thoreau also came away from the Maine woods with a better understanding of the Native American, especially through his two guides, Joe Aitteon and Joe Polis. He got along well with both, but especially with Joe Polis. The two enjoyed each other's company and engaged in many hours of banter. As a result, at the end of his trip with Polis, he had obtained a clearer understanding of the Native Americans' relationship with the natural world, and he saw the protection of their way of life as related to the protection of their environment, including the Maine woods.

Perhaps the most important insight Thoreau gained on his trips was his own relationship to the natural world. His thinking about wildness was certainly challenged on Katahdin during his attempts to reach its summit. He also learned in the dense, dark boreal forest that the woods can be intimidating when he and his companion, Edward Hoar, lost their way on the Mud Pond Carry and can also produce fear, such as he experienced when Hoar got lost on their carry through the burnt land near Webster Brook. He was also put off by the waste he saw in the killing of a moose and how little of it was used.

Thoreau, however, found his Maine journeys a source of renewal for his love for nature, as evidenced by his many eloquent descriptions of the beauty he saw in the land with its lakes, streams, mountains, woods, and wildlife and the mystery that the dark woods held. Without a doubt, the Maine woods had a decided influence on his view of nature during the few years he lived beyond his trips. In that short time, he left us a written record of one man's relationship with the natural world that remains with us today, and still makes many of us pause to consider our own relationship to that world of which we are an inextricable part.

Appendix A. Conservation Areas in Thoreau's Maine Woods

Adapted from Conservation Lands in Maine, Maine Bureau of Parks and Lands

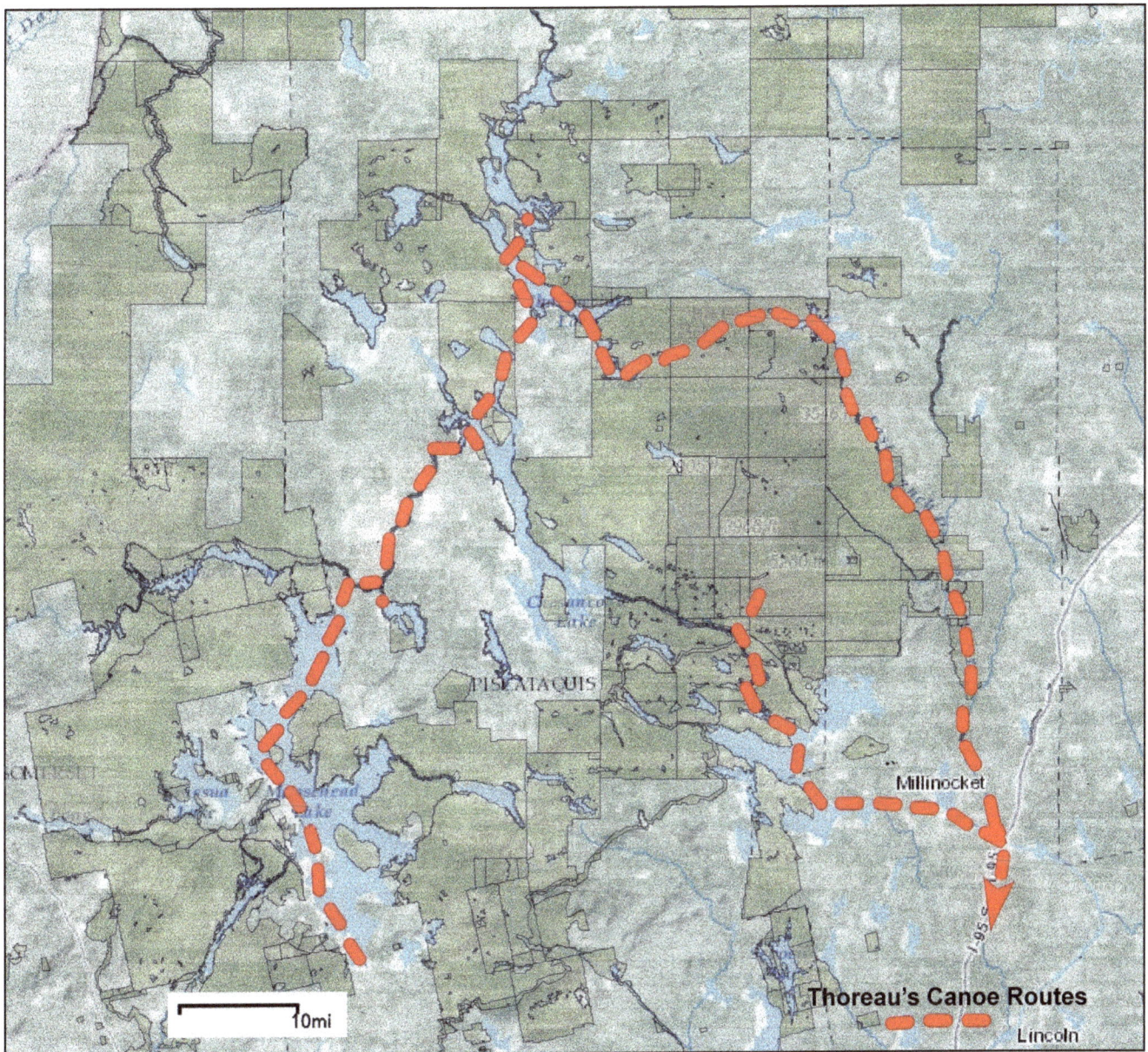

Appendix B. Key to Map Conservation Information

Note: Base maps are adapted from Conservation Lands of Maine, Maine Bureau of Parks and Lands. www.maine.gov/dacf/parks/publications_maps/conservation_lands_maine.html.

1. **ATCF**   Appalachian Trail Corridor
2. **ATCF/E**   Appalachian Trail Corridor
3. **AWWF**   Allagash Wilderness Waterway
4. **BCF**   Beaver Cove
5. **BCGEF**   Bowdoin College Grant
6. **BMF**   Baker Mountain
7. **BRFPF**   Big Reed Forest Preserve
8. **BSERF**   Big Spencer Ecological Reserve
9. **BSPF**   Baxter State Park
10. **BSPATCF** Baxter State Park Appalachian Trail Corridor
11. **BSPE**   Baxter State Park
12. BSPF   Baxter State Park
13. **BSPSMAF** Baxter State Park Scientific Management Area
14. **CLBMF**   Chamberlain Lake-Bear Mountain
15. **CLF**   Chamberlain Lake
16. **CUF**   Chamberlain Unit
17. **DAGF**   Days Academy Grant
18. **DMF/E**   Debsconeag Matrix
19. **DMKFF**   Debsconeag Matrix-Katahdin Forest
20. **EPIAAF**   EPI Access Agreement
21. **FIF**   Farm Island
22. **GIF**   Gero Island
23. **HLE**   Haymock Lake
24. KFE   Katahdin Forest
25. **KIWF**   Katahdin Iron Works
26. **KLF**   Katahdin Lake
27. **KWW**   Katahdin Woods and Waters
28. **KWWNMF**   Katahdin Woods and Waters National Monument
29. **LBSPF**   Lily Bay State Park
30. **LLF**   Lobster Lake
31. **LMR**   Little Moose Restricted
32. **LMUF**   Little Moose Unit
33. **MFF**   Marble Fen
34. **MKHF**   Moosehead Kennebec Headwaters
35. **MKSPF**   Mount Kineo State Park
36. **MRCE**   Moosehead Region Conservation
37. **MRE**   Moosehead Region
38. **MRPF**   Moose River Preserve

39. MWBE	Moosehead Wildlands Brassua	
40. NF	Nahmakanta	
41. PE	Pingree	
42. **PRCE**	Penobscot River Corridor	
43. RSEDF	Rockwood Strip E Doyle	
44. RSPE	Ripogenus Storage Project	
45. RSWF	Rockwood Strip W	
46. SAGF	Sandwich Academy Grant	
47. SF	Seboomook	
48. SIF	Sugar Island	
49. SRGPE	Seboeis River Gorge	
50. TE	Telos	
51. TRCEF	The Roaches CEF	
52. USJLF	Upper St. John Lands	
53. WBE	West Branch Easement	
54. WF	Wassataquoik	

Appendix C. Maps and Artwork

A Word about the Maps

Today, more than a century after Thoreau toured the Maine woods, conservation areas surround a large part of the routes he traveled. They can be seen in the maps that accompany the images in this book. The maps name fifty-four different conservation areas now protected by various legal mechanisms. It is also noted that a named area may occur in several locations. The maps were adapted from maps created by public and private entities and placed on the internet by the Maine Bureau of Parks and Lands under Maine Conserved Lands. The conservation areas surrounding Thoreau's routes are colored green and labeled by lettered keys placed on maps in their approximate locations. For a general view of conservation lands surrounding Thoreau's routes, see Appendix A: Conservation Areas in Thoreau's Maine Woods. Appendix B: Key to Map Conservation Information lists each conservation area with its name and kind of protection, whether by easement or fee or both. For example, the protection of Baxter State Park is labeled BSPF for Baxter State Park Fee. The capital "F" at the end stands for fee, or fee simple, meaning that the land is owned outright. Labels that end with a capital "E" are easements. A conservation easement is a legal agreement between (1) a land owner and a private organization, such as a land trust, or (2) a government agency, that limits use of the land in order to protect its conservation values.

The website Conservation Lands in Maine may be reached at the following address:
Maine.gov/dacf/parks/publications_maps/conservation_lands_maine.html
At the website, the Bureau of Parks and Lands notes the following: "The Maine Conserved Lands map contains conservation lands ownership boundaries at 1:24,000 scale for Maine land in federal, state, municipal and non-profit ownership with easements or long-term protection status. The ownership lines do not represent legal boundaries nor are the ownership lines a survey. Conserved lands is an inventory of approximate property boundaries."

The website also provides the following Access and Use Constraints—Disclaimer:
"Information provided on this site is accurate to the best of our knowledge and is subject to change on a regular basis. While the Maine State Conservation Editors of the Geographic Information Systems makes every effort to provide useful and accurate information, we do not warrant the information to be complete, factual, or timely. Information is provided on an 'as is' and an 'as available' basis. The State of Maine disclaims any liability, loss, injury, or damage incurred as a consequence, directly or indirectly, resulting from the use and application of any of the contents of this web site."

Depicting the Natural World

Nature is complicated, ever-changing and so is its effect on emotion and the human spirit. Illustrating the complex character of the north woods in writing is difficult and challenging. Creating revealing, imaginative photographic images and illustrations also demands artistic interpretation, skill, and patience.

To artistically depict the places in this book that Thoreau passed by, I drew on my collection of several thousand photographs. When we photograph a natural scene outdoors, we see through layers. What our eyes see most sharply is the layer on which the eyes or the camera is focused. We seem to see through the closer layers, which can appear transparent or blurred, while the other layers beyond the layer of our focus are also blurred. To achieve this effect in an image in this book, I digitalized selected photographs to make up the layers in each scene, and, with other photographs, I added details and layers of design objects, such as trees, stumps, rock outcrops, and animals. I then changed their transparency, blurredness, abstractness, color, and other factors to create the final piece as the eye might see the scene in nature.

From my digitally-produced images, I sometimes created watercolor paintings, using traditional wash, masking, and transparency techniques in place of digital methods. Watercolors can produce surprise and spontaneity, abstraction and realism, transparency and depth, movement and flow, and softness and sharpness—much like what I see and feel in the natural world. After a watercolor painting was completed, I added digitally-produced details. This book contains combinations of digital images of both photographs and watercolor paintings for the purpose of presenting an artistic impression of the nature that Thoreau and all of us see in the Maine woods—an impression of nature that is ephemeral, evanescent, elusive, esthetic, and suggestive of an ethical dimension. It is this picture of nature that I wish to draw viewers into with the hope that for them a new reality will emerge that produces, first, interest, then connection, and finally the dawning of responsibility.

Appendix D. Scientific Names

MAMMALS

Beaver—*Castor Canadensis*

Black bear—*Ursus americanus*

Caribou—*Rangifer tarandus caribou*

Meadow mouse—may also refer to meadow vole or *Microtus pennsylvanicus*

Moose—*Alces alces Americana*

White-tailed deer—*Odocoileus virginianus borealis*

Wolf—*Canis lupus lycaon*

BIRDS

American robin—*Turdus migratorius*

Bald eagle—*Haliaeetus leucocephalus*

Belted kingfisher—*Ceryle alcyon*

Blue jay—*Cyanocitta cristata*

Canada jay (gray jay)—*Perisoreus Canadensis*

Cedar waxwing—*Bombycilla cedrorum*

Common merganser (Sheldrake)—*mergus merganser*

Loon (common)—*Gavia immer*

Osprey—*Pandion haliaetus*

Pileated woodpecker—*Dryocopus pileatus*

Raven—*Corvus Canadensis*

Ruffed grouse—*Bonasa umbellus*

Spruce grouse—*Canachites Canadensis*

Water pipit—*Anthus spinoletta*

FISHES

Atlantic salmon and **landlocked salmon**—*Salmo salar*

Brook trout—*Salvelinus fontinalis*

Lake trout (togue)—*Salvelinus namaycush*

Minnow—family Cyprinidae

Pickerel—*Esox niger*

Yellow perch—*Perca flavescens*

TREES AND SHRUBS

Alternate-leaf dogwood (alternate cornel)—*Cornus alternifolia*

American white birch (canoe birch)—*Betula papyrifera*

Arborvitae (white cedar)—*Thuga occidentalis*

Balsam fir—*Abies balsamea*

Balsam poplar—*Populus balsamifera*

Beech—*Fagus grandifolia*

Big tooth aspen (poplar)—*Populus grandidentata*

Black ash—*Fraxinus nigra*

Blue berry—*Vaccinium angustifolium*

Choke-cherry—*Prunus virginiana*

Eastern hemlock—*Tsuga Canadensis*

Highbush cranberry (tree cranberry)—*Viburnum trilobum*

Hobblebush—*Viburnum alnifolium*

Jack Pine—*Pinus banksiana*

Moosewood (striped maple)—*Acer pennsylvanicum*

Mountain ash—*Pyrus Americana*

Naked viburnum—*Viburnum nudum*

Quaking aspen (poplar)—*Populus tremuloides*

Rasberry—*Rubus strigosus*

Red maple—*Acer rubrum*

Red osier dogwood—*Cornus stolonifera*

Red pine—*Pinus resinosa*

Red spruce—*Picea rubens*

Sugar maple—*Acer saccharum*

White pine—*Pinus strobus*

White spruce—*Picea glauca*

Yellow birch—*Betula lutea*

WILDFLOWERS

Cardinal flower—*Lobelia cardinalis*

Clintonia—*Clintonia borealis*

Creeping snowberry—*Gaultheria hispidula*

Joe-pye weed—*Eupatorium maculatum*

Rough wood aster—Eurybia *radula*

Slender rush—*Juncus subtilis*

OTHER

Crayfish—*Cambarus bartonii*

Old man's beard lichen—*Usnea* (genus)

Notes

Preface

1. Milton Meltzer and Walter Harding, *A Thoreau Profile* (Concord, Mass.: Thoreau Foundation, Inc., 1962), v.

2. Edward Wagenknecht, *Henry David Thoreau: What Manner of Man?* (Amherst, Mass.: The University of Massachusetts Press, 1981), 130.

3. Meltzer and Harding, *Thoreau Profile*, v.

4. Ibid., 3-6.

Introduction

1. Henry David Thoreau, *Wild Fruits*, ed. Bradley P. Dean (New York: W. W. Norton & Company, 2000), 236-237.

2. "Establishment of the Katahdin Woods and Waters National Monument—A Proclamation," *Bangor Daily News*, 26 August 2016.

3. Ibid.

4. Bradley P. Dean, letter to author, 24 May 2000.

5. www.penobscotculture.com

6. Henry David Thoreau, *The Maine Woods* (Boston, Mass.: Ticknor and Fields, 1864), 162, 202, 297.

7. Thoreau, *The Maine Woods*, 160.

8. Ibid, 171.

KTAADN

The 1846 Trip

1. Henry David Thoreau, *The Maine Woods* (Boston, Mass.: Ticknor and Fields, 1864), 1.

2. Ibid., 63-64.

1. Quakish Lake

1. Thoreau, *Maine Woods*, 32.

2. Ibid., 32-33.

3. Lucius L. Hubbard, *Woods and Lakes of Maine* (Boston, Mass.: Ticknor and Company, 1883), 210.

4. Thoreau, *Maine Woods*, 32.

5. Joe Rankin, "Field Work: At Work Mining Timber with Tom Shafer," *Northern Woodlands*, Winter 2014.

2. North Twin Lake

1. Thoreau, *Maine Woods*, 38.

2. Ibid., 40.

3. The Nature Conservancy website, https://www.nature.org/ourinitiatives/regions/.../KatahdinForestProject

3. Moose Tracks

    1. Thoreau, *Maine Woods*, 51.

    2. Ibid., 37.

    3. Ibid., 69.

    4. Ibid., 101.

    5. David W. Lime, *Moose as a Nongame Recreational Resource* (St. Paul, Minn.: North Central Forest Experiment Station, 1975), 113.

    6. Ibid., 114.

    7. *Baxter State Park Annual Operational Report* (Millinocket, Maine: Baxter State Park Authority, 2012), 82.

    8. U. S. Forest Service website, "Respect Wildlife," (Highlight Topic). https://www.fs.usda.gov/detail/r10/recreation/society/ethics

4. The Lakes

    1. Henry David Thoreau, *Walden* (Princeton, New Jersey: Princeton University Press, 1971), 186.

    2. Thoreau, *Maine Woods*, 36.

    3. Ibid., 81.

    4. Jodie J. Jones and Holly Dominie, *Scenic Lakes Character Evaluation in Maine's Unorganized Towns*, Planning Report no. 82 (Augusta, Maine: State Planning Office, 1987).

    5. Maine Department of Environmental Protection website, www.maine.gov/dep/water/lakes/

    6. Circle of Blue website, Codi Kozacek, "Biggest Lakes in the World Under Pressure from Human and Environmental Threats," June 3, 2015. www.circleofblue.org/2015/world/biggest-lakes-in-the-world-under-pressure-from-human-and-environmental-threats/

5. Loons

    1. Thoreau, *Maine Woods*, 32.

    2. Ibid., 169.

    3. Ibid., 229.

    4. Maine Audubon website, www.maineaudubon.org/2017/03/results-of-the-loon-count/

    5. Maine Audubon website, informational sheet, "Loon Protection." www.maineaudubon.org.

    6. Thoreau, *Maine Woods*, 270.

6. Debsconeag Falls

    1. Thoreau, *Maine Woods*, 45.

    2. Ibid.

    3. Janet McMahon, *Maine's Whitewater Rapids and Their Relevance to the Critical Areas Program*, Planning Report No. 74 (Augusta, Maine: Critical Areas Program, Maine State Planning Office, 1981); and *Maine's Waterfalls and Their Relevance to the Critical Areas Program*, Planning Report No. 60 (Augusta, Maine: Critical Areas Program, Maine State Planning Office, 1988).

7. Pockwockamus Deadwater

    1. Thoreau, *Maine Woods*, 50.

    2. Ibid., 50-51.

    3. Ibid., 51.

    4. Ibid.

5. See BDN (Bangor Daily News) Blogs, Act Out with Aislinn, "1-minute Hike: River Pond Nature Trail Near Millinocket," (Pockwockamus Deadwater), www.actoutwithaislinn.bangordailynews.com/tag/river-pond-nature-trail/

8. Pockwockamus Falls

1. Thoreau, *Maine Woods*, 56.

2. This note on the meaning of the native name of Pockwockamus came from: Lucius L. Hubbard, *Woods and Lakes of Maine* (Boston, Mass.: Ticknor and Company, 1883), 209.

3. Alvin K. Swonger and Thomas Brewer, *Maine's Waterfalls* (Augusta, Maine: Critical Areas Program, Maine State Planning Office, 1988), 185-186.

4. Ibid., 186.

9. Abol Deadwater

1. Thoreau, *Maine Woods*, 52.

2. Ibid., 53.

10. Trout

1. Thoreau, *Maine Woods*, 53-54.

2. Maine Department of Inland Fisheries and Wildlife website, "Maine Brook Trout. www.maine.gov/ifw/fishing/species/Maine'sWildBrookTrout.htm

3. Maine Council of Trout Unlimited website, www.tumaine.org/brooktrout.htm

11. Moose Skeleton

1. Thoreau, *Maine Woods*, 55.

2. See Maine Department of Inland Fisheries and Wildlife website, www.maine.gov/ifw/wildlife/species/mammals/moose

3. Wickipedia, the free encyclopedia website, *Parelaphostrongylus tenuis* (brainworm).

4. National Wildlife website, John Carey, *The Deepening Mystery of Moose Decline*, September 29, 2014.

5. Scientific American website. Shannon Hall, "Will Moose Thrive or Die Because of Climate Change?", April 29, 2016.

12. The Unbroken Forest

1. Thoreau, *Maine Woods*, 80-81.

2. Aldo Leopold, *A Sand County Almanac* (New York: Sierra Club/Ballantine Books, 1970), 262.

3. Public Law 88-577, *The Wilderness Act*, 1964.

13. Gray Lichens

1. Thoreau, *Maine Woods*, 32.

2. Henry David Thoreau, "Natural History of Massachusetts" (*The Dial*, July 1842, 19-40), 36.

3. Ray Angelo, "Thoreau as Botanist: An Appreciation and a Critique," *The Thoreau Quarterly*, Volume 15, 1984.

4. Wikipedia website, *Usnea.*

5. Steven B. Selva, "Lichen Diversity and Stand Continuity in the Northern Hardwoods and Spruce-Fir Forests of Northern New England and Western New Brunswick," *The Bryologist*, Vol. 97, No. 4 (Winter, 1994), 424-429.

14. Diversified Country

1. Thoreau, *Maine Woods*, 81-82.

2. "Biodiversity."

3. Maine Natural Areas Program website, About MNAP. www.maine.gov/dacf/mnap/

15. Overlooking the Country

1. Thoreau, *Maine Woods*, 1-2.

2. Ibid., 55-57.

3. Ibid., 60-62.

16. Thoreau's Katahdin

1. Thoreau, *Maine Woods*, 63.

2. Ibid., 64.

3. Ibid., 63-64.

17. Beyond Reach

1. Thoreau, *Maine Woods*, 63-65.

2. Ibid., 65-66.

3. Ibid., 70-71.

CHESUNCOOK

The 1853 Trip

1. Thoreau, *Maine Woods*, 101.

2. Ibid., 159.

3. Ibid., 160.

1. Moosehead Lake

1. Thoreau, *Maine Woods*, 91.

2. Ibid., 93.

3. Henry David Thoreau, *Wild Fruits*, ed. Bradley P. Dean (New York: W. W. Norton & Company, 2000), 236.

4. Natural Resources Council of Maine website, "Plum Creek's Massive Moosehead Proposal." www.nrcm.org/projects/forests-wildlife/plum-creek's-massive-moosehead-proposal/

5. Maine Department of Agriculture, Conservation and Forestry website, "Moosehead Region Management Plan: Final Draft." www.maine.gov/dacf/parks/get_involved/

6. Forest Society of Maine website, "Moosehead Region," www.fsmaine.org/conserved-lands/moosehead/

2. Northeast Carry

1. Thoreau, *Maine Woods*, 94-95.

2. Mrs. William Starr Dana, *How to Know the Wild Flowers* (New York: Charles Scribner's Sons, 1902), viii.

3. U.S. National Park Service website, "The Value of Wildflowers," https://www.nps.gov/plants/cw/variety.htm

4. Glen H. Mittelhauser, et al., *The Plants of Baxter State Park* (Orono, Maine: University of Maine Press, 2016), 2.

3. Red Maples

1. Thoreau, *Maine Woods*, 95-96.

2. Ibid., 98.

3. National Wildlife Federation website, "The Value of Autumn," https://www.nwf.org/News-and-Magazines/NationalWildlife/The-Value-of-Autumn.aspx

4. Climate Central website, "Drought, Climate Impact Fall Foliage in Complex Ways," www.climate-central.org/news/drought-climate-impact-fall-foliage

5. David Cole and Steven Boutcher, "Wilderness and Climate Change," U.S. Department of Agriculture, Forest Service, Climate Change Resource Center. 2012. www.fs.usda.gov/ccrc/topics/wilderness

6. Henry David Thoreau. "Autumnal Tints," *The Atlantic*, vol. 10, no. 60 (October 1862).

4. Lobster Stream

1. Thoreau, *Maine Woods*, 98-100.

2. Wikipedia website, "Lobster Lake (Maine)", https://en.wikipedia.org/w/index.php?title=Lobster_Lake_(maine)&oldid=759325367

3. "Lobster Lake Survey Sheet," Maine Department of Inland Fisheries and Game, July 1958.

4. Jodie J. Jones and Holly Dominie, *Scenic Lakes Character Evaluation in Maine's Unorganized Towns*, Planning Report 82   (Augusta, Maine: Maine Department of Conservation and Maine State Planning Office, 1986), ii, 17-20.

5. A Small Island

1. Thoreau, *Maine Woods*, 100-101.

2. Ibid., 101.

3. Ibid., 102.

4. Maine Department of Agriculture, Conservation and Forestry website, "Central Penobscot Regional Plan," https://www1.maine.gov/dacf/parks/get_involved/planning and acquisition/management_plans/docs/central penobscot plan context.pdf

6. The Moosehorn

1. Thoreau, *Maine Woods*, 102-105,

2. Ibid., 105-106.

3. Maine Department of Inland Fisheries and Wildlife website, "Moose," www.maine.gov/ifw/wildlife/species/mammals/moose.html

4. Maine Department of Inland Fisheries and Wildlife website, "Wildlife Management Districts (WMSs)," www.maine.gov/ifw/wildlife/land.wmd/index.html

See also "Moose," www.maine.gov/ifw/wildlife/species/mammals/moose.html

7. Ragmuff Stream

1. Thoreau, *Maine Woods*, 108-109.

2. C. W. Martin, D. S. Noel, and C. A. Federer, "The Effect of Forest Clearcutting in New England on Stream-Water Chemistry and Biology" (Durham, New Hampshire: N. E. Forest Experiment Station, U. S. Forest Service, 1981), 1-8, 11-12, 47-49.

8. Big Island

1. Thoreau, *Maine Woods*, 110.

2. Ibid., 112.

3. Ibid., 200.

4. Fannie P. Hardy, "Trip Down the East Branch via North East Carry," 1888, pp. 63-64, Journals of Fannie (Hardy) Eckstorm Collection, Special Collections Department, Raymond H. Fogler Library, University of Maine, Orono.

5. Richard Judd, "Route to a New Frontier: The Allagash River and the Creation of a Wilderness Concept," *Habitat: Journal of the Maine Audubon Society* 3, no. 6 (June-July 1986), 20.

6. See *Seboomook Unit Management Plan* (Augusta, Maine: Maine Department of Conservation, Bureau of Parks and Lands, 2007), 18.

7. See Forest Society of Maine website. www.fsmaine.org.

9. White Pine

1. Thoreau, *Maine* Woods, 123=124.

2. Ibid., 19.

3. Ibid., 110-111.

4. Ibid., 148.

5. Ibid., 218.

6. "White Pine Forest Fact Sheet," Maine Department of Agriculture, Conservation and Forestry, Maine Natural Areas Program. www.maine.gov/dacf/mnap/features/communities/white_pine_forest.pdf

7. Maine Department of Agriculture, Conservation and Forestry website, "Regenerating White Pine Stands in Maine (Information Sheet 22).

8. Maine Department of Agriculture, Conservation and Forestry, Maine Forest Service website, "White Pine Blister Rust." www.maine.gov/dacf/mfs/forest_health/diseases/white_pine_blister_rust.htm

10. Pine Stream

1. Thoreau, *Maine* Woods, 112.

2. U.S. Department of the Interior, U.S. Fish and Wildlife Service, and U.S. Department of Commerce, U.S. Census Bureau, *National Survey of Fishing, Hunting and Wildlife Associated Recreation*, 2011.

3. Ibid., *Survey*.

4. Maine Department of Inland Fisheries and Wildlife website, "IFW News—Maine Moose Permit Auction Raises Over $133,000 for Scholarships," January 30, 2017.

11. Moose

1. Thoreau, *Maine Woods*, 112-113.

2. Ibid., 115.

3. Ibid., 121-122,

4. Ibid., 123.

5. Maine Department of Inland Fisheries and Wildlife website, "2016 Maine Moose Hunters' Guide," 11-12.

12. White-tailed Deer

1. Thoreau, *Maine Woods*, 142.

2. Maine Department of Inland Fisheries and Wildlife website, Gerald R. Lavigne, "White-Tailed Deer Assessment and Strategic Plan 1997 (May 1999)"; and F. Polvin and J. Huot, "Estimation of Carrying Capacity of White-Tailed Deer Wintering Areas in Quebec," *Journal of Wildlife Management* 47 (1983):464-475.

3. Don C. Stanton, *A History of the White-tailed Deer in Maine* (Augusta, Maine: Maine Department of Inland Fisheries and Game, 1963), 23.

4. Ibid., 24.

5. Ibid., 27-28.

6. Joe Wiley and Chuck Hulsey, "Living on the Edge: How Deer Survive in Winter," 2010 Newsletter, Small Woodlot Owners   Association of Maine and in *Maine Fish and Wildlife*. www.mefish-wildlife.com

7. See *Guidelines for Wildlife: Managing Deer Wintering Areas in Northern, Western and Eastern Maine* (Augusta, Maine: Maine Department of Inland Fisheries and Wildlife, 2010); and Daniel Harrison and Stephen Sader, "Effectiveness of State Regulations to Protect Deer Wintering Habitats in Maine" (Orono, Maine: The University of Maine, School of Forest Resources, Department of Wildlife Ecology, 2013). PDF available at https://www.google.com/#g=effectiveness+of+state+regulations+to+protect+deer+wintering+habitats+in+maine

8. See Andrew Whitman, et al., *Climate Change and Biodiversity in Maine: Vulnerability of Habitats and Priority Species*, Report SEI-2013—03 (Brunswick, Maine: Manomet Center for Conservation Sciences,2013).

13. Mountain Ash

1. Thoreau, *Maine* Woods, 88.

2. Ibid., 59.

3. Ibid., 98. 99. 108.

4. Henry David Thoreau, "Natural History of Massachusetts," *The Dial*, vol. III (July 1842): 117-121.

14. Chesuncook Lake

1. Thoreau, *Maine* Woods, 126.

2. Ibid., 326, 328.

3. See "Chesuncook Lake (lake survey)," Maine Department of Inland Fisheries and Game, 1960. https://www1.maine.gov/ifw/fishing/lakesurvey_maps/piscataquis/chesuncook_lake.pdf See also "Chesuncook, Maine," Wikipedia, the free encyclopedia. https://en.wikipedia.org/wiki/Chesuncook,_Maine

15. Chesuncook Village

1. Thoreau, *Maine Woods*, 126-133.

2. See "Chesuncook Lake," Wikipedia, the free encyclopedia website. https://en.wikipedia.org/wiki/Chesuncook,_maine and Natural Resources Council of Maine website. http://www.nrcm.org/explore-maine-map/by-county/piscataquis/gero-island-public-reserved-land-unit/?share=google-plus-1&nb=1

16. Chesuncook Shore

1. Thoreau, *Maine* Woods, 132.

2. Maine Department of Agriculture, Conservation and Forestry, Maine Natural Areas Program website, "Ecological Reserve Fact Sheet, Gero Island, 2009"; and *Juncus subtilis* E. mey., "Slender Rush, 2013."

17. Osprey

1. Thoreau, *Maine* Woods, 134-135.

2. Henry David Thoreau, *Journal*, June 13, 1853.

3. See John K. Terress, *The Audubon Society Encyclopedia of North American Birds* (New York: Alfred A. Knopf, 1982), 644-645.

4. The Cornell Lab of Ornithology, All About Birds, Osprey, website: https://www.al-laboutbirds.org/guide/osprey/id

THE ALLEGASH AND EAST BRANCH

The 1857 Trip
    1. Thoreau, *Maine Woods*, 270.
    2. Ibid., 203.
    3. Ibid., 281.
    4. Ibid., 282.
    5. Ibid., 281-82.
    6. Ibid., 267.
    7. Ibid., 233.
    8. Ibid., 245.

1. Mount Kineo
    1. Thoreau, *Maine* Woods, 168, 173, 176-177.
    2. Ibid., 178-182.
    3. Wikipedia website, "Mount Kineo." https://en.wikipedia.org/wiki/mount_kineo
    4. Ibid.

2. Phosphorescent Wood
    1. Thoreau, *Maine* Woods, 185.
    2. Ibid., 184.
    3, Helmut Brandl, "Luminescent Wood in Coal Ore Mines: A Historical Review," *Fungi* 4, no. 2 (Spring 2011), 6, 8.
    4. Thoreau, *Maine Woods*, 185.
    5. Ibid., 185-186.

3. Mud Pond Carry
    1. Thoreau, *Maine Woods*, 217-218.
    2. Ibid., 218-229.

4. Chamberlain Lake
    1. Thoreau, *Maine* Woods, 227, 230-231
    2. Ibid., 233-234.
    3. Ibid., 235-236.

5. Eagle Lake
    1. Thoreau, *Maine Woods,* 236.
    2. "Eagle Lake," (Augusta, Maine: Maine Department of Inland Fisheries and Wildlife, 1990).
    3. Philip W. Conkling, *Old Growth White Pine (Pinus strobus L.) Stands in Maine and Their Relevance to the Critical Areas Program*, Planning Report No. 61 (Augusta, Maine: Maine State Planning Office, Critical Areas Program, 1978), 32; and Dean   Bennett, *Allagash:Maine's Wild and Scenic River* (Camden, Maine: Down East Books, 1994), 60-63.

6. Pillsbury Island
    1. Thoreau, *Maine* Woods, 237-238.
    2. Ibid., 242-243.

7. Chamberlain Farm

1. Thoreau, *Maine* Woods, 245.

2. Ibid., 245-246.

3. Ibid., 246.

4. Ibid., 245.

5. See "Chamberlain Farm Insurance Policies," June 1858 and July 1869, E. S. Coe Chamberlain Farm Papers, Captain Myron H. Avery Collection, Maine State Library, Augusta.

6. A. G. Hempstead, "A Visit to Chamberlain Farm," *The Northern* 7, no. 8 (November 1927): 714-715.

7. For an account of the history of the Allagash Wilderness Waterway and the effort to protect it, see Dean B. Bennett, *The Wilderness from Chamberlain Farm: A Story of Hope for the American Wild*, (Washington, D. C.: Island Press, 2001).

8. Red Pine

1. Thoreau, *Maine* Woods, 247-249.

2. Ezekiel Holmes and Charles H. Hitchcock, "Preliminary Report upon the Natural History and Geology of the State of Maine: 1861," *Sixth Annual Report of the Secretary of the Maine Board of Agriculture: 1861* (Augusta, Maine: Stevens & Sayward, Printers to the State, 1860), 344, 346.

9. Sheldrakes

1. E. Lawrence Palmer, *Fieldbook of Natural History* (New York: McGraw Hill Book Company, 1949), 483.

2. Birds of North America website, "Common Merganser." https://birdsna.org/Species-Account/bna/species/

3. Thoreau, *Maine* Woods, 256.

4. Ibid., 254.

5. Animal Diversity Web, University of Michigan, Museum of Zoology website. animal diversity.org/accounts/mergus_merganser/

6. Palmer, *Fieldbook*, 483.

7. Edward Howe Furbush, Merganser," *Birds of America* (New York: Doubleday & Company, Inc., 1917), 111.

10. Burnt Land

1. Thoreau, *Maine* Woods, 261-262.

2. Ibid., 262-268.

3. Maine Department of Agriculture, Conservation and Forestry website, "Maine Forest Service, Programs and Services." www.maine.gov/dacf/mfs/forest_protection/programs_services.html

11. Grand Pitch Webster Brook

1. Thoreau, *Maine* Woods, 266-267.

2. Alvin K. Swonger and Thomas Brewer, *Maine's Waterfalls and Their Relevance to the Critical Areas Program*, Planning Report no. 60 (Augusta, Maine: Maine State Planning Office, Critical Areas Program, 1988), 1-7.

3. Ibid., 108-109.

12. Second Lake

1. Thoreau, *Maine* Woods, 270-271.

2. Ibid., 271-272.

3. Ibid., 273-274.

13. Jack Pine

1. Thoreau, *Maine Woods*, 277.

2. Ibid., 274.

3. Ibid., 275.

4. See International Society of Arboriculture website, ISA. www.isaontario.com/content/jackpine

5. George L. Goodale, "Botanical Notes on the New Lands," in Holmes and Hitchcock, "Preliminary Report," 364.

6. *Jack Pine* (Pinus banksiana) *in Maine and its Relevance to the Critical Areas Program*, Planning Report 77 (Augusta,   Maine: Maine State Planning Office, Maine Critical Areas Program, 1983), 20.

7. Ibid., 23.

14. East Branch

1. Thoreau, *Maine* Woods, 277-278.

2. Ibid., 278-279.

3. Matagamon Lake Association, Inc., website, "Matagamon Dam." www.katahdinoutdoors.com/dam/

15. East Branch Country

1. Thoreau, *Maine* Woods, 279.

2. See "Establishment of the Katahdin Woods and Waters National Monument, A Proclamation," *Bangor Daily News*, p. C8, 26 August 2016.

3. Ibid., C8.

4. Ibid., C8.

5. Ibid., C8.

16. Haskell Rock

1. Thoreau, *Maine* Woods, 285.

2. "Haskell Rock Is Named After William M. Haskell," *Baptist Church Bulletin*," West Poland, Maine, 21 July 1841. (photocopy in possession of author)

3. For information on the geology of Haskell Rock, see Maine Geological Survey: Haskell Rock, East Branch of the Penobscot River. www.maine.gov/doc/nrimc/mgs/explorer/bed-rock/sites/oct05.htm

4. Fannie P. Hardy, "Trip Down the East Branch via North East Carry," 1888, p. 80, Journals of Fannie (Hardy) Eckstorm Collection, Special Collections Department, Raymond H. Folger Library, University of Maine, Orono.

17. Grand Pitch East Branch

1. Thoreau, *Maine* Woods, 285-287.

2. Swonger and Brewer, *Maine's Waterfalls*, 107-108; and Maine Trail Finder website. www.mainetrailfinder.com/trails/trail/grand-pitch-trail

18. Oldhamia

1. Thoreau, *Maine* Woods, 287.

2. "Oldhamia," Wikipedia website. https://en.wikipedia.org/wiki/oldhamia; and "Thomas Oldham," Wikipedia website. https://en.wikipedia.org/wiki/thomas_oldham

3. Robert B. Neuman, *Bedrock Geology of the Shin Pond and Stacyville Quadrangles Penobscot County*, Maine Geological Survey Professional Paper 524-I (Washington, D. C.: U.S. Department of the Interior, 1967), 15.

4. "The Poetry of Fossils: John Joly," *Not Just Science* (A Blog by Anthea Lacchia), January 092, 2013.   https://anthealacchia.wordpress.com/2013/02/the-poetry-of-fossils-john-jolly

19. Seboeis River

1. Thoreau, *Maine* Woods, 289-290.

2. Wikipedia website, "Seboeis River." https://en.wikipedia.org/wiki/Seboeis_River

3. *Maine River's Study*, Final Report (Augusta, Maine: State of Maine, Department of Conservation and U.S. Department of the Interior, National Park Service, 1982), 57.

4. Dean B. Bennett, *The Forgotten Nature of New England: A Search for Traces of the Original Wilderness* (Camden, Maine: Down East Books, 1996), 213-214.

5. Maine Natural Areas website, "Focus Areas of Statewide Ecological Significance, East Branch Penobscot-Seboeis River-Wassataquoik Stream. https://www1.maine.gov/dacf/mnap/focusarea/east_branch_penobscot_focus-area.pdf

20. The Wassataquoik

1. Thoreau, *Maine Woods,* 290.

2. Ibid., 292.

3. Maine Natural Areas website, "Wassataquoik Stream." https://www1.maine.gov/dacf/mnap/focus-area_branch_penobscot_focus_area.pdf

About the Author

Dean B. Bennett began painting and photographing the north woods in his home state of Maine in the late 1950s and early 1960s when he began canoeing the Upper West Branch of the Penobscot River and the Allagash Wilderness Waterway and backpacking in Baxter State Park. Since then, while pursuing a varied career, he has retraced much of each route Thoreau traveled in the Maine woods. After completing a four-year apprenticeship in cabinetmaking through the Maine State Apprenticeship Council, he went on to receive a bachelor's degree in industrial arts education and a master's degree in science education, teaching both subjects in the Yarmouth, Maine, school system. Later he received a Ph.D. in Resource Planning and Conservation from the University of Michigan with a special emphasis in environmental education. Since then, much of his professional life has been devoted to teaching, writing, and illustrating books in the fields of science and environmental education, natural history, and human relationships with nature. He served as the first environmental education school curriculum specialist in the Maine State Department of Education, and later, he spent many years at the University of Maine at Farmington as a professor of science education. He was among one-hundred educators selected by Unesco to participate in the first world environmental education conference in Belgrade Yugoslavia, and at the organization's invitation, he wrote a book on evaluating environmental learning for teachers. He received the Percival Baxter Award for Leadership in Wilderness Preservation from the Maine Chapter of the Sierra Club, the Environmental Activist Award for protection of the Allagash Wilderness Waterway from the Natural Resources Council of Maine, and the Teacher of the Year Award from Maine Audubon Society. In 2014, he and his wife Sheila K. Bennett jointly received from the Conservation Voters of Maine the Harrison L. Richardson Environmental Leadership Award for '... inspiring all of us to care for the nature of Maine and its wild places.'" This is his eleventh book in the nature/environment field. His other books include: *Maine's Natural Heritage: Rare Species and Unique Natural Features, Allagash: Maine's Wild and Scenic River, The Forgotten Nature of New England: A Search for Traces of the Original Wilderness, The Wilderness from Chamberlain Farm: A Story of Hope for the American Wild, On Wilderness: Voices from Maine* (in collaboration with Phyllis Austin and Robert Kimber), *Nature and Renewal: Wild River Valley and Beyond, Ghost Buck: The Legacy of One Man's Family and its Hunting Traditions* (a memoir), and three children's books, which he illustrated in watercolor. He enjoys playing jazz and ragtime music on his plectrum banjo and continues to hike and canoe with his wife in the north woods of Maine.